Learning to Teach: Teaching to Learn

Routledge Education Books

Advisory editor: John Eggleston
Professor of Education
University of Keele

Learning to Teach: Teaching to Learn

Gwyneth Dow

Routledge & Kegan Paul
London, Boston and Henley

First published in 1979
by Routledge & Kegan Paul Ltd
39 Store Street, London WC1E 7DD,
Broadway House, Newtown Road,
Henley-on-Thames, Oxon RG9 1EN and
9 Park Street, Boston, Mass. 02108, USA
Set in IBM Press Roman by
Hope Services, Clifton Hampden
and printed in Great Britain by
Lowe & Brydone Ltd,
Thetford, Norfolk

British Library Cataloguing in Publication Data

Dow, Gwyneth Maude

Learning to teach: teaching to learn. – (Routledge education books).
1. Teachers, Training of
I. Title
370'.71   LB1715   78-41307

ISBN 0 7100 0093 6

Contents

Acknowledgments   vii
Introduction What *Learning to Teach: Teaching to
                Learn* is about   1

1 Thinking about education   17
2 Who am I?   54
3 Being at risk   81
4 Methods: where the 'what' and the 'how' most
   readily meet   117
5 Assessing oneself?   153
6 A course for radicals?   172
7 School teachers as educators of teachers   197
   Conclusion   241

   Notes   247
   Booklist   249
   Index   253

Acknowledgments

If special research funds had not come my way this book would not have been written, for the experiment it examines would not have existed. It was Federal money from two sources that enabled me to launch a radical experiment in teacher education in 1973 at the University of Melbourne — to run what was called Course B, which was based on principles that most of my colleagues either doubted or opposed and would certainly not have underwritten. Thus my first acknowledgment is to the Federal policy which funded innovations at my University and to the New Developments Committee (now the Development Grants Sub-Committee) that awarded Course B one of the very first grants. It provided, among other things, a senior lecturer's salary for four years and a lecturer's salary for three.

Bernard Newsome had already been temporarily employed towards the end of 1972 from Faculty funds made available by the then Dean, Professor A. G. Austin, to help me with the final planning of the Course. The New Developments grant enabled us to employ him as a senior lecturer and Assistant Director. For three years Bernie was unstinting in the help he gave to organizing the Course, to schools and to students. He played an inspirational part in helping both staff and students to develop and clarify the principles underlying Course B — principles of far-reaching educational importance that are the subject of this book. Rod Fawns was appointed to the lectureship for a year, after which he gained a permanent position in the Faculty and continued to work part-time for the Course, and has acted as its Director for 1978. Rod's boundless energies were spread over all the Course's activities, but in particular he pioneered the development of a relationship with student-teachers and supervising teachers in our practice schools, where he became an influential promoter of, and participant in, innovatory teaching projects. Rory Barnes, who succeeded Rod full-time (1974-6), Doris Cosopodiotis (1976-8) and Ron Toomey (1976), who succeeded

Bernie, each on a part-time basis, were also employed from New Developments funds and all made a selfless, creative contribution to the Course.

It seems invidious to have to distinguish between those people who helped the Course and those who helped the book, though I must do that if the acknowledgments are not to become too unwieldy. Many members of school and University staff sent written contributions or are referred to in students' diaries and so will appear in one form or another in the book itself — my apologies to colleagues who by chance do not, despite their value to the Course. Above all, for diplomatic and ethical reasons, I am unable to acknowledge by name the major contributors to the book, the students who provided voluminous material that either directly (in quotations) or indirectly (in helping to give me their interpretation of the course) I drew on in writing the book. It is to the students that the greatest acknowledgments are due, for the book is an attempt to see things through their eyes.

Much of the thankless, behind-the-scenes recording and collating of material for the book was done by an array of variously brilliant secretaries who worked with us for short or relatively long periods, usually en route to higher qualifications themselves. They formed the nerve centre of the Course — Bronwyn Hughes, Janie Larkins, Nadine Dalgarno, Jan Malley, Joy McDonald. Each was alertly sensitive and responsive to students and staff, and they all contributed to policy-making as well as keeping those demanding records that a publicly-funded experiment demands. The Australian Advisory Committee on Research and Development in Education (later to become the Educational Research and Development Committee) provided a yearly grant to cover the first three years of the Course and to pay for the secretarial/research assistance (carried on in 1975 by the New Developments grant) that I have indicated was so extraordinarily talented and helpful.

I am also indebted to the AACRDE for the funds that subsidized the evaluation of the Course. This work was undertaken by the University's Centre for the Study of Higher Education, whose investment in the work greatly exceeded the contribution the Course could make. I have drawn on the Centre's published report and much of its unpublished, but carefully recorded, documentary reports. *Learning to Teach: Teaching to Learn* owes a great deal to the Centre, notably to Barbara Falk (its then Director), and to Torrey Orton and Cleo Macmillan who researched and wrote the evaluation, showing in the process how participatory evaluation could be worked out. The AACRDE and a small grant from the Buckland Foundation made it possible for us to buy resources and software both for our teaching and for the evaluation of the Course.

Study leave, granted me in 1977 by the University, made it possible for me to write *Learning to Teach: Teaching to Learn*, while Rod Foster ably took over from me as Director of Course B, supported by Co-Director Karel Reus-Smit and other friends in the Faculty and the State Department of Education.

I am grateful to Professor Brian Simon for inviting me as a Visiting Research Fellow to the University of Leicester, where I wrote the bulk of the book, and was lucky to meet Denise Spence, who undertook all the typing from chapter 3, the earlier chapters having been typed by Nadine Dalgarno, who also helped me with advice during the difficulties of deciding what style and shape the book should take. The book was finished in London, where Mrs Margaret McGill allotted a Nuffield flat to my husband and me for three months, and this was of immeasurable help.

It remains to express sentiments of deep friendship to the five people who read the manuscript and encouraged me while giving constructive criticism. Bill Hannan of Melbourne (though in County Limerick at the time in question), Peter Wright and Douglas Holly of Leicester all reassured me that I was unorthodoxly sane, not the reverse, and this, with their other help, I really needed as I was writing. Since my return Gwen McDowall of the University of Melbourne has helped me with the final stages of the book in more ways than I can mention. My husband, Hume, had the most thankless and possibly often unthanked task of reading what I was writing throughout. He has the infuriating habit of usually being right in his judgments, for which, retrospectively, he must be fully credited and affectionately thanked.

The author and the publishers are grateful for permission to reproduce the two poems by Bertolt Brecht in chapter 7, translated by Michael Hamburger, taken from Bertolt Brecht, *Plays, Poetry and Prose: Poems 1913-1956*, ed. John Willett and Ralph Manheim, London, Eyre Methuen, 1976, pp. 105, 252. 'Of Poor B.B.' — 'Hauspostille', Copyright 1927 by Propylaen Verlag, Renewal Copyright 1968 by Helene Brecht-Weigel, Berlin; 'Questions from a Worker who Reads' — *Svendborger Gedichte*: Copyright 1939 by Malik-Verlag, London. Due acknowledgment is also made to Suhrkamp Verlag, Frankfurt.

Introduction

What *Learning to Teach: Teaching to Learn* is about

At first glance it might appear that this book is a case study of a particular experiment in postgraduate teacher education. Narrowly speaking, this is true: the book is indeed based on one experiment, a radically innovative course (known as 'Course B') begun at the University of Melbourne in 1973. In broader terms, however, the book is, or certainly attempts to be, an account of educational principles in action, with the intention throughout that the reader, like the students in Course B itself, be invited to consider the applicability of those principles to education in general.

My concern in this introduction is to indicate what those principles are; to show how Course B – and this book – came into being; and thus to provide the context in which the rest of the book is set. That setting is within a traditional faculty of education within a university that is proud – I think justifiably – of its academic standards. Thus the book is local in a purely fortuitous way: the University of Melbourne's being Australian, the illustrations drawn from students must have the stamp of the Australian postgraduate student and of Australian idiom.

Within this idiosyncratic context problems arise that are by no means local or special – problems that transcend national or local differences in being basic to the very nature of teaching and learning. What may make the story unusual is that it is told largely by students, and is a deliberate search for the student's viewpoint. The main characters in the book, therefore, are the postgraduate students undertaking their Melbourne Diploma of Education year (a Diploma that qualifies them to become secondary school teachers); others with important roles in the account are University staff, school teachers and school pupils. It would, of course, be ludicrous to suggest that the problem of learning to teach (or, for that matter, learning to learn) is the same in Nairobi, Canton, Leeds, Stockholm, Chicago, Leningrad, or even Melbourne and Sydney (for, in Australia, education comes under State, not Federal,

1

legislation and administration, and so one cannot talk about an Australian system). But, for all that, the book's attempt to see what student-teachers go through, when they and their staff are seriously trying to produce effective future teachers, may be assumed to have some universality.

It should nevertheless be made quite clear that at no time is there any suggestion that what one can do with a graduate student body that shares a professional purpose is exportable and generalizable to vastly different groups of learners. All that *is* being suggested is that what we learned, what our students taught us, has relevance beyond the Course itself and might at least provoke thought and enlightenment on wider educational issues.

Many of the points that emerge are valid beyond the professional education of teachers and might apply, for example, to professional education in medicine, nursing, law, social work or engineering. Certainly, students' preoccupation with understanding themselves and the image they present — with what is fashionably called their sense of identity — is not unique to student-teachers. Nor is their problem as simple as that. In trying to acquire a teaching style that fits them well, they have to face up to defining, living with and learning to act according to values that deeply satisfy them. Their attempts to do this — to answer what I call the 'Who am I?' question — have significance beyond teaching for each of them, and applicability for those learning other vocations. A great part of the early chapters of the book is devoted to this question, and the emphasis given to it reflects the emphasis that students gave to it themselves. Learning to teach intensifies one's awareness of the importance of learning about oneself, as the title of this book suggests; but learning about oneself is of course not unique to student-teachers. If my thesis is right — that students, in learning to teach, also learn to learn in both a personal and academic sense — it would seem likely to follow that all professions which entail human relationships may also be valuable sources of learning in a way that might help to breach the destructive division in so many professions between theory and practice.

Again, the book may be read as an exploration of the hazards, successes and failures inherent in any attempt to innovate within an established framework. This particular case study is concerned with teacher education, but many of our problems would arise in any educational innovation, and some of them in any innovation of any kind.

The book is not a tightly organized documentary studded with explicit or implicit statements of the 'we did this ... we did that' kind. It is an exploration of how various principles were tried out. It is necessary, therefore, to tell here the story of how the Course came about, and the principles on which it was based. How it worked out is told in the chapters that follow.

Before Course B was introduced in 1973, the characteristic Diploma of Education at Melbourne consisted of lectures and some tutorials or laboratory work in educational psychology, philosophy of education and sociology of education. In addition, in the traditional course, for one morning a week, students attended sessions on their two teaching subjects (it is customary in Victoria for students to offer two teaching subjects). Three times a year students would be placed at a school for teaching practice, each time for three (or at most four) weeks — totalling from nine to ten weeks in the year, each 'teaching round' usually being at a different school.

Some ten or so years ago, before Sociology of Education was offered, I had introduced an interdisciplinary first-year subject that was closely tied to current educational problems and practices. I pinned my faith on catching immediate interest rather than on trying to initiate students, especially science, mathematics and music students, into new and complex intellectual structures at the beginning of the year, when they were preoccupied with the task ahead — that is, with learning to become teachers. While, by and large, the students seemed to think this decision right, the ones who blossomed most dramatically were the weary, often listless, evening students, many of them primary teachers who did the Dip. Ed. to gain a qualification for secondary education. What distinguished them from the full-time, less heavily-pressed students was that the Course enabled them to draw on their experiences and to relate their study and written work to what they were already doing daily in schools.

The conclusion was obvious. Experience was the spur to academic endeavour, and academic endeavour became a further spur to better practices, even to interesting innovations in the evening students' daily teaching. But how could one contrive to give sufficient and timely experience to those who were newcomers to teacher training? Theory and practice simply *had* to be interwoven. One of the obstacles was that the time students did spend in schools gave them too little responsibility to see, let alone to face and analyse, the consequences of the teaching they did. They usually took over a supervisor's class for a period here and there; they had to be slotted into his programme, and so had little scope for planning their own; the class management was indirectly the supervisor's, and only minimally the student's own; and the students left the schools with little consecutive teaching of any class, almost no chance of getting to know pupils, and little feedback from pupils to guide them in examining their successes and failures.

It had meanwhile become increasingly urgent for student-teachers to gain experience in policy-making and curriculum planning in the schools. In Victoria, the State Department of Education had (pressingly) invited schools to plan their own curriculum and to innovate — in short, had given secondary schools a degree of autonomy quite unprecedented in

Victoria, indeed in Australia. The teachers' unions, particularly the Victorian Secondary Teachers' Association, were taking an increasing interest in professional matters and helping to create lively interest and often heated debate in the teaching world.

By the late 1960s there was widespread criticism from the schools that teacher-training institutions were failing to educate students to meet the new, exacting demands made of teachers. Pilot schools had been set up under the aegis of the State Education Department and a newly-formed representative body, the Curriculum Advisory Board (CAB) to innovate in curriculum planning and school organization. I was an inaugural member of the CAB (founded in 1966) and so was closely associated with the experimental pilot schools. By the time I left for study leave in 1970, the influence of the State Education Department, the pilot schools, the CAB and the unions had led to a ground-swell of curriculum change throughout Victorian schools, but they were starved of sufficient supportive guidance in their endeavours.

Three things were now obvious. Teacher training must find a way of relating theory and practice for its students; schools must be able to turn to teacher-training institutions for practical as well as academic help; and teacher-training bodies had to inform themselves of the new realities in the schools.

What I saw Harvard doing in 1970 in its Master of Arts in Teaching (MAT), funded by Federal money from TTT (Trainers of Teacher Trainers), suggested some ways in which schools and universities could work profitably together. Harvard staff and higher degree research students worked with a network of schools in fostering and monitoring innovation. A virile partnership existed in which schools inspired the University and the University helped the schools with innovations and planning that could be jointly undertaken, examined, developed and evaluated. Why could we not at Melbourne also help schools in shared ventures with our staff, and with our research students and trainees? Why should we not encourage school teachers more actively to pursue their practical concerns in a university context? There seemed to be great scope in the University's offering real help to those schools which trained our students, so that student-teachers would become valuable to schools and not just a necessary evil that schools endured out of a sense of professional duty.

Moreover, the gap between schools and universities needed to be breached: for example, as my active memory of school teaching receded, and I became increasingly preoccupied with historical research, I was in danger of feeling phoney as I sat in the back of classes watching students trying to teach. But our research, too, needed to be conducted with the smell of the classroom in our nostrils, and this was as true of empirical research as of philosophy or history. There was, moreover, great scope for action research to be undertaken by schools and universities together.

Late in 1970, on my return from study leave, a Faculty committee was set up by the Dean (Professor A. G. Austin), consisting of a small group of University staff who were anxious to foster the ideas I had on radically changing teacher training. We worked towards preparing a submission seeking external funds for a pilot scheme. I was assisted in drawing up the submission by Kwong Lee Dow (subsequently a Professor at Melbourne); Morris Williams, the Sub-Dean who was in charge of teaching practice, helped in 1972 to try out the idea of continuous teaching practice within the traditional course by placing a handful of students in two schools, Sydney Road Community School and Trinity Grammar School, for two days a week throughout the year; both schools were anxious to try out the new procedure. In 1973, Course B began with our students being placed in these two schools and in Swinburne Community School.

As a member of the CAB, I had already had some connexions with these schools. I had worked with Trinity Grammar, an independent boys' school, in introducing an experimental 'General Studies' course at fifth form (eleventh grade); and in 1971 Sydney Road was started as an annexe of Moreland High School, with which I had worked for some years, since Moreland was one of the important pilot schools chosen by the CAB. I was also familiar with the work of Swinburne Community School, set up (also in 1971) as an annexe to Swinburne Technical School.

Sydney Road and Swinburne annexes were both small — each of a hundred or fewer pupils. They had adopted the term 'Community School', but, in other countries, might equally have been called 'free school', 'alternative school', or even 'school without walls', although both operated in church halls and were part of the State secondary system. They were planned to be run on democratic lines and to provide small groups for study so that individual children did not get lost, as they so often did in large institutions. Like Trinity, they both preferred our two-days-a-week-throughout-the-year programme to intermittent 'teaching rounds'. The community schools in particular found student-teachers useful in helping to reduce the size of teaching groups, and all three schools encouraged students to work with individual pupils needing special help. We, for our part, needed above all to have schools that were our friends and welcomed our students. We needed flexible schools to work in. And we needed schools that were rethinking their practices. It could be argued that we should have started Course B in schools more typical of the whole system; but the considerations mentioned outweighed all others.

Towards the end of 1972 we had been notified that the University of Melbourne would provide two extra lecturers for the experimental Course out of a Federal 'New Developments' grant given to inject a shot in the arm of older universities. The Australian Advisory Committee for Research and Development in Education (AACRDE), to which I had first applied for Federal funds, also made a grant that enabled us to contribute money to an external evaluation of the Course and to pay for research/secretarial help in the massive records that this would make necessary.

The external evaluation was undertaken by the Centre for the Study of Higher Education at Melbourne University. Barbara Falk (then the Director), Torrey Orton (engaged on the evaluation full time from 1974 to 1976), and Cleo Macmillan from the Centre became valuable colleagues while firmly retaining the necessary detachment. Their task was an extraordinarily difficult one. They recognized that a new course, run on new principles of the kind we planned, could not be evaluated by the usual instruments and techniques. Our project would have to be regarded as an example of action research and could be judged only by descriptive and analytical methods of a clinical rather than a quantitative kind. This was a problem that not only concerned Course B but also importantly concerned all educational innovation. The AACRDE obviously had had early reservations about helping to fund a venture that did not lend itself to tight, traditional means of evaluation. The Centre was to make its contribution not only to current thinking about the place of participatory, 'formative' evaluation of educational innovation but also to Course B itself, as this book in part will show, though the fuller story is to be found in the Centre's official report.[1]

The condition on which the 'New Developments' funds were made available was that the parent body, in my case the Faculty of Education, had to absorb the experiment into its normal funding after three years — or else wind it down as a failure. The constant worry of seeing how we could ever be absorbed, no matter how successful we might be, hung over us right through the early years. By 1974, when our numbers more than doubled, we functioned on a normal or below normal staff-student ratio, despite the funds we were contributing to the Faculty. Education's staff-student ratio was abysmal at the best of times, and the strain on Course B, with endless reporting to donors, vast recordings for evaluation, and constant meetings, either to keep the course going well or to argue our case politically, put us under severe strain. We were promised the help, part-time, of a psychologist, a sociologist and a philosopher. Except in the case of philosophy, however, every staff member we were given was temporary, and so we had the services of people often for only one year, and it naturally took months before a newcomer could begin to understand our unusual approach and contribute usefully. Even so, our numbers rose to fifty in 1974 and thereafter to sixty, which led to the schools attached to us being increased to thirteen or more.[2]

Fortunately, we had one other supporter, A. E. Schruhm, the then Director of Secondary Education in the Victorian State Department. I knew from working with him, in my capacity as chairman of the steering committee of the CAB, that he was stolid when in opposition and staunch when in agreement — and he could be both at the same time to the one person. After putting me through a gruelling cross-examination about my proposed experimental Course, he supported my application for funds and promised that one supernumerary (that is, additional) teacher would be given to any high school that joined the scheme, and would be appointed jointly to the school and the Course. This was an extraordinarily generous offer made at a time of severe teaching shortage. His reason, he said, was that a scheme of teacher training that was closely in touch with schools, and helped them, instead of being divorced from them, would obtain his full co-operation. Unfortunately, Mr Schruhm had retired before his generous offer was fully taken up. (But Dr Ray Maddocks, newly appointed an Assistant Director-General of Education, did come to our help later when Lloyd Jones was jointly appointed to Flemington High School and Course B in 1976.)

With the grant of outside help, without which the Course could never have been set up, Bernard Newsome, Rodney Fawns and I began the Course in 1973. The students were largely self-selected; but since there were more applicants than places we tried to get an equal mix of men and women, and of pass and honours graduates, and to select according to the Methods that we could offer, beginning with history, social science, English and science, which our trio itself could man. For other Methods we needed help from the State Department of Education, school teachers, and other members of the University.

Having received external funding, we were committed to the principles and plans advocated in my various submissions. The danger of introducing a new orthodoxy bothered me in the early stages of the experiment but, once constant action became necessary, we were in danger of becoming too adaptable, too greatly influenced by immediate and perhaps passing problems, but certainly never static. Nevertheless, our basic underlying principles, though variously interpreted from time to time, remained constant.

Since the chapters that follow are dictated largely by how students tell the story in the diaries they agreed to write, and they seldom wrote a connected narrative (that was not the point of the exercise), the framework of the Course is best given now.

As has already been mentioned, the overarching principle on which the Course was based was the cross-fertilization of theory and practice. To bring this about, and for other reasons already explained as important in themselves, our relationship with schools was centrally important. For Course B the schools were the linch-pin of the experiment from the outset, and the school teachers who worked most closely with us were indispensable; but as chapter 7 will show, there were often pulls between schools and University, and our success in becoming accepted by schools in full trust was slow and chequered, sometimes for reasons quite beyond the control of either — such as the turnover of school staff. Even so, in some schools an excellent working partnership developed both in teacher training itself and in fostering action research. Many of the teachers from schools affiliated with the Course play a large part in its academic programme, and some of them are, at the same time, engaged in research degrees with us. Our ex-students, now teachers, have also contributed importantly to our work and to the parternship between schools and the Course.

Before the Course began, the Faculty set up a Schools' Committee, with deliberative, advisory and policy-making powers about the conduct of school practice in Course B. This has been a vigorous body and an important link. Each school that takes Course B students is represented on the Committee, as are students and various groups from the University staff. Many imaginative suggestions from the Committee have been adopted and have become part of our policy and practice.

Looked at from the students' point of view, there were three postulates that guided our thinking and planning. The first was that for each student the problem of becoming a teacher was an intensely personal individual matter. The second was that to become an effective teacher, the student needed to be scholarly not only in his teaching subjects but also in his approach to education. The third was that graduate students, especially those who were to be teachers and therefore needed to think about democratic school practices, should have as much experience as we could give them in thinking and acting autonomously during their training year. I shall look at these three postulates in that order.

We considered that, to the extent to which teaching is an art — an imaginative, empathetic engagement between teacher and learner — it is ill suited to mass methods of instruction by precept. Our first postulate was that students had to discover an appropriate teaching style. In doing so, each had first to ask the questions 'Who am I?' and 'How do others, especially children, see me?' This sort of personal knowledge could best be fostered by feedback from children and sensitive support from University and school staff, as well as from fellow-students. The initiation into the classroom could be gradual and carefully planned; but when a student is sheltered for a whole year of training from facing these questions realistically, it merely postpones the shock until the first year of actual employment — when fewer supports are available. We knowingly accepted that for our students the Dip. Ed. year would put them at risk; but we could not possibly have foreseen in detail what that would mean, and precisely what sorts of problems would arise. Chapters 2 and 3 tell something of that story, largely as students saw it.

In postulating, second, that, for teachers to be effective, they had to face the task in a scholarly manner, we were favoured in one sense, in that all our students were graduates, and most of them came from the University of Melbourne, which is a highly selective university; but there were two major dangers in this that were associated with the tasks before us. It was not good enough to be knowledgeable in one's teaching subjects; it was also necessary to be informed and thoughtful about the role of education in a particular society, about the social pressures that affected various kinds of children's responses to formal education, about the way in which children learn, and about the moral basis of a teacher's authority. Some of these issues meant, for each student, a totally new introduction in a very short time to a complex world of thought. There was no shared realm of ignorance, either, that we could take for granted. Some had a strong academic background in political theory, some were strong in psychology, some in philosophy, some in none of these things, and all were weak in at least some of them. To find a programme that was equally suitable to all was quite impossible. I know of no other university faculty that faces a problem of quite this magnitude — that is, of a student body so utterly diverse in its background. We decided that students must help to teach each other from their own particular strengths, and this meant encouraging group learning. We also decided that the best time for tackling theoretical questions was when they arose in actual teaching. It would have been almost valueless to tell people in advance what problems we foresaw as the ones they would face: it was much better for them to formulate their own questions from their own experiences. Beyond this, we ourselves had to learn the hard way. Given our assumptions that the solution to this problem did *not* lie in trying to teach educational philosophy, educational psychology or educational sociology as separate academic studies, we were not quite sure about the best way to tackle the interdisciplinary course that we called 'Curriculum Studies'. I had said in my submission for a grant that I could not commit myself in advance to a definite view of how to fuse the various branches of educational studies, but that I hoped experience in running the Course would help us to clarify this. And that is what chapter 1 is about.

When it came to the side of the academic work that was concerned with the students' preparation for classroom teaching, we seemed to be on firmer ground. They were all graduates: they were all formally certified as being academically proficient in the subjects they were to teach, though possibly many of them were somewhat arrogant about their scholastic 'know-how'. This, we thought, made it particularly difficult to have to treat them as novices in education studies and theories, but gave us a great starting point for a rigorous programme in teaching methods. Our rigour should come from building upon existing strengths, in a way that we could not do in Curriculum Studies. It was, we thought, in our work in 'Methods' that we could break down the notion that Dip. Ed. was 'a soft option', or, as one of my colleagues (not then in Course B) had put it, a year that seemed to students like the morning after the night before.

In Victoria, for the students' two 'Methods', the common combinations are English and history (or social science), and science and mathematics; but there are many variants that include geography, economics or modern languages.

Our major emphasis in Methods was to lead students to reflect upon the nature and teachability of the subjects they had specialized in at university. Methods, as we predicted, never gave us the same sort of trouble as Curriculum Studies; but there were some tensions, most notably the pull between some students' demands for 'tips for teachers' and others' delight in taking flight into highbrow intellectual discussion, both of which we had to resist. There was also the necessity to break down subject-mindedness and over-specialization, without overlapping with what was being done just for that purpose in Curriculum Studies; but this was a relatively minor problem in a small and tightly-knit course. These and other questions related to Methods are the subject of chapter 4.

We placed great emphasis on the Methods courses, often giving a whole morning or afternoon to each. Whereas in the traditional course at Melbourne much Methods work is taken by teachers seconded part-time from the schools, in Course B four of the biggest Methods courses were taken by the core University staff (English, science, history, social science); and when we added part-time school teachers to the staff we tried to do so from the schools that were affiliated with us: they became very closely attached to the core staff at the University and actively engaged in planning our policies. There was of necessity (and certainly not by design) more chopping and changing than we liked in some Methods because we could not obtain for lengthy appointments all the staff we needed.

To discuss the Course under the headings 'Teaching Practice', 'Curriculum Studies' and 'Methods' is quite misleading, since, by its very nature, the Course did not fit into nice neat slots. Both Curriculum Studies and Methods were closely tied in to the students' practical teaching. Every member of staff, particularly every member of Methods staff, like every student, was concerned with teaching practice. A lecturer had not only to know what was happening in the schools: he had also to be able to help students to see and to formulate consequent theoretical questions. There were great advantages in having graduate students, but for the most part they were so accustomed to learning the skills of answering other people's (their lecturers') questions that it took a great deal of relearning for them to begin to *ask* significant questions for themselves. Moreover, the ways in which they had learned as undergraduates, even their whole concept of the subjects they had studied, were often quite unsuited to school learning. An extraordinary number of them had managed to complete successfully three or four years of study of, say, history or a science, that left them with a very shadowy and arid idea of the nature of their subject. This difficulty is recurrently illustrated throughout the book. As staff, we could do little about it unless we saw what happened when these students were teaching.

This was a severely testing problem for some of the staff that joined us, especially those whose experience of schools was slight — as can happen even in an education faculty. But no one volunteered to teach in Course B without being willing to work with our students in the schools and with the schools' staff and pupils. Contact with schools, especially with supervisors in the schools, and the constant debates about the Course that went on in our frequent staff meetings, enabled us to learn from each other; and an attitude of serious professional concern did characterize the whole Course. This was one of the most valuable consequences of the Course that had not been fully foreseen in the planning of it, and something of the effect on staff is told in chapter 6.

The third postulate, to which we were immediately committed, was that graduate students (and I quote from the submission for a grant) 'can and should play a major part in constructing their own professional studies' and that they would be responsible for self-evaluation. The most radical thing about the Course was that it was an experiment in student autonomy. Paradoxically, as chapters 5 and 6 will show, student assessment was the least difficult part of the experiment for us, although it was one that gave us great trepidation in the early stages and that caused most raised eyebrows. Since many schools were trying out co-operative methods of assessing pupils, as well as involving pupils in school management and decisions about educational policy, it was essential, we thought, that student-teachers be given first-hand experience in these practices. What must be borne in mind in applying our practices more widely is that our students were relatively mature; they were already graduates who must have had at least some experience in taking responsibility for their own studies; and, whether enthusiastically or reluctantly, they were in the Course to learn a profession, which of itself imposed some self-discipline and often very strong motivation, even dedication.

Given all these warnings about the dangers of generalizing from a

11

special example, we make one small claim confidently. There is much loose talk about 'competition as the necessary incentive to endeavour', or put more crudely, it is said that 'students will not work except for marks'. Course B can claim to have disproved these two statements. This is not to say that competition and marks can *not* be incentives, only that we have shown that they are not always indispensable ones. More than that, Course B graduates will certainly have thought about these questions as well as about pupils' participation in and responsibility for their own learning. They will not all have reached similar conclusions — far from it. Many, probably most, leave the Course still undecided about how they can and will act in these matters when they become full-blown teachers; but at least they will have been encouraged to be open-minded, and their responses will not, we trust, be automatic.

The Course was a total reconstruction of teacher education based on integrating theory itself and relating it to action, on working towards a close partnership with schools, and on experimenting with student autonomy. It was the totality and attempted consistency of the Course that may be regarded as truly innovative. We can find courses, such as Professor Paul Hirst's at Cambridge University, that have integrated their education studies around questions of major concern to trainee teachers. On the other hand, we can find education faculties with a long tradition of close relationships with schools. I have already referred to Harvard's MAT (though I understand that it no longer exists in that form), and Professor John Goodlad is widely known for his insistence on, and demonstration of, the importance of school-based academic research in education. In England, especially in universities where the emphasis on Methods work tends to have a higher status than in Australia, there are many examples of close work with schools — for example at London, Sussex, Bristol, Leicester, Keele, York, and no doubt many others that I have not visited. But even in England, Oxford's recent moves in this direction are regarded as extremely innovative. Some teacher-training institutions have abandoned examinations (Melbourne University has, to a large extent) and experimented with other forms of assessment; but self-assessment is rare indeed, and rarer still is the course in which theory and practice, planning and assessment have all been deliberately reformed to be consistent with the educational principles governing the running of the course.

One reason why reforms tend to be patchy is the difficulty, within an established institution, of introducing root-and-branch changes, and even many of the new universities tend to be timid. What gave us the freedom to make total changes was that we started with a small group and independent money, which meant we did not have to ask favours or make basic compromises; and it is interesting that, in recent years, Melbourne has tended to break into smaller units for Dip. Ed., though the 'theoretical' subjects usually remain intact. It is the totality of our attempted revamping of teacher education that we must be judged by. And it is that which makes this book so difficult to organize.

It is worth repeating that every feature selected for attention flows over into others, and therefore to make too discrete an organization of the material would be false. As soon as one talks about Curriculum Studies, for example, it leads to what is happening concurrently in Methods, to what different students are looking for because of the particular problems they are experiencing in their schools, and to what each of those schools and its supervisors are like. The picture is ever-changing and will not stand still for the observer. This is not to say that the Course was unstructured but rather that the structure could never be precisely anticipated — experiences never occurred in neat, separable compartments, and students' writing about their experiences seldom took the form of a still, hard look at one thing in isolation from others. The recognition of this distinguished the Course from others, and to force the account into a tightly ordered narrative would distort it. Nevertheless, major themes could be extracted, as has been indicated, though at no point could any one of them be tidily isolated from related ones.

The Course *looked* clearly organized enough. On Mondays and/or Tuesdays there were two long Methods seminars. On Wednesdays and Thursdays students were in school. On Friday mornings they were back at university for Curriculum Studies. But in practice it could never work quite like that. There were conflicting pressures on students' time that forced them to work out their own priorities in organizing their lives. At school there might be a crucial staff meeting on Friday morning, or missing the lesson with 2C on Tuesday meant breaking the whole continuity of a series of lessons, or little Pat had run away from home after being beaten up by her drunken father, or Johnnie was in court for shoplifting just when he was beginning to show progress, or there was a school camp that simply could not be missed: at university depth study or a seminar paper had to be worked on at the expense of some school commitment, or a two-day seminar on multi-cultural education or remedial reading would be most valuable, or there had to be an extra planning session before a team-teaching project could be begun.

Teaching is like that, and made a thousand times more difficult by a sudden loss of morale, or a crisis with 4D, or an ill-prepared lesson after staying up until dawn trying to swot it up, or a personal disaster that makes concentration impossible. To pretend that it is otherwise would make a neater but less true book, and I have tried to let many students tell their truths. They undertook to keep diaries that might form the basis of this book, and they chose to hand in either their spontaneous outpourings or a version they censored for us — or nothing at all. I write with their permission. Sometimes I have quoted from their mini-research (their depth studies, which are described in chapter 1), and occasionally from educational autobiographies which we often asked them to write at the beginning of the year. There are other sources, too, such as minutes of meetings, and special reports.

What I trust distinguishes this book from many others on education is that I have sought to select material that would give readers the perspective of the students — of various students enrolled in each of the first four years of the experimental Course. There have been consequent problems, indeed dilemmas, in writing the book. An extract from a student's diary might be chosen because it illustrates one particular point most aptly; but, because the diary extract had been written as often as not to let off steam or to try to sort out a problem by putting it into written words, it would seldom be making one main point — it would rather be a spontaneous expression of a complex set of closely interwoven experiences and events. For a reader to share and understand the students' experiences, and so to re-live what it might feel like when trying to teach, or to learn, it was necessary for me to avoid imposing some preconceived order of my own on their writing — and certainly to avoid censorship.

This is not to say that I claim to be the neutral transmitter of others' views. I believed from the outset that students' accounts would be more lively, more moving, and certainly more authentic than anything I or anyone other than the students themselves could write about what happened to them and to the Course they were in. The selection of themes naturally reflects my own priorities, and there can be little doubt that anyone else writing this book would have made different choices and have given different interpretations. Within the choices I made, I took care not to suppress criticism of the Course and, if anything, I might have erred in presenting unrepresentative adverse criticisms. To some extent the book must be unrepresentative anyway in that many students wrote far more than others (some, indeed, wrote no personal diary at all); a few were dull and uninformative; and the most prolific, interesting writers were often prompted to write at times of greatest distress or irritation. On several occasions a student handed me a diary during the year, and as soon as I read it I realized that this was the least frightening and most effective way for the student to say, 'I need help urgently.' Many times diaries were distressing, and the writer was astonished to discover how upset I was by what he had been through. One example will do. Jenny, who is quoted in this book, so worried me that I rang her immediately and asked her why she had not let me know sooner how painful it had all been, so that we could have done something about it. She laughed apologetically, saying, 'Gwen, don't take it so seriously. When I was miserable I cried on my own shoulder by writing in the diary. When things went well, you wouldn't know. I'd give a dinner party, drink wine and rejoice.'

In basing a book on students' diaries, there is a risk of giving an exaggerated view of the ups and downs, especially of the downs, and this should be borne in mind. As Leonard Woolf put it in volume 2 of his superb autobiography:[3]

> Diaries and letters almost always give an exaggerated, one-sided picture of the writer's state of mind. He is concerned to reproduce as vividly as possible − to make the reader feel as deeply as possible − a mood, only one of many moods which chase one another all day and all night long through our minds and bodies. Even to ourselves we habitually exaggerate the splendours and miseries of our life and forget in the boredom of Wednesday the ecstacy of Tuesday − and vice versa.

The point to be remembered is that the moods are true, though not necessarily representative; and the value of diaries lies not only in the record they provide for those who want to evaluate a course such as ours − the sort of record that no hard-nosed evaluation can provide − but also as a memory of each student's way towards self-knowledge.

Another problem in basing a book on what students say or write is that one is constantly torn by three conflicting aims: the literary value of building up character sketches of the various students, the necessity for anonymity, and the difficult task of sticking to a theme when each student is speculating on something very personal that introduces many themes because that's the way of life. Although I have often chopped the student's writing into bits, noting that bit one is for chapter 2, and bit two is for chapter 5, I have tried to keep enough in each to evoke something of the reality that the student saw and something of the student too. This sometimes makes for a leisurely pace and even an apparent digression. To compound this difficulty, I have written for the layman, not just for the professional, and so when students are saying important things about, say, learning theory, alienation, or autonomy, I have deliberately avoided in my comments theoretical signposts or jargon that would be quickly picked up by the academic in education and would show him where the argument was going. The beauty of students' writing is that most often it is direct, personal and alive, which so little educational literature can claim to be. If students can do it, I thought, I can and should be able to do it myself whenever I intervene. Thus the book may seem deceptively simple, discursive, and lacking in theoretical framework or quotation from authorities.

The students and I agreed that their contributions should be anonymous. Names given them are fictitious almost always, and, when I

15

thought it necessary, I have made the circumstance unrecognizable. I seldom disclose accurately the actual school, the teachers or the pupils concerned in the quotations; but with University staff and with supervisors in schools who were most closely identified with the Course I give proper names, except occasionally as a matter of tact. This was one way of metaphorically footnoting and giving some small part of the recognition due to the staff, whose story this is, just as much as it is mine.

Note

I had intended not to alter a single spelling mistake or infelicity in punctuation in quoting from students; but I found that often this would make intolerable demands on the reader and have done an injustice to the student, who, often writing quickly, informally, and under great stress, would make uncharacteristic slips. All but minor alterations in phraseology are indicated by square brackets, and some of the writing remains as clumsy as the original, for I have tried very carefully never to distort meaning.

To avoid confusion I always call school children 'pupils', though I am well aware that it would often be more proper, correct and dignified to call them 'students'; but I had to reserve that term for the Course B students. The term 'teacher' is confined to school teachers and supervisors, to distinguish them from University staff. These formalities, which are also followed in the quotations from students, are solely for clarity and are by no means indicative of any real or imagined hierarchy — indeed, some of the most inspired and scholarly contributions came from school 'pupils' and 'teachers'.

Sexism in the English language was one of my most intractable problems. After trying various ways of giving 'her' or 'she' equality with 'him' or 'he', I gave the language best, reluctantly adopting the masculine form. Even if I could have found a better formula on those points, I defy anyone to show me how to make 'fellow-student' a neuter.

Melbourne, 1978   GMD

Chapter 1

Thinking about education

Experience is the teacher

Those of us who planned Course B sought to provide a training year that was a thoroughgoing attempt to blend theory and practice. First of all this meant that if the University staff running the Course held particular values or had convictions about how learning most effectively takes place they had to be living examples of their beliefs and not merely to talk about them in the abstract. Second, it meant that student-teachers had to be given a year in which they could find their own way towards values and convictions not only that they could live with, but which they, too, were prepared to exemplify in their own teaching. Hence the year was to be a study of action accompanied by further action refined by reflexion. Continuous teaching practice of at least two days a week throughout most of the academic year was designed to give the students a foothold for their academic educational studies so that they were thinking about, reading about, and discussing what they were doing and became less dependent on what we, as staff, were thinking up for them. We wanted them to formulate their own questions and not merely to answer questions that we formulated for them.

But where to begin? Experience could not be manufactured or forced quickly. Most students came to us as subject specialists, but as novices in educational studies. Some of them were not convinced that they really wanted to be teachers; but most, probably all, cared very personally about what sort of a showing they would make in the classroom. This shared concern was the obvious starting point.

It would have been brutal, and indeed it was impracticable, to place all students in school at the beginning of the academic year. We began the Course with a fortnight spent at the University. This enabled us to try to make the University a social and intellectual centre. It gave us a chance to see as best we could that students were suitably placed in

17

particular schools — a thing that could not be effectively done on paper or even on the basis of introductory interviews.

That first fortnight served as a very early reminder of how vapid educational discussion can become unless it is rooted in experience. The only experience that students could call upon was their own education. Years of book-work and lectures had given them an impatient urge to be tested in action, and possibly their closeness to their own education untested against a wider reality left them with a distorted memory of what they had gained in the process. The typical graduate (if there is such a being) was quite out of touch with ordinary pupils, and usually had little understanding of severe learning problems or of the all-too-common view found in school pupils that education had little to offer them.

We planned the first fortnight more carefully than any other part of the University work. We took our students to schools; we brought school children to meet our students at the University; we set up small teaching projects with pupils that we, as staff, undertook with the students; we showed and discussed carefully chosen films; we introduced stimulating books, and we gave what we thought were seminal papers on some of the central educational problems. Often we were raising what seemed like remote problems, or ones that were uncomfortably pressing and consequently — rightly — agitated the students. That was perhaps no bad thing. It was bad only when the students remained unmoved, and our questions were seen as non-questions.

After the first fortnight, each student was attached to a particular school for Wednesdays and Thursdays. It was a firm conviction of the schools affiliated with us that students should be attached to the one school throughout the whole year. In our first year we moved most students to a new school in third term to give them a wider knowledge of the school system; but at the request of the Schools Committee (see p. 8), we decided against this after 1973 except when there were special reasons for transferring a student. The Schools Committee, on balance, were right. Their request suggested the schools' keen sense of commitment to the students who were with them and indicated that, as the year progressed, students came increasingly to be counted as assets rather than liabilities at their schools. What was sacrificed in breadth and variety of experience was compensated for in the acceptance of growing responsibility. We also deliberately fostered a widening of experience by encouraging students to work with some of their fellow-students in other kinds of schools, and by various school visits.

For their part, the affiliated schools gave serious thought to inducting students gradually and purposefully into teaching. Usually, at first, one teacher was primarily responsible for one student, and students began by observing a few lessons (prolonged observations would have only added to anxiety, for they were too inexperienced to be astute observers) and by sharing small-group teaching with the supervisor in his particular classes. Students also were given care of particular pupils who needed extra help. Gradually students took over, first, small sections of a lesson and then a full lesson. Eventually they took whole units of work with one class, and gained experience of teaching throughout all age-ranges. It did not always work as smoothly as this; but it often did.

Curriculum Studies – a problem-centred approach

On Friday mornings the students returned to the University for Curriculum Studies – an interdisciplinary course in educational theory and literature. But the division into theory and practice was by no means as clear cut as the timetable suggests. Many of the most fruitful theoretical enquiries took place in schools with supervising teachers or with fellow-students or in school staff meetings, not to mention in the 'caf', at parties or in pubs. Curriculum Studies, however, brought together students of diverse academic backgrounds – from all the diverse faculties from which the students graduated – and tried to ensure that some insight was gained into the main contributions that various educational studies (empirical or theoretical) could make towards solving educational problems. Since students came to us pretty blasé about their intellectual and scholarly acumen, but babes in matters educational, this was our great challenge, and it manifested itself most sharply early in the year. Almost everything that one tried at this stage seemed to need something to precede it. If one started by putting students into the classroom, they seemed to need some foreknowledge of what to expect, and they needed a neutral base to belong to at University. If one started in the seminar room, one was quickly driven to draw on experience in the classroom. Students' fears about teaching were intensified by their fears about getting to know each other when coming in to what was expected to be a fairly tightly-knit group, and their fears about what sorts of monsters the staff might turn out to be.

I had always argued that, because students entered the Course at the end of years of intensive academic work, we should start on a pretty high academic tack. I was soon proved wrong in this. It might have point in Methods work (see pp. 9–11), where students with a fairly homogeneous background were together, but Curriculum Studies was another matter altogether. Piaget, say, might have been a psychology graduate's meat but was an English graduate's poison, especially early in the year. Christina Stead's *The Man Who Loved Children* might throw great light on human relations of educational importance for the literary student but be baffling to the maths graduate, whereas the maths student could obviously more readily converse on factor analysis of intelligence than could the English or history graduate. Such is the problem in any first year of educational studies.

We were convinced that we should ease students into the study of educational questions and the vast literature, to which they were new-comers, not by introducing them to the so-called foundation educational disciplines (psychology, sociology, philosophy, history, and the like) as separate subjects, but rather by centring our studies on such problems as seemed urgent to them. Since students came to us not only with different academic preparation but also with different personal experiences and influences arising from their own education, our first task was to gauge what preconceptions and anxieties preoccupied them. It was then up to staff and students to respond to the problems that arose as the students gained teaching experience. This, we thought, was the best approach in itself. Added to this was the pragmatic consideration that it is utterly unrealistic to believe that students can be initiated into educational psychology, educational sociology, philosophy of education, history of education with any degree of adequacy in a one-year course, a good half of which is spent in schools.

Of course there are different kinds of thinking that are appropriate to different kinds of learning. At a purely common-sense level one would not talk about measuring free will, or feeling compassion for the Second Law of Thermodynamics, or feeling ashamed about sunsets, or learning the facts that would enable a woman to say she wants to have children, or looking for the evidence when someone asks to go to the lavatory. Nor would one look for the same kind of verification of the statements: 'the car won't run because it has no petrol'; 'educational standards have fallen because of permissive teaching methods'; 'Tolstoy is a better novelist than Waugh.' One might wonder, however, whether subject specialization is the best way to guide students to discriminate between when it is appropriate to look for hard evidence, or to be rationalistic, or to be spontaneous in judging, or merely to respond to what is before them. It is hard to say which bedevils us more – super-stition or a witless pressing for scientific methods.

Certainly the most difficult educational problems that students face can seldom be answered by reference to any one subject, and insistence on introducing educational studies by teaching the foundation 'disci-plines' as separate subjects can cause myopia as well as fragmented thinking in approaching real problems. On the other hand, education is the victim of platitudes and jargon that mask, or are attempts to mask, absence of systematic, sustained thought.

Course B's concern with this problem is shared by many educationists throughout the Western world. At this stage I shall concentrate on one, though many more could be cited. In a paper presented to the English

University Council for the Education of Teachers in January 1976, 'The P.G.C.E. Course: its Objectives and their Nature', Professor Paul Hirst pointed to the limitations presented by having only one year in which to prepare graduates for teaching. It would be 'a deceit', he maintained, if the 'prime aim' in such a year was not to prepare students for their first teaching jobs. He regarded it as illegitimate for a postgraduate course to take upon itself the responsibility for giving students a 'liberal or general education' *per se*:

> I do not doubt that any satisfactory training year will necessarily contribute significantly to students' liberal education, but it seems to me a simple confusion of priorities if elements are introduced into the course for this explicit purpose.

The sort of inappropriate response to questions of different kinds, such as the ones I have just illustrated with deliberate exaggeration, may reveal an inadequate general education — a lopsidedness in a student's preparation. We shall find many examples of this in various chapters of this book. We shall find scientists pressing hard for evidence or data that humanists think out of place. We shall find humanists arguing from hunches or conviction, when scientists rightly point out that empirical evidence is needed if it can be found. More fruitfully, we shall find many examples of students' becoming aware of deficiencies in their own education when it comes to facing practical problems or teasing out theoretical ones in dialogue with students with quite different academic backgrounds.

If we tend to agree with Hirst, this is as it should be. Our programme was designed to focus on educational questions that were central to good performance. The broadening of the students' education grew out of reflecting on professional concerns: it did not follow a blueprint for a theoretical curriculum that tried first of all to ensure that everyone was absolutely comprehensively educated. Hirst asserts that

> There are vast areas of educational psychology, educational administration, sociology, philosophy, history of education, comparative education, and even curriculum theory which have no really justifiable place in a [postgraduate] course. We need to filter out the elements in these areas that are in fact significant for the practical business of teaching and to restrict ourselves to these.

This suggests a reversal of emphasis, which Course B certainly exemplifies. I would add to Hirst's plea for a different focus determined by professional concerns, that the *way* in which they are examined should always be 'liberal' in that it should always be guided by opening up to students as many different ways as possible of looking at the problems and as many ways as we can find of providing insight into

21

them. Thus the concern for our students to be liberally educated will be integral to everything we do and the results are likely to be better, for, as Hirst reminds us:

> theoretical knowledge becomes significant for the practical activities of teaching only if it is in fact applied in the interpretation of teaching situations and in the formation of practical judgments. Studied purely academically there is no reason to suppose even the most relevant theory will in fact be applied; indeed there is much evidence to suggest that it will not be ... Mere experience does not itself provide the concepts needed to understand what is going on ... I conclude that both schools and training institutions have a proper contribution to make to the students' professional development in its intellectual aspects.

How, then, do we go about it, and where do we begin?

The Curriculum Studies programme was our attempt to find the answers to those questions. We chose as our content at the beginning an examination of successful and unsuccessful learning. We drew on students' reflexions about when in their own education they had learned most, when they had drawn blanks, and why. We all wrote educational autobiographies — staff, students and sometimes (when they were interested to join in) the Course's secretaries. The task itself was a profitable and illuminating way to begin the year. It sounded so easy compared with most university assignments. There was no reading required, no one would notice poor organization or expression, for the submissions could be anonymous, and we made it clear that we were not in the least interested in judging any of the submissions except in terms of the enlightenment they might provide; yet we all found the task exquisitely difficult. Masses of fascinating material were handed in, and to deal adequately with it and its potentialities as a teaching/learning device would require another book. We learnt from bitter experience in 1974 that we had to be very careful and tactful about how to use the material (see pp. 101–2), and certainly it could not be used to full effect except in small groups who knew and trusted each other, and so it offered no solution to how to start the year's seminars. We could, without doubt, have derived much more value from the autobiographies if we had used them for more sustained work; but that is something we still have to explore much further and to develop more fully.

Again, there was a time gap before we could effectively draw on students' teaching experience to provide *the* major source of systematic study. We believed that the act of thoughtful teaching can and should be the integrating and generative discipline in a course such as ours; but we had to allow the students time to acquire the necessary experience.

Underlying every decision that was taken about what we should do and how we should do it was the assumption that the Course staff were constantly under inspection and that, if we forbore to preach, our beliefs could be inferred from our practices. Hence, to take the example already used, since we ran Curriculum Studies as an interdisciplinary course, we did so partly to encourage students to consider the very question of subject specialization as against teaching around themes or problems. Could the students see, as well as being told, that in the emphasis we gave to teaching Methods, an apparently subject-based extension of their undergraduate specializations, we used an existing and shared starting point for moving out to curriculum and learning as a whole? By contrast, were the students aware that we merged the main 'educational disciplines', where there were too few common starting points, into our Curriculum Studies programme as a means towards moving inwards to the complexities of educational practice and the relevance of different lines of academic enquiry?

The second line of approach was pedagogically by far the harder one. If we could find no common starting ground, we had to create it. This we decided to do by introducing students literally and vicariously to children and schools. Our choice of books was guided by several criteria. A well-written book, we thought, had already the means of capturing interest and in addition would show that educational writing need not be dull and clumsy; if it was also popular, it indicated that it expressed something of the mood of the times. Each book, in addition, had to throw some light on why and when learning/teaching succeeded or failed. Some books such as *Letter to a Teacher*, written by the pupils at the School of Barbiana, met all these criteria; Herbert Kohl was another obvious choice, whereas Paulo Freire gripped many students' imagination despite the stylistic difficulties that, in translation at any rate, he presents to the reader. But we were never on target with all students at the one time, as some diary entries early in the year indicate:

> I suppose I'm no real judge, but I view such books as vaguely uninteresting – something about which I can talk heatedly if and when prodded, but not otherwise. *Dibs* I liked. Kohl I felt I could as a teacher have most in common with. *Young Teachers and Reluctant Learners* was something I did feel had a lot to say. What, I don't know, but it was relevant. To what? Lord, I don't know. The School of Barbiana I felt removed from my situation ...

Well, really! One sighs with agreement when he concludes: 'I suppose I'll have to prepare to ask myself demanding questions.' It is *not*, apparently, that he found the books too simple, but even the reading that he liked seemed 'vaguely uninteresting'. This sort of muddled reaction was common in the first few weeks:

> I found a lot of the Friday seminars fairly irrelevant at this stage
> although they were quite interesting in themselves ... I felt that none
> of us knew enough about teaching to really know what the books
> were talking about (none of the Dip. Eds., of course). [Thanks for
> that backhanded compliment to staff.] I think that it would prob-
> ably have been better if we'd left this until 2nd or 3rd term & done
> learning theory in first term.

Yes, second or third term would have been better. The longer the year
went on the easier it became to teach anything — practical or theoretical — for the basis had been laid. Our problem was how and where to
begin — and we *had* tried learning theory with disastrous results. How
can you talk about how children learn until students know some children
and watch them learning — or not learning? Again, clearly written and
popular books were not being criticized for being too simple, but rather
for raising new problems.

If *we* had a problem in finding common ground among our students,
although all of them were united in preparing to be teachers, what
problems would *they* face in finding common ground among their
pupils? The plea for learning theory, I suspect, was a desperate plea for
a quick recipe to be used to make children 'learn' and thus to help
teachers teach first up. Another student, Jill, who had graduated with
psychology as a major study, knew that it was not so simple:

> I really began the course thinking that I couldn't learn to teach & I
> think if I'd been through ... any other course I could still think
> that. There's just no way of relating structured subjects like philos-
> ophy of ed, psych etc. to kids if you're not there teaching them ...
>
> The thing which characterized the year for me was thinking again.
> Something I'd forgotten how to do at university [as an undergrad-
> uate]. One of the things which helped this most was the breakdown
> of barriers between traditional subjects. Another was working with
> people with very different interests.
>
> I'm stunned at how much I've internalized of our conversations &
> curriculum studies seminars. All those psychologists I'd poured shit
> on for years turned out to have something to say to me. Not so
> much in the seminars themselves — I often felt at a loss then. But the
> continual reference to them, the sudden moments of awareness that
> they were on about questions I am too, as I looked at the world
> around me, & people, especially at school, talked about the parts
> they found relevant to them in our informal talks — often just sitting
> in the middle of the hall.
>
> That goes for theorists too as well as Kohl & the Letter to a
> Teacher & others I can't name. It horrifies me that other dip edders
> from other courses haven't ever heard of some of the writers/books I

consider absolutely essential to our course — eg Freire, Lost for Words, Language & Learning, Basil Bernstein, Kelly, Bruner, Myth of the Deprived Child ...

I've decided I want to teach more ... And if a course can bring me from a position of never wanting to teach to becoming committed to it —it's just got to be good.

It should be noted that this diary entry was made late in the year while reflecting on the year as a whole, and there is a lesson to be learned from taking too seriously every minute criticism that students utter at the time of their seminars — or their own teaching! If they are all 'turned off' by everything, there is something wrong with the everything. It is perhaps asking too much for total success, just as it is ludicrous to expect anything to grow out of total boredom and consequent withdrawal, intellectually speaking. Some ideas are immediately fruitful; some lie dormant and take time and change before they germinate, like Jill's reaction to psychology in her first degree; some are still-born, or, even worse, sterile to begin with. But it is romantic, if one longs to have a child, to hope that every act of intercourse will produce pregnancy.

No teacher and no student can, by definition, know what seeds have been planted until they become fertilized. One student, Prue, had something to teach us and herself on this score. She made the staff feel they had completely failed with her, for she often missed University classes in first term, sometimes for weeks on end. For her the heart of the Course was found in her school. 'I'm a "doer" rather than a "thinker",' she wrote at the end of the year, 'and for this reason, I placed more emphasis on teaching practice than on attending method and curriculum sessions for a more theoretical approach.' But how could we be confident that she was learning anything from her year? In second term she turned to us — to Bernie Newsome — for help when she had what she called a 'discipline problem ... aggravated by my inexperience'. When Bernie visited her, he 'gave me an over-all perspective on what I was doing, at a time when I was too submerged in classroom activity to sort this out for myself.' Even so, this gave us little confidence that the year was working for Prue. As she said, 'I was teaching at and above them. There was too much giving out of information which was dull and useless, and appeared to be given for its own sake.'

It was not until the second half of the year that we began to feel reassured. She had good supervisors and they gave glowing reports of her teaching, describing her as probably the best student they had ever had. By this time, too, she had become deeply involved in an option on Children's Literature as part of Curriculum Studies. Prue wrote at the end of the year:

What I did not gain from the year was more the fault of my personal limitations rather than of the Course or its staff. I have always tended to work and solve problems by myself ...

I suppose my first concern in teaching was simply to get through classes in a reasonable manner — to develop basic teaching skills and strategies and to get to know something about kids. I now find that I need to have a theoretical grasp of, and an over-all framework of ideas ... on which to base and improve my practical teaching. In the earlier part of the year I couldn't make much sense of the theoretical works we were presented with. Some of them struck me as common-sense, but even these tended to go in one ear and out the other. Many of the discussions about these lacked depth and seemed too hurried. It was only after quite a bit of personal teaching that their relevance sank in properly. For instance, I found myself promoting 'banking' education* but had to face the disastrous results. I had read Freire previously and at the time I had thought 'Yes, that's true' ... His message only came through loud and clear when I had to face these problems in my own teaching.

Prue's account raises more important issues. Despite our anxieties and doubts, the Course had given Prue room to move, and showed that while she had pushed aside much of what we offered at the beginning, she had unconsciously tucked away a good deal that she subsequently found enlightening when she came to clarify her thinking and teaching. Perhaps if we had driven her harder she would have acquired more intellectual resources to turn to: perhaps, on the other hand, she would have 'backed off', to use her own term, even more.

How students learn

Important questions arise for us from Prue's account. There is the very subtle and elusive question of when the teacher ought to push and when he ought to let go. The reactions of serious students like Prue also led us to wonder what, if anything, was fundamentally wrong with the way we started the Course.

In Prue's case, although we did not know it for some time, we had been successful in offering some ways of looking at things that later clicked into place when she was wrestling with a real problem. Although

---

*She is referring here to Freire's characterization of much education as a one-way activity in which the teacher deposits knowledge in a passive receptacle — the student. His scathing metaphor indicates that knowledge is being treated as a materially valuable possession.

much of what teachers offer is permanently cast aside by their learners, some of the important things that are what Freire would call 'generative' are stored away and called forth to refine and develop thinking at a later date. This is what Michael Polanyi would call 'tacit knowing' and Jerome Bruner would call intuiting concepts before we can verbalize them. Once we verbalize them we further order our thinking and can proceed to even more subtle, refined and abstract thinking, and this we can express economically in more abstract codes, a sort of verbal short-hand. Being introduced to Freire began the process for Prue. Although we could not manipulate or in any way control when and why Freire would fall into place for Prue, suddenly one of his basic concepts, 'banking' education, gained personal meaning for her. No doubt we had made mistakes in our introductory sessions, but, by introducing ideas that we knew (better than novice teachers could know) could throw light on teaching, and by constantly relating ideas to the practice that students were undergoing, we had a better chance of hitting the mark than a purely practical or a purely theoretical course could have.

And then there is the reverse side of the process, and this I am less confident about explaining. Many 'successful' students and pupils become adept at playing intellectual games with ideas that they can manipulate at will and verbalize with great articulateness but from which they remain personally detached. The worst example of this is the slick use of jargon, seen all too often in 'successful' essays or exam papers. Sometimes the process of genuine learning and structuring that has gone on is forgotten, and when they have to communicate with more ignorant, less sophisticated people, students cannot re-embody their thought processes. Those processes often have lost their meaning and become submerged. This is an exquisitely difficult problem that novice teachers are forced to face. They have lost their commitment to their ideas — if indeed they ever had it. This is seen when the simple question flaws the 'wise' man and shows the emptiness of his abstrac-tions. This, too, had happened to Prue when she found herself doling out 'dull and useless' information whose value she failed to question. In effect, she found herself talking to herself, and not very interestingly at that. We can and shall see many examples of that happening. There can be no better form of experience in re-embodying ideas, of revitalizing thought processes, than the practice of teaching. Until the teacher learns to ask himself, 'How did I get here?', he has no hope of taking the uninitiated with him by similar paths. Once he does that he enriches his own thinking. Hence we find, to take extreme cases, many teachers who say, as I did about economics (although I had passed university economics subjects), 'I realize I had never understood it until I came to teach it.'

Hence much of the vague and fashionable opposition to compelling children to study should be an argument against force-feeding predigested concepts; and when phrases like 'starting where the children are at' are used, they should not be interpreted as an injunction to start in the child's backyard, metaphorically or literally speaking, but as an injunction to build on existing intellectual structures or sub-structures. The child who has failed to order or structure any of his thought processes is rare and indeed deprived. He is, to be tautological, a disordered child; but the much more common phenomenon is the child whose meaningful experiences are foreign to the teacher's, and the teacher has a twofold, interrelated task of finding what does make sense to that child as well as imaginatively recreating how he, the teacher, has made meaning of his own world so that he can retrace his steps using a frame of reference different from his own. Perhaps this is a counsel of perfection and, as such, is one that teachers can only approximate. Certainly, if one accepts it, it gives the lie to the notion that teaching is a cushy profession. It also throws light on why new teachers often find their way into teaching most effectively by working in the early stages with individual or very small groups of children. It cannot be done *en masse*, but with a normal-sized class that they know well, teachers can become very skilful at 'reading' their children and finding meaningful starting points.

One student, Ralph, began to see this point a month after the Course began, when he was reflecting on his reading, especially Freire. We tend, he said, to scan 'superficial surfaces and facts', and he cited as an example how we might teach that Canberra is the capital of Australia before we bother to find out if pupils have any notion of what a capital city is, which is far more important than the surface fact about Canberra. Once we concentrate on the children's underlying perceptions and skills, aiming at uncovering the 'themes of their reality', we can no longer as teachers 'be justified in feeling completely knowledgeable or authoritative', for we must necessarily engage in dialogue with our pupils. He then footnoted his speculations:

> It just occurred to me that this ... is a fundamental & essential part
> — the initial step — in all education ... It is in fact the answer to the
> ... old questions of 'how do you find out what the kids really want
> to learn if you don't want to [push them into new stuff they are not
> at first] interested in?' ... a possible approach for our hopes of team
> teaching ...

If my somewhat simplified account of the nature of thinking is right, it also follows that refining thinking and applying concepts to embrace wider and wider meanings or truths is essentially a structured business, although fickle and at crucial points not subject to a contrived act of will. The moment of enlightenment, when everything one has been groping for seems to click into place — what some people call the

'Eureka!' of learning — is something that nobody can do for anybody else. We can foster it, we can help to set up preliminary structures that will lead there, but we can never do it for another person, and we can never foretell when we shall get there ourselves; nor can we force some-one else to absorb even the preliminary structures that we build up. Prue, we saw, had been given room to move, and she was able to move because at critical times we kept out of her way, whereas at other times she needed us.

Perhaps room to move is simply giving people time for reflexion, which a lot of schools are very bad at. I can recall watching a Course B student giving a second-form class a number of useful and interesting tasks to perform about their own locality — aerial photographs of an area today to be compared with early sketches of the same place, with a number of leading questions to be answered, and things of that kind. One girl did them very quickly, and the faster she went, the more new tasks were given her until she plaintively whined: 'Oh, come on, Miss, I've done a lot of work, just give me time to please meself now. You've no idea how I love to day-dream and what I day-dream about.' It was meant to be funny and a bit cheeky; but it *was* funny because she really had a point. First, she was weary of doing too many tasks (all rather slickly) and the tasks did not become increasingly challenging; and second, she was irked at being fussed over, and possibly might have benefited by being allowed to drift for a while.

Diaries

We often positively discourage reflexion in our teaching, and perhaps it is hard to provide for it within a structured programme; but this is where students' diaries often came to be invaluable for them. We put some pressure on them not only to be active, but to ponder over what they were doing. Diaries were one way of deliberately encouraging this. We discussed them and they agreed (indeed initially the suggestion came from them at the beginning of our first year) to keep a diary which would prompt them to consider what they saw in schools, what they did in schools and how well it worked, what we did in the Course and how well it worked — in short to discover the sources of their own learning throughout the year. This was to help them to think consciously, through evaluating their own experiences, about the nature of learning: it was agreed upon as a means to help us to evaluate the Course, and most of the material in this book is drawn from those diaries.

As Ralph put it, after we had had our first discussion in our first year about whether or not diaries would be desirable:

In the afternoon we talked about assessment both of the course and of ourselves. The usefulness of keeping some kind of journal — perhaps like this one [he had already written, unasked, twenty-five pages] — seems to have been largely agreed upon. Particularly the possibilities of being able to look back over the documented development of our own course — an investigation into our own learning processes. Just how does each of us develop? If we have a journal of thoughts to look at perhaps we can draw conclusions from it. As well as that is of course the advantage to be obtained from trying to distil our vague thoughts and inspirations into a writable form.

He did just that — groped for meaning as he tried to put down his 'vague thoughts and inspirations'. Stewart, a scientist, who also wrote a very lengthy diary, paused after several months to write:

I lent this diary to a friend ... to read yesterday and the major criticism was that it is too chronologically precise — virtually listing in point form what I did. Thus there is a general lack of critical reflection and questioning of action.

I think this criticism is justified. So I intend from now on to include more criticism and general reflections as far as my changing philosophy of education goes. I believe my idea on the role of the school and my role within the school has changed quite radically from what it was two or three months ago ... What really matters is whether you're helping kids to be interested and alive in their outlook. This doesn't necessarily mean a total rejection of conventional teaching methods and predigested subject matter — but definitely a realization of the total perspective and aims of education.

Diaries became a way, not only of getting a lot out of one's system, but also of thinking aloud in an attempt to clarify one's ideas. Many students switched from what had happened in their classrooms to what they read, to what they had discussed with friends or in a seminar, and then back into the classroom. Susie was an excellent example. She had been teaching second-form maths when she went to a seminar on Bruner. Could children successfully learn the sign rules for multiplication by doing tasks that led them to discover the rules for themselves, she asked herself. At first she thought the idea might be too 'romantic', for 'there are certain subjects (if not all) that require basic facts before we can proceed with the formation of concepts and principles.' This seemed a reasonable doubt about the appropriateness of learning everything by discovery. And so then she considered using games to acquaint children with the sign rules:

I do not think Bruner's approach would have worked ... If the students know the sign rules for multiplication, they would stop at that and take them for facts, which they are not. However, there is a logical follow-up from a game to the establishment of the sign rules for multiplication. Some of the students still revert back to the game stage when multiplying – perhaps I've failed to go beyond the first stage ... I don't know! I get more confused as I think about it! No! I've worked it out ... The rules of the game were the basic information. Then, as I abbreviated the written rules with signs, they formed their concepts. From then on, they combined the concept and formed principles and this enabled them to advance to the next notch.

Three weeks later – and Bruner would be relieved if he knew:

Read two of Bruner's books. 'Towards a Theory of Instruction' and 'The Process of Education'. These helped me change my previous views on the present educational system. Also, during this time, I compiled a questionnaire booklet for my depth study [on a related topic].

Diaries, then, were a medium for reflexion, not only about the students' evaluation of their teaching and about what they were reading and discussing in terms of its applicability to what they were doing, but also about their own development – their own learning.

Depth studies

As staff, we also thought that, during the year, the students should undertake some work that required concentrated and sustained effort to give focus to their study and thinking. Examinations can give this sort of focus to some students. Such educative value as examinations have probably comes from the pressure put on students to integrate, to get a conspectus of, the various elements that have gone to make up their year's or half-year's work; but this does not always happen, by any means, for reasons that have already been implied – that no one can *make* complex ideas click into place meaningfully for anyone else, let alone predict that it will happen by a particular time, like the time of the examination. Nevertheless, it is at the time of formulating and articulating one's thinking that disciplined effort is required, and it is the formulation that triggers off new and deeper explorations which at the outset may be only dimly perceived.

A good teacher will not only challenge a student to feel itchy about a problem, he will also push the student to persist with it; but ultimately the clarification, though enlightened by the teacher's personal understanding, must be the student's own. Otherwise, the student will, at best, produce logically presented material, even the sophisticated

31

juxtaposition and comparison of ideas that passes for understanding, but in reality is only at one remove from plagiarism. University students and even school children become adept at this display of pseudo-discipline. What distinguishes genuine from specious exposition is that the student should be committed to his search for understanding and not merely to displaying his ability to juggle with ideas. Ron Toomey, who was a lecturer in Course B for a year, saw one important key to this difficulty as the constant testing of ideas against experience – in a teachers' training course, against actual teaching. This came to him strongly when he subsequently found himself marking assignments in a theoretical course:

> As I read I get flashes of the contributions studes made in class or at schools & detect dissonances between those and the plagiarized bull-shit that's so nicely typed in their papers ... I'm sure they would not be saying, for example, 'music can be taught creatively' and leave it at that, if they had been out in schools more and spending less time reading second-hand accounts of what it's like out there. (Not that music can't be taught creatively; they just don't know very much about schools or teaching & live in a permanent fairy-land.)

In an attempt to push students to think some things through we suggested that they undertake a depth study – a piece of sustained work, mini-research if you like, that would enable them to formulate and to pursue, with help, questions that most seriously stirred them. It was to be an all-year interest that we hoped would be devised during the first term, and would replace set essays or examinations. It did not have to be exclusively written work, and indeed one student carried out the most exacting task in organizing children's drama workshops – an experience that led him into a career in that speciality. Another student taped interviews with children who chose to move from a small community school back to its big parent school. She also interviewed their teachers in both schools. Her written evaluation of this was disappointing, but we accepted her reason that she 'ran out of puff' because it was so time consuming. And, as she wryly put it, 'You say that this is to benefit us, not to be done just to impress you. It was the most enlightening thing I have done at university and you will just have to take my word for it.' One's faith is not always vindicated in ways that one might hope for, but in this case, she gained a teaching post in a community school; she had a clear idea of her role as a teacher and of the role of such schools in a school system; and in subsequent years she was able to work with our students and to discuss such problems with real point.

Most students did choose written work of some kind or another, and we tended to expect this. Few failed to complain bitterly from time to time. Some of the complaints arose from sheer practical difficulties

– of time, tiredness and conflicting pulls. But many of the complaints, I believe, bear out my earlier point – that the discipline required in persistent, and often apparently unrewarding, slog comes from having to think a thing through to a conclusion, however tentative. Some sort of coherent formulation is part of the process of clinching one's understanding and of seeing its future significance in generating further thinking. A written formulation has great value here.

Some of the students' diary entries bear out this thesis. Margaret's are a good example:

> The pressure of work sickens me. I can't get it out of my mind and I'm worried about it. Well this afternoon I did get some depth study work done ... I covered all the depth study work re Flemington High School's individualized Maths Programme, and even, believe it or not, began work on Dienes and his theories behind individualization. I must admit this is the first time I have been to the Baillieu [University Library] this year and from the useless information I obtained from the books taken out, the last. I just don't seem to be able to find anything of relevance ...
>
> It's the first day for a long time you know that I have worked with pen and paper (and it was great) for a significant length of time ... I went to bed very much pleased with myself and my effort.

The next day she bemoaned her inability to find any book to help her work, 'so I had to resort to other resources'; and the following day, commenting on her contribution to the work that three of the students were to do, she wrote:

> I nominated myself to write up the Introduction in the hope that I will be able to work out exactly what I am striving for in *my* research. Every time I talk to Rod [Fawns – her supervisor] my mind is changed. It has gotten to the stage where I don't know what I'm doing. I hope I can get my study done in the two weeks to come ...

A week later:

> I've managed to complete the Introduction at last although I had difficulty in putting words together especially after not having written an essay for years literally.

Then came the vacation, and after two weeks of solid work, Margaret decided that she had to have a break by going home 'rather than go round the bend'. Where she had first found library books 'useless', she now complained that relevant written work seemed inexhaustible. This is a nice illustration of how impossible it is to tell the student in advance of where her exploration will take her. Even the experts in the books she first read could not get their message across, and she had to take

33

different routes, in a kind of bleak faith, until they could talk sense to her:

> It is really bad news for I found that the more I read ... the more I had to and wanted to read. The time factor ultimately drew the line for me. I think the most difficult decision that I did have to make was one of deciding what it was that I was going to write: a mini-thesis or an essay of so many thousand words. Surprisingly it was good to get into some theory work for a while. It was a change and a novelty! ... I only hope all the work was worth it. I know that it proved an invaluable experience to myself. It broadened my ideas and outlook on the whole theory of individualization and consolidated it as well.

This diary has been quoted at some length because for Margaret it did precisely what we hoped for. The detailed, week-by-week comments on what went on serve to illustrate the points I have tried to make. At one time she needed to get away, to give her time to drift and let things lie fallow. Just what sort of gestation went on subconsciously then, we cannot know and she could not tell us. Just how much help she gained from the reflexions recorded in her diary — far more extensive than the quotations indicate — is also conjectural; but when she returned from her holiday she settled down to the writing and found that the problems it presented meant that she had to impose some sort of order on her thinking, which she found a difficult but rewarding learning experience.

We hoped that students would see for themselves, through their own efforts, that just 'fun-learning' is no learning at all; and that they would remember this in their own teaching. Margaret provided something of a model in that everything we hoped for and planned, and too often failed to achieve, seemed to work in her case. Our intention was that students should be grouped to pool the results of their depth studies, which should become an important element in the Curriculum Studies programme in third term. One reason why this worked less than perfectly was that too many students took too long to get started, and others got tied in knots at the last moment and failed to hand in their work in time for us to read it and make it most usefully available to others before the year ended. In Margaret's case there were two other students involved; they met the deadline, and Rod Fawns arranged a session in which their work was the basis of a seminar. Margaret commented:

> This depth study session proved to be the most valuable part of the work ... Rod was most reassuring and destructive at the same time. Well that is the end of that. I only wished we could have somehow

got copies of some other depth studies. My study for me was one of the better things about the course.

We can but hope that, although Margaret didn't see it at the time, the conclusion of this work was *not* 'the end of that'.

Lou Soccio, who for present purposes will be given no pseudonym, did a quite different sort of depth study, and one which, to his and my delight, was immediately accepted for publication in *Melbourne Studies in Education 1977*.[1] Although his topic is so different from Margaret's — in that he wrote a family history, tracing his parents from a peasant community in southern Italy and the development of their two groups of children — those born in Italy and the 'Kangeroni', like Lou, who were born in Australia — he made many points in his diary similar to those made by Margaret about what went into the project:

> Another worthwhile aspect of the course has been my depth study. It wasn't until I had finished the essay that I realised the worth of it ... It gave me an opportunity to sort out, and try to explain many issues concerning my family and migrants in general. It was the first time that I have ever really studied something which has an intimate relevance. The actual writing of it was exceptionally difficult; at times painful. I have never written anything vaguely creative, and the essay was a novel experience. But, I felt that years of formal primary, secondary and tertiary education have somewhat blunted the little writing talent I was able to muster up. It was a constant struggle to try and make the essay say something original and not to rehash the trendy concern for migrants that has blossomed in the past few years. After I had researched for the essay and put it together, I sat on it for a long time trying to work out how to approach it, how to write it. I really don't know if the essay tells a pleasant story or if it really says something about migrants living in a foreign community. Ever since I handed the essay in I have been very eager about the comments.
>
> It was really exciting doing something like this. The whole idea about a depth study is great as long as one basic criterion is met; that is, the topic must have a real, personal interest which is sufficient to motivate a sincere, emotional effort. Academically, the depth study has been everything three years of university has not been.

The people who gained least from the depth study were the ones least likely to have written much in diaries. Those who were most vocally opposed were usually so for ideological reasons — they believed the requirement a betrayal of our claim to offer self-determination and self-evaluation. At meetings with students about assessment they agreed that there ought to be requirements and there ought to be evaluation, and they consented, with varying degrees of conviction, that the depth study was as good a means as any other. It was always suggested that they could put forward other propositions if they personally preferred something different, but they never once, I think, took up our offer by suggesting some alternative. Often their objection was prompted by our being too indefinite about what we had in mind by a depth study — though samples were always available and lists of topics made up. I found it extremely difficult to explain what I predicted to be the value to them of such a project, for the value could emerge only in the course of their doing the work, and I know of no way of giving a foretaste of such a claim.

Probably objections came, too, from finding moments of great difficulty, such as both Margaret and Lou described. Be that as it may, at the end-of-year review session in which we took stock of the year's programme by seeking students' opinions as a basis for changes in the Course in future years, nearly all students agreed that they were glad they had eventually done the work, and they thought in the end that it was a good idea — even the most vehement critics agreed with this, sometimes very sheepishly. There was always a strong recommendation that more end-of-year time should be given to group discussions of the depth studies than had been done, and in this they were unquestionably right, though the administrative difficulties already referred to made it more difficult to carry out than it should have been. When really sustained and thoughtful work has been done, one of its most important values should lie in its being shared with colleagues. Enquiries based on classroom observation — notably by Nancy Martin's team at the London University Institute of Education — show that an overwhelming proportion of children's writing is done 'for the teacher', very little is done for their colleagues and almost none for their own satisfaction.

We tried to reverse this order, and when students did give seminars based on their depth studies or on other questions they had been studying, they showed a great respect for their colleagues as an audience — far more than they showed for us as staff present, and that is how it ought to be. The disciplinary value of exposition is enriched by having to take into consideration an audience with a variety of points of view, quite apart from the fact that students can very effectively learn from each other.

Freedom of choice

There were morals for students to draw from their experience with their own depth studies. First, if we were right in insisting that enjoyment or even engagement were insufficient in fostering learning; that difficult, even bad, patches had to be struggled with; that the results of fruitful effort cannot, by definition, be foreseen — here were some principles that students might bear in mind when their turn came in schools for making curricular decisions. The Catch-22 for 'progressive' education is that if you know in advance what you are to find out there is nothing to find out. Looked at another way, until you understand something of the nature of the work entailed in options, how can your 'choice' be more than a blind guess? A failure to see this produces a good deal of the nonsense that is talked about pupils' freedom to choose their own curriculum — a failure that gives the Black Paper people the best ammunition that they can muster. But to say that is not to say that force will work either or that hard and painful effort is good for you simply because it *is* hard and painful. In retrospect, to revert to Prue who presented us with this dilemma, I think that we should have pressed her harder early in the year; but to have done so effectively we needed to know at the time what was 'turning her off', and this did not emerge until we read her diary at the end of the year.

Second, when students reflected on their own work, as they often did in their diaries, they gained insight into their own moments of satisfaction or frustration, into their own successes and failure in learning, which they could and often did apply to their thinking about their pupils' responses.

Third, when students pressed us to justify our suggested requirements and watched our discomposure or listened to our explicit commitment to a task, it took little imagination for them to see themselves in the same position with pupils in their own classes. In challenging us, in meeting our expectations and constantly evaluating us (as well as themselves), they would, we hoped, be made to think of the expectations and demands they could properly make of their own school pupils. Where we failed, they might fail: where we succeeded, they might succeed. There is no need for simulation games as a means of encouraging role-switching if the Course itself consciously leads its members to identify themselves with staff, fellow-students and pupils.

I am not sure whether the small minority who handed in work that appeared to have been useless to them (and their colleagues) analysed the reasons. We tried to discuss the work with each student individually; but this important exercise was sometimes frustrated by work being handed in at the last minute and having to be returned with nothing but a detailed written comment after students had disappeared from the campus. Once we had experienced the difficulty, we made regular times for each supervisor to discuss progress reports with his students, but this fell down with the more dilatory students. We were left with the small consolation that, in our experience, the proportion whose work was superficial, half-hearted or inept was considerably lower than the proportion who handed in this sort of work in other courses requiring traditional essays or examinations.

Indeed, why I felt such attachment to the depth study, despite all the difficulties that it caused, was the result of chance. Two years before the Course began, I had several classes enrolled in sociology of education. The room I was allotted for my teaching was atrocious — a corridor which was used as a passage for people going to other classes; and there was no ventilation because to open a window meant that the antiquated gas heating from the ceiling blew out, and the atmosphere became suffocating. I refused to go on teaching in it. Instead, I arranged to take groups of a few students (about four or five were all that could be fitted in) in my small study. In these sessions we worked out together individual or group projects which the students pursued, meeting regularly, but less than once a week, for discussion of the work in hand. The result at the end was so good, so vastly superior to the work I was used to receiving, that I did this again the following year, and started Course B the year after with a strong prejudice in favour of the method. Most of the staff fancied the procedure, and the students were always consulted before it was agreed upon. Had they been determinedly opposed, we should have had to drop the practice and use more normal methods.

In addition to the merits already outlined, the depth study encouraged students to *find* their own topic — to discover what they liked to call 'their own thing'. Its weakness lay not, I believe, in the idea, but in the fact that staff, who were already overburdened, nearly always gave first priority to helping students with problems in their teaching, and so the time required to make the depth study really successful was simply not available. It amounted to a question of whether we should have bent more to the limiting reality. By and large, I still think not; and apparently my successors agree, for the requirement continues, although an alternative to it is offered.

As one might expect with graduates, many students had no difficulty in 'going it alone'; but many needed far more support than we could give once our numbers doubled. Here was an ideal opportunity to help those students whose undergraduate courses had required little independent reading or sustained writing. Here was an opportunity for us to help balance the education of the mathematician, scientist, even economist, geographer and psychologist. For the more 'literary' graduates our encouragement of concern with practical issues was an antidote to the too theoretical bias that many of them had acquired.

The most difficult part of all for staff was to provide the richness of interests early in the year that would enable students to get over 'problem blindness'. Lou was absolutely right: death to a depth study was pursuing a question in which there was only a token interest. Everything, said Stephen Spender, is work except inspiration; and if teachers are to push for hard work, as I have advocated they should, they must first try to ensure that students have the fire that kindles the intellectual process. But spontaneous combustion (inspiration) does not occur in a vacuum. Catch-22 again.

Participatory planning and team-teaching in integrated studies

I think that we were right, at the beginning of the year, to try to create some common ground as a starting point, and to do this through direct contacts with schools and children as well as indirectly through reading and discussion. The way in through separate educational subjects taken 'bookishly' would not in itself have solved the problem — it would only have masked it. That some of the problems we raised seemed remote was inevitable; that they hit home with some more than with other students was also probably inevitable; that they created tensions was desirable provided that the tensions and irritations were stirring and not dulling. But when our approach to problems seemed 'bitsy', that was bad, though remediable.

There are problems inherent in running an integrated or cross-disciplinary course, especially one that is based on the principle of participatory planning with students. It is easier to gain coherence in the study of a single subject, though paradoxically such specialization itself contains its own dangers of fragmentation, not to mention remoteness. An integrated course usually suggests team-teaching of some sort or another, and this becomes increasingly difficult with the size of the student group and with the size of the team of teachers. The individuality and special interests of each teacher must be respected, yet the logical development of thinking and the coherence of content are held in the mind of each teacher and conveyed to, though not necessarily imposed on, the learning group. Thus it is easier for one teacher to obtain continuity in an integrated study unit than for five; but, on the other hand, there is more likelihood of needing to draw on the expertise that various teachers can give. Coherence and structure must reside within the teachers, yet each one is probably idiosyncratic and there is virtue in having diversity within the team. These apparent contradictions can be reconciled by the way the team plans. We had successes and failures in team-teaching.

We nearly always planned carefully; but sometimes an apparently tightly-knit, closely connected series of classes on a topic, given first by one lecturer and then by another, though it looked fine on paper and all staff concerned could see the connexions, looked to the students as if we were playing musical chairs. Rod Foster, a philosopher, might give a lecture attacking behaviourism. By citing studies of animal behaviour he showed that some animals displayed problem-solving abilities beyond anything that could be explained by conditioned learning. Terry Werner, a psychologist, would give the next lecture putting behaviourism in its best possible light as expounded by some of its foremost thinkers and their research. Both lecturers were utterly clear; but to the students each lecture stood as a thing in itself, and they needed time, study and guidance to compare and contrast the two approaches, to disentangle what lay at the centre of the controversy. What was wrong with the planning here was simply that we assumed too much and should have pursued the topic far more intensively. The two lecturers (though with different views) had a common focus that students could have come to share. The principles of the planning were sound, but we let the matter drop before the students had been given the chance to grasp fully and explore more thoroughly the ideas that had been introduced.

In another example, the principles of planning were less sound, although the plan looked good until we carried it out. One of the themes taken at the beginning of one year was children's language development. We began with a paper given by Bernie Newsome that centred on one of his main interests – the exploratory use of language in young children, the development of this into expressive language, all splendidly illustrated with written work and with tape-recordings of children's soliloquies and discussions. This was then contrasted with the sort of formal writing that tends to predominate in the work secondary school children mostly do.

Following this, I gave a paper in which I took the School of Barbiana's *Letter to a Teacher* and compared it with Freire in that both saw language development as a means towards self-liberation and as a necessary release from oppression. In the third session, small groups discussed one author of their own choosing – Herbert Kohl's *Reading, How to*, or Labov on the speech of working-class black children in Harlem, or the School of Barbiana, or Freire.

This programme looks connected enough; but in retrospect, as teachers, we all 'did our own thing'. Bernie emphasized one point; I emphasized another; and my guess is that each of the seminar leaders in the third session took the discussion in different directions yet again. Certainly they were all about children's language development, but there was no focus, even though, as teachers, each of us knew the links between the various topics. The links were far more tenuous and diffuse than the links between Rod's and Terry's lectures on behaviourism, and it would have taken us down innumerable paths before our connecting ideas could have become more than disparate, embryonic (though possibly interesting) separate topics. In our concern to indicate the totality of, and interconnectedness of, the 'Big Problems' of education we left the students without any structure to focus on or work towards.

A team of teachers, I think, needs to concentrate on some manageable central theme or themes, and not to be diffuse.

Behaviourism was potentially a good topic for integrated study. It is itself a serious, organizing, explanatory concept, whatever one may think of its merits. Moreover, most students were already familiar with some forms of the philosophical view of which it was an expression — historians, scientists, students of literature or language. In later discussions with individual students or with small groups it was obvious that they were familiar with many of the ideas though they were puzzled by the significance of the lectures. Possibly a better first step would have been to encourage the students to try to articulate the philosophy as they recognized it in reflecting upon their own knowledge. They could then more readily have applied this understanding to learning theory, and would have had a firm basis for grasping the significance of behaviourism and critically evaluating the new material to be presented in lectures.

One of the points of integrated studies is that they lend themselves to the study of important organizing ideas and to widening students' ability to develop their own powers of generalizing. When one sees a topic such as 'Living in Cities' as the topic secondary school pupils will study in a general studies programme, the first reaction is to groan inwardly, for a broad content area in itself is unlikely to benefit from so-called 'integration' but rather to lead to a smattering of bits of disconnected information. Yet 'Living in Cities' can be more successful than the title suggests, when teachers have decided to elicit from it one or several main themes. 'Children's language development', by contrast, as we taught it, had too many large and complex themes that we touched upon and dropped too quickly. For different reasons, our treatment of this, too, resulted in a disconnected smattering of ideas backed up by too *little* information; but at least it stimulated many students to pursue some of the questions raised, even if it left others bemused.

Our failure to see quickly where we were going wrong was no doubt a reaction to the highly structured, undeviating approach that has characterized much subject teaching in the past — a tendency to 'push on regardless' in the hope that in the end it would all add up for the learners in just the way it presumably already had for the teacher. If we began with a highly structured, cut-and-dried programme, we feared that students would charge us with hypocrisy in our promises of participatory planning — as indeed they sometimes did. But the very diversity of the student body and their ability to influence us in where we were going was the real safeguard needed. When what we did seemed to be 'all over the place', their contributions tended to be tangential. When we knew where we were going, their contributions tended to be relevant and we could afford to encourage and profit from the different views and experiences that they offered. Their contributions could then genuinely change the plan and lead it in a better direction. This seems to be the essence of student participation — that it can and should lead to changes in direction. And for the teacher to be happy that that should happen, and not thrown into confusion, he needs to have some clear idea of his own direction from which he sees point in diverging. Whether staff taught singly or in groups it was assumed that they would not panic when students led discussion and enquiry beyond their competence (and the 'their' can be used ambiguously since it applies both to staff and to students). We were willing to say, 'We can swot this up' or 'We must bring in an expert, for it is beyond any one of us.' The second alternative is rarer.

Professor Hirst, famed as the upholder of distinctive Forms of Knowledge, at a staff seminar at Melbourne University in 1976, proudly confessed that, in his teacher-training courses, he was often forced to make unexpected visits to the library to read some psychology or sociology because of questions that had arisen in his seminars. Many members of the audience were shocked, especially when he added that he found it very good for *him* to have to do so. Such a statement presupposes that exploring educational problems inevitably leads one into unexpected paths, and that the specialist benefits from becoming more of a generalist. I am inclined, too, to agree with the Crowther Report's contention that intensive study, even of a specialist kind, ideally leads beyond 'subject-mindedness' to an awareness of the relevance, indeed the indispensability, of allied subjects. The ideal is often almost entirely missed in a subject-centred curriculum, just as superficiality is a hazard in a problem-centred one; but it ain't necessarily so in either case.

One of our troubles in the early years of the Course was an undue fear of superficiality, resulting from the assumption of our critics that this is what we were bound to be, and an undue sensitivity to students' evident boredom, especially when this was not explicitly stated. We sometimes failed to recognize when they were out of their depth, and we often interpreted signs of boredom as being due to our being too obvious or simple. Hence we too readily switched to something different in an attempt to be more interesting when we should have persisted in clarifying the bothersome question in hand, and we were rightly charged with skating over issues when really we were afraid of risking disaffection.

This over-sensitivity of staff to students' reactions is inherent in a course based on participatory planning, and only experience could help us to overcome it. Whatever errors we made, the broad introduction in first term Curriculum Studies did give students a base from which to decide what they wanted to explore more thoroughly. Towards the end of first term, we called students and staff together in an attempt to break Curriculum Studies into options in second term. By second term, too, the students had faced their first teaching ordeals and had vastly more experience on which we could draw. Their choice was necessarily influenced by what staff cared most to offer as special studies; but by this time the students were able to make real, not just fanciful, choices − to exercise real freedom.

Everything favoured a better second term than first term in Curriculum Studies. The groups were smaller, we knew each other better, and therefore students were much franker with us − a thing on which we depended greatly. They were also much less threatened by each other, and were thus franker with each other. When we did offer options by team-teaching, as many of us did, there was far more soundness in our planning. With a definite topic to be pursued, we were not forcing integration, but as a team we tended to work together on the central ideas that we wanted to explore, and to plan with an eye to the special contribution each of us could make to any particular idea. Our approach was cohesive and focused, and yet we were flexible enough to be greatly influenced by the way that seminars worked out and to be guided by what we sensed were the matters of over-riding concern to the students. This seldom led to incoherence or chaos, no matter how radical the change in direction might be. It is in staff's being prepared to change structure, rather than in avoiding structure at the outset, that students get proper experience of autonomy.

Theories in action

Broadly, the options studied tended to be politically or pedagogically flavoured, though obviously there was considerable overlap, as some of the titles will indicate: Freedom and Authority; Ideology; Equality; Children's Literature, Language and Thought; Scientific Language, to name but a few. Each attracted students with different academic backgrounds, and all of them were interdisciplinary in approach. In nearly every year students formed a group themselves to discuss ideologies in education, which seemed to be of gripping interest to many by third term and usually became a major theme towards the end of the year, based sometimes on depth studies and sometimes arising from discussions led by students who had formed their own group.

Early in the year, however, ideological questions met a mixed reception, and I think we were sometimes too quickly responsive, too sensitive, in moving to less troublesome ground. It is especially difficult, until staff and students know each other well, for staff not to misinterpret signs of indifference, let alone irritation: for example, the

43

popular books that we chose for preliminary reading were soaked with concern about class differences between teachers and pupils, about the privileges that university education bestowed at a cost that impoverished other sections of the system, and about whether or not there was a 'deficit' in working-class families – in short, with questions of equality. For various and very different reasons, these issues sometimes threatened the students personally or misfired altogether.

One student, already quoted, noted that he felt 'removed' from the Italian peasant children who, as pupils at the School of Barbiana, wrote *Letter to a Teacher*. It was small wonder that he did feel removed since he had been to an exclusive independent school and chose to go to another during his year with us; yet the chances of his teaching children in Australia from whom he *was* indeed removed were very great, for he held a studentship with the State Department and was bound to teach in the State school system.

For another – John – A. S. Neill was all right, for Neill fitted his vague sort of radical mood and didn't appear to raise important issues of social class. 'Enjoyed Rory [Barnes]'s presentation of Neill,' he wrote. 'Following discussion was good.' He was happy about the question of freedom, but was deeply unhappy when that afternoon I hit the wrong chord in introducing Ivan Illich:

> Afternoon annoyed me. After introd. to Illich much of class began to set up barriers between themselves and others believing that they could not fully appreciate the life of 'working-class' people & their values and thus could not communicate with them. They're people aren't they? [I trust I did not suggest anything to the contrary.]
>
> I couldn't sit and watch this fashionable class consciousness develop. We can always divide people with socio-economic status standards, such as occups. & money etc, but stopping communications between us and --- I don't believe there is a 'them'.
>
> Found group of like-minded people going to Clyde [Hotel] – joined them. Discovered that out of these eleven, only one student had tertiary educated parents, ie on both sides [!] Most indeed had working-class ... backgrounds. Didn't need to drown feelings of guilt at being [middle-class] uni. students ...
>
> I've 'had' talks & seminars ... some topics could be left until later in the year eg. ideology of education.

Yet Freire's ideas oddly enough didn't raise the same hackles about class consciousness in John. Freire and Neill make strange bedfellows, but not for this student whose first impression of the school he was placed at made him look forward to retreating from his school back to the University with all its 'talks & seminars'.

By God, Freire would destroy this school in one breath. Integrated studies in this school, I feel a mere reorganization of <u>directed</u> studies — a way of getting students to do something different.

The looseness of structure ... is on the side of the teachers, and not for the students to work within ... Why read Freire, see his truth if we are unable to practise what we then believe? It will be a relief to return to uni. tomorrow.

A week later he added:

When I read Freire [*Pedagogy of the Oppressed*] I found an articulation of how I wanted to approach 'teaching' as well as why I wished, in some respects, to be a teacher ...

I become very tired & bitter at having to justify to fellow students my belief in children 'learning' without curriculum.

Here was a student who was taking his reading very seriously but was more touchy about Illich's class consciousness than about Freire's, which for the moment he saw as an indictment less of inequality than of authoritarianism. While Freire is rightly interpreted as attacking teacher domination, I suspect that he would be amazed to learn that he meant there to be no curriculum at all. But John's confusion was fruitful and probably a desirable step towards clarification. What was wrong was that in sensing that I had disturbed or even hurt students in presenting Illich to them I kept off Illich from then on. What I should have done was to continue to face such students with the difficulties of reconciling freedom (which gripped this student) with equality (which repelled him).

Other students had deeply personal reasons for quick and sympathetic responses to anything that touched on equality. Antonio, for example, came to the Course with a fairly strong background in politics in his undergraduate degree and was immediately interested the moment any of the introductory seminars and books dealt with equality, for his father had been a factory labourer. Antonio, unlike the students referred to above, had no fear of being unable to talk the language of working-class children and no sense of guilt about his background. He found other issues difficult to grasp, such as a session run by Rod Foster based on a film showing conditioning and machine-controlled education taken to extremes in the twenty-first century. 'I was fascinated,' he wrote. 'Yet the link between the seminar and school activities seems quite thin. Admittedly an understanding of what direction educational methods are heading for is a valuable long-term concept to ... meditate upon'; but he was bothered because he found it difficult to relate 'the practice and theory'. Not so when we discussed equality. His diary is studded with early conjectures, thoughtful concern, about the response of working-class children to education, and in second term he joined the Equality option without a second thought:

> The Curriculum Studies Equality Seminars have been rewarding. The lively discussions have been stimulating. The topics all have a relevance to my teaching experience at school and seem to complement my teaching perfectly. The seminars have been important because I felt that before I could teach history and geography there were some issues that I needed to consider. Issues, such as, what is the aim of teaching working-class children? Do we educate them to be middle class? *Education and the Working Class* and *Letter to a Teacher* look at these questions and come to some significant conclusions.

Antonio was in conflict, but it was fruitful conflict even though he remained somewhat confused as he swung between what he was reading and discussing and what was happening at school. He discovered in one of his classes a Turkish boy who, for three years, had sat in classes without 'understanding anything that was going on'. Antonio formed a friendship with the boy and tried to teach him English. He asked himself what he could do about the boy:

> He wants to be a technician. It's obvious he won't succeed in his ambition. He should have been given remedial English as soon as he came to the school. But what do you do? Do you tell him to lower his aspirations, down to the assembly-line level? Or do you let him go on and find out for himself that he has been cruelly rejected? It is a sad story.

Antonio was in a dilemma about the relationship between equality and social mobility. A little later he described his reactions to a class that misbehaved. It should be mentioned that he was teaching in an industrial area, surrounded by council housing estates, with a group of pupils he could understand better than most of our other students could:

> Today, I had my first serious trauma. In true melodramatic fashion I walked out of the class I was taking and went home. On reflection, it was a very stupid thing to do and simply involved not being able to handle ... a group of 'naughty boys'. But the whole thing was partly a response to the equality seminars at university. In the seminars we had been discussing how we should make working-class children articulate and literate and free them from dehumanising factory-work etc. However, I just could not cope with blatant refusals to work, and I feel it would be easy to ignore those that are not prepared to study (or 'learn'). It's all very frustrating and all so easy to forget and go on teaching history and geography to the passive minority who will absorb it all on their way to middle-class status. I tried to be logical; to tell them they would end up in factories, etc. etc. but

they would not respond to my middle-class concept of logic. I became nasty and sarcastic and walked over to the 'naughty boys' and told them they had succeeded in giving me the shits and walked out.

I suspect that Antonio's last remark would have got through to the 'naughty boys' much more immediately than the earlier attempts at reasoning. At that stage he was so close to his own background that he saw education for working-class children as being primarily to equip them for 'better' occupations. His father and older brothers and sisters had worked in factories and saved until they could open a shop, after which the younger children could be put through university when they were old enough. He placed great store in the power of education to lift underprivileged children out of what he regarded as their rut.

That Antonio believed in the power of education to increase children's sense of their own worth when most things in their lives conspired to convince them of their powerlessness and worthlessness was fine; but what he seemed not to have grasped was that if, by some miracle, education equipped all children for higher education and the professions, some people would still have to do what he called, and knew from his family's experience to be, dehumanizing work. Even if he had grappled with this curly political problem, there was still the immediate classroom problem that, if the goals he was proposing succeeded with some pupils, the difficulty of what to do with the rest, who were not convinced, remained just as intransigent as ever.

What bothered him with the pupils he taught was his ability to interest them but his inability to persuade them to think things through — their readiness to give up as soon as real effort was required. He had, for example, given the class a simulation game that they enjoyed and discussed sensibly, but he thought they should have been guided to probe further:

It is easy to experience something but much harder to analyse and understand it. I do feel that traditional methods of education lack stimulation, involvement and interest, yet I feel there is a place in education for serious, academic work and that learning to analyse, articulate and understand are valuable skills.

He went on puzzling over this, being uncertain in his own mind about how much pressure he could and should apply. Some time later he was still in a quandary. As he reflected on why he had walked out of his class he noted, 'I could have entertained them sufficiently to superficially earn the title of "teacher". Until I demanded solid work from them I was getting on quite well.' It was then that he reverted to his reading in search of an answer:

I want to teach, not entertain. I want to be a teacher, not a friend. It's all very confusing. The only solace I have found has been in *Letter to a Teacher*. This book seems to solve the problem of equality in education within an unequal society very well indeed. Furthermore, it does not wait for the 'Revolution' to do so. Yet the ideals expressed in *Letter to a Teacher* are very hard to implement.

But Antonio's outburst to his class about their ending up in factories was, of course, quite alien to the way of thinking of Father Milani and his School of Barbiana. Milani was messianic in giving his boys pride in their own class (and anger at their subjugation) — a pride that was a spur to their determination to learn, and through learning, to gain power and self-respect. But social advancement was seen by them as a corrupting motive.

Antonio's girlfriend, who had been at secondary school with him, shared many of his views, and, indeed, shared some of his confusion. She wrote:

My impulse to push the students very hard comes from my own experience in a working-class school — I saw so many students fall away just for lack of a teacher demanding work from them. At the same time I think that for me education was a way of asserting myself — I could say that I was as intelligent as anyone, regardless of my class — and I wanted these kids to prove themselves and their class. I know there are other ways, but for me education seemed the only way, and I want others to feel the power that education gives them over their background.

My sixth-form lit. class clearly feels disadvantaged coming from Brunswick [an industrial suburb] , and love to hear me say I was in the same position, and 'made' it.

And so we have seen that issues that turn some students on, to use the students' terminology, turn others off; but if we take an example like Equality, as we have just done, it would be grossly misleading to suggest that it had instant success with working-class students while being threatening to middle-class ones. It was by no means as simple as that, since what students bring with them is the result of very complex factors. John, for example, had found the question of class consciousness and the reactions of his fellow-students distastefully personal; Kate did not, though she came from a professional family:

Gwen gave an account of Milani and the School of Barbiana after which we broke into groups ... We talked about classes mixing ... (socially & at school) ... I was surprised and heartened by the fact that people talked about themselves, & a bit less suspicious & apprehensive (both about being exposed, & that this wasn't wasting time). I began to understand how going about 'learning' in this way is the deepest if scariest way of really 'growing up' — my supposedly academic mind/training still posits it has limited usefulness & application. None the less ...

For Gita, however, who had been in the same seminars as Antonio, much of the discussion must have washed over her, and it was not until she moved from an academic high school to teach in a difficult technical school in a very poor area that the problems became starkly real:

Well — it was a real experience just to come in contact with a type of life which was completely unknown to me — I had always lived in a middle-class suburb, and so things that were accepted as an everyday happening there just did not happen in my corner of the world. I was completely unaware of the life-style in these working-class suburbs ...

I can remember one day when I became terribly frustrated as I could not get the boys away from the coloured TV set into a classroom — I started jumping up and down and getting very upset, yelling such things as: 'You're completely irresponsible! You don't even have a pen or a book: how do you expect to be able to read and write! What are you going to do later on when you have a family???!' They all looked at me, with a meaningless stare upon their faces, as though I hadn't even spoken; then one boy looked up at me & answered coldly, 'I already have two children, miss!!!'

I — well I just did not know what to say or what to think!! — and only then I realized how foolish I had been to try to impose my standards upon them — those kids knew very well, by experience, that they could not raise a family by learning to expand on their reading and writing. They know that they will have to work hard to keep their families — present and future (eg. drive a truck, become a bricklayer or a cleaner). If they want to know what is going on in the world they don't have to read a paper — they can switch on the television set; and if they want something, they'll steal it.

But what came as a worse shock to me was just how passively they had come to accept their situation!

For the first time Gita began to see that life and job expectations have a direct bearing on the meaning that children derive from education, though she was still pretty naive about occupations. One might wonder, for example, how the poor truck-driver would survive if he couldn't read a map, let alone signposts.

The same things touched off different responses, excited different nerve endings in different people. For Susie, for example, the problem of authority and authoritarianism hit hardest because she had been educated in an autocratic school. When she read *Young Teachers and Reluctant Learners* she immediately asked herself two questions: Could she, with her own special background, be anything but an authoritarian teacher? Had being at an authoritarian school had the results that the authors described? In answering the second question, she agreed with them:

> This [the writer's description of an authoritarian school] is true of my school ... There was no cooperation ... We always worked alone and only your best friends lent you anything. Not that we fought or anything. It was just that the sense of competition was so great that we forgot we were supposed to learn in a school — facts and reasons from the teachers and how to live from the other students. Reflecting back, I went through all the 3 stages listed:
> 1. hostility (I stole in 1st grade)
> 2. withdrawal (between 2nd Grade and 2nd Form)
> 3. submission (2nd Form onwards).

In wondering whether she could adopt a 'relaxed, informal approach, with voluntary contributions from the floor', she thought she would find it difficult 'after having 10 years of highly structured teaching'. For that reason she found the Course itself difficult, especially learning to participate in discussions:

> 1. I cannot think quickly (in the structured system you were fed the bare facts). I have to 'brew' on the question in hand.
> 2. I find my concentration wanders and the topic in discussion is easily lost (in the structured system, this can be done easily without attracting attention ...)
> 3. I accept most things I read as true, I very seldom question anything written down.

If her third point was accurate, she had learned very quickly, for few students pondered over, questioned and tried to make sense of what they read in the way that she did in her diary.

Other students, like Kate, also reflected on their own learning processes in an attempt to apply what they learnt to how they taught. After first term Kate was one of a group who attended a Bruner workshop and then continued with a study of Bruner as their main option. Kate noted:

> Something also happened between the end of term & the end of the Bruner workshop. I think partly it was seeing informal groups working with lots of materials & ostensibly all over the place, still working & having some coherence & direction. It was important that by the end we could see we had moved on from where we'd begun ... as

though various aspects of life ... knitted together ... Lots of concern about how kids would 'learn', react & respond, not just ... worries for teachers over whether this stuff threatened their established style.

With Chris, our most vocal critic (in his diaries at least) in four years, everything we did was misguided. A few weeks after the Course began, he wrote:

An easy 7,000 bucks next year.
    I'm not in the least disillusioned, as all the idealistic theorizing nearly led me to be. Practice not only makes perfect, it is perfect, or as near as we can get to it ... the mind crap is the put-off ...
    Well now, it turns out everyone else was disappointed with their initial school experience. I blame it on their getting their praxis all buggered up (to use a Freireanism, which I will, as I want to get onto him in a bit).

And then a few weeks later:

I feel I'm learning a lot in my own way, so stop with the moral pressure to get me continually into the classroom ... I will be a good teacher next year, though a bad Dip.Ed stude this year if I do things my way ... I don't care a stuff about being a good Dip. Edder. One is important, the other a gaining of a piece of paper. God bless SELF-ASSESSMENT, because I'll hold you to it.

Later again in the first term:

Yes, well I've been reading this fellow Illich ... The trouble is, he's an intelligent sort of fellow, and he seems to have convinced me he's got something there in what he's raving about. Which makes it a little awkward for me, as it answers the burning question – Why are we educating kids? with – We shouldn't be.
    Here am I stuck in Pooksville.
    Do you know what you're doing, issuing introductions to such books ...? Is it meant just as an indulgence, a dip into attractive theory, a taste intended to sate, but not intended to be followed up ...?
    I mean, if We shouldn't be, why am I? I do wrong. So I'm only in it for the money, I have been bribed/bought. Which is fine by me, but is it what you intended? Strikes me, you've got more problems ... than me. I'm only fighting it, calling it names so as to avoid getting fucked up by it, but you are actually fucking up people.
    ... Why an introductory skim through Recent Educational Theorists Who Are 'In' to Read?

Towards the end of the year, the cynicism and bitterness were as strong. Education, Chris says, neglects the fantastic, the funny, the creative, the artistic, the beautiful, the good, the real, all the important stuff ... and the best products are the machines which make sense; but not think ... love doesn't make sense either, it too is a thought.

Love is a thought
Not taught,
Jokes are a thought
Not taught.
Goodness,
Gracious,
Me, is a thought
Not taught.
Life, a slack rope,
Not taut
Is a thought
Not taught.
School
Is a fool
Nothing's taught.

Right at the end, perhaps to mollify us, he wrote that second term was *the* term for work in the schools, presumably implying that university work was thereby all the more redundant: 'I apologize if any of my comments at about this time cause offence – I felt it at the time, not now.' He then mentioned the limited coverage in the diary. 'The Simulation option, for example, doesn't receive all the mention it should.' I take it that this is an indirect way of telling Rod Fawns that he ran a good option – and in second term, by the way.

Covering the whole diary was a postscript marked 'please read this first' in which Chris mentioned that he followed a strict rule of never changing anything once written:

The angers and delights of a day appear untempered by any hindsight or cooling off period. This is fine for the delights, but the angers come out a bit too naked and passionate. I must trust to the reader to temper them. They are the genuine reactions of me at the time, they are not considered.

I apologize sincerely for any offence any of these remarks cause anyone. I do not intend any now.

On reflection, it's not a very good diary.

The YOU and THEY continually mentioned throughout refer sometimes to the reader in general, sometimes to Course B staff, and often to the legendary THEY of myth. The diary was written with only itself in mind, I was not talking to anyone in particular.

At least we irritated and stirred Chris, and it is pretty characteristic that students tended to talk more about, and probably to remember better, what annoyed them than what worked with them. Even Prue, for example, failed to mention that, despite her erratic attendance in first term, she was one of the most enthusiastic members of the second-term option on Children's Literature, run by Stephen Murray-Smith, and that it inspired her to do a quite splendid depth study of an Australian author, once very popular with children, but now seldom mentioned. Prue thought the author ought to be reinstated, and argued her case with a keen sense of literature and children.

The fact is that our gravest problem was finding generative starting points at the beginning of the year. We made mistakes in having large groups when our numbers doubled, and we added to the early difficulties the extra problem that some students clammed up whereas others hogged the discussions and caused further clamming up. It was this, rather than our adopting an interdisciplinary approach, that aggravated our difficulties. But apart from the remediable errors we might have had, our early difficulties have a wider significance. For us, as for all teachers, introducing students into new territory, when they all bring different background knowledge and experiences with them, is a subtle and ineradicable problem, especially if one is committed to respecting their individuality and to being guided by their concerns.

One of our greatest assets in the long view, our ability to relate theory and practice throughout, was one of our especial difficulties at the outset. When Maureen noted in her diary in first term what seemed to her to be our greatest problem, she was speaking as many students felt:

> There seems to be a great amount of resentment among the kids
> about any sort of theoretical discussion. I think the school experi-
> ence is hanging over everyone's head at the moment. Tension is
> building up over how each student is going to perform as a teacher,
> so the theoretical dialogue seems irrelevant. I think these books are
> really relevant and important — perhaps they could be left for a later
> date ...

Perhaps they could have, but that would have only created other problems. But Maureen was unquestionably right: the thought of having to teach hung over nearly all of them acting either as a source of motivation or as a paralysing threat.

Chapter 2

Who am I?

Finding oneself

'It's so hard, so exhausting, trying to be a *person* all the time', one of the students complained to a friend on the Course; and so it is if one of the main targets in a one-year training course for teachers is to help each student to find out what sort of teaching style and ideology is the one for him. There is no stereotype of The Good Teacher, we kept telling our students, perhaps partly to conceal our inability to work out our own criteria. We knew that very different kinds of people make good (or bad) teachers, but we hadn't pinned down the common characteristics.

Our original intention was that the full year should revolve around the experiences students had in learning to teach. From the students' point of view, our own experience told us, nothing could compete in intensity during that year with the challenge that teaching presented, and built into that challenge was the anxiety most felt about their 'image'. 'How do I look to others?' is a question that any sensitive teacher has to face sooner or later, and one that he alone can discover answers to. Hence, if it weren't for plagiarism, this chapter could well use Virginia Axline's title, 'In Search of Self', or, even better, Gore Vidal's remark, 'Selves are hard to come by'. The search, by its very nature, must be private; but if we were to be of any help and if the Course were to be supportive in the right way, the chances were great that problems would be more public than was normally the case. There were risks for students, we knew, perhaps the greatest being an undue encouragement of introspection and public soul-searching — of being 'on show' to each other, to staff and to pupils. But we sensed that there were greater, though different, risks in courses that cushioned for the student the impact of learning to teach. There were risks too for staff and schools since we put ourselves in an exposed position in 'practising what we preached', and in cutting the preaching down so that our beliefs were proved in action.

Through experience in the classroom and in school life students were meant to discover what were the most important questions to ask of their studies. But there was a prior question for most of them. The prospect of teaching set up an agitated anticipation of how they would be seen as persons in the classroom. The first taste of schools often intensified this to such an extent that there was no room for a while for anything else. It was all-absorbing.

While this preoccupation tended to blunt students' response to theorizing unless it was seen as immediately helpful to their early anxieties, those anxieties provided very powerful motivation which we welcomed. Educationists overseas were, at the same time, paying attention to the importance of personal involvement in showing how students profited (or failed to profit) from preservice training. At an OECD conference it was reported that the experts were unanimous in their opinion that a student's commitment to teaching could spring only from the student himself, but 'initial training could facilitate the capacity of the student to identify his commitment and, having found it, to develop it with guidance from the training institution' (see S. J. Eggleston in *New Patterns of Teacher Education and Tasks*,[1] p. 27). They made the further point that 'Students who had developed, at an early stage, the capacity to diagnose and respond to a situation were clearly to be preferred to those who had been trained to defer all decisions to seniors' (p. 22).

Professor Hirst in the article already referred to in chapter 1 points to three inter-related elements in learning to teach. Every practical judgment the student has to make, he suggests, requires an intellectual grasp of the problem and of appropriate ways to handle it, executive skills, and a 'disposition' to carry out his deliberations and to exercise his skills. Dispositions are 'stable and established patterns within the human personality'. I take it that he has in mind the acquisition of guiding, almost governing, 'right' or desired responses that one acts on even when caught off guard — that become part of one's personality and the values it subsumes as the result of reflective experience. We may know what should be done but be unable to do it; or we may have skills but fail to make 'a progressive intellectual critique' of our use of them. 'Left to himself a student can develop his capacities only in so far as he has the understanding to monitor his own teaching and the objectivity to carry out the task. These are huge demands ...'

School and teacher-training staff working together can help the student towards this self knowledge; but perhaps the first step towards it is in the relationship the student establishes with children. In discovering his commitment to teaching (or his inability to be committed) and to the values that will guide him as a teacher, the student must first of all acquire a commitment to children and their learning.

Being ill-at-ease with children

Although we had expected students to be scared of children, we had not expected the fear to be so often paralysing; and the more scared they were, the more introspective, sometimes egocentric, they became. It has already been pointed out that we had some sort of formula for easing students into teaching (see pp. 18–19), and many of the supervisors were very good at this.

In the first year we took groups of students to the schools affiliated with us so that they gained the opportunity of getting the 'feel' of various schools and of talking to some pupils before they were placed in a school. In our second year we gave even more emphasis in the first fortnight to talking to children. We brought classes from schools into the University and we went into schools too, wherever possible setting up some shared task that would provide a point of contact between pupils and students – for example, seeing and discussing a lesson we had videotaped the previous year and bringing in some of the pupils to assess it with the students and staff.

It was by bringing in children that we discovered to our surprise how inarticulate and shy students in their twenties were with youngsters in their early teens. Only those who had younger brothers or sisters or had some experience in working with younger people seemed to be at all at ease: for example, I took a group of about five pupils and four students on a tour of the University. Much to my amazement, I was the only adult who could talk easily and naturally to the schoolchildren. Many of the staff had similar experiences. It might be thought that having University staff present inhibited the students, but this is not altogether true, for we noted that great silences occurred when students were alone with pupils.

It became clear to us what the ordeal must have been like to face a blur of thirty faces while still being afraid of one individual child. What a false basis for teaching. It also dawned on us that many practising teachers had slipped into their role with little but a generalized understanding of children *en masse*. We began to note how many experienced teachers had built up defences against their fear of children – or, looked at in another way, of themselves. It took even more time and experience to discover that there was an opposite danger in informal, small schools – that students could all too readily become friend, adviser or 'facilitator' (I think that was the 'in' word) as an escape from facing the implications of being a teacher and of positively engendering learning.

To some extent the first reactions of the students to the pupils they had tried to talk to vindicated us in our attempts to introduce literature that dealt with 'reluctant learners' from impoverished homes. It was a new world and one that most students would soon have to enter. One group of students who had taken five children to coffee talked of their astonishment that only one in the five had any ambitions, and wanted to stay to sixth form to become a primary teacher. How could you hope to teach the other four, they wondered.

Wanda was astonished at the cynicism and gaucheness of one of her colleagues when they were showing pupils around the University:

> One thing which really annoyed me, was one co-student's comment to a Flemington High student, whom we were showing around the Uni. After visiting the Beaurepaire [Sports] Centre, the Union and the billiard room, the pupil commented, 'Don't you do any work around here?' I commented that you should try and strike a balance … My friend then told the pupil that you could muck around the first two terms at Uni and you'd pass O.K. if you borrowed lots of other people's notes and worked pretty hard in 3rd term, which I reckon is a stupid thing to say − it really irked me (some people need to work all year to pass).

Wanda's friend touched a sensitive spot in her and so she failed to see that the bravado, the showing off, indicated how ill-at-ease her friend was. He needed a great deal more contact with individual children who would quickly have shown him that they saw through his pretences. Within a week of joining her school Wanda noted that the pupils seemed 'really lively and happy' and she enjoyed spending a morning with them 'feeling more relaxed … and a bit more confident with them', whereas her friend spent the year never being sure whether his pupils were ragging him or having crushes on him.

Nothing illustrated the students' awkwardness with children better than the difficulties in finding a common language. Most students, though warned repeatedly in advance, took a long time to grasp that their normal vocabulary was incomprehensible to their pupils. This is just one example of 'the tricks of the trade' that can *not* be taught from the lecture platform or the seminar room. Angela, writing after nearly a month in school, complained of her difficulty in discussing the Declaration of Independence with a fourth form:

> their vocabulary was so bad that nearly every word had to be explained. This gave me a fright because I could sense it was totally above their heads yet I couldn't explain the words!! You <u>use</u> so

many words in history easily enough out of habit, yet come to give a precise meaning —!

A bit later, her fears had intensified and it is difficult to know if it was the children or adults or both that unnerved her: 'I'm so scared of people. Really scared. I don't think I have anything intense to give — [my teaching] is just crap. I don't have views or opinions — I run dry.' It had been, she said, 'Really a terrible day at school ... I feel so dumb.'

Adrian, the staff had predicted, would have had far more trouble than Angela. He seemed much less outgoing and far more tongue-tied; but within a week of being in the school he had come to know some pupils by doing menial chores like handing out paper and thus moving among the boys. He helped the one teacher who was prepared to take soccer, and he joined an excursion to the local court and to Parliament House. When he came to prepare his first lesson — on the price mechanism in the economy (even more difficult, I should have thought, than the Declaration of Independence) — he decided to start with the decision made in the court case they had seen. 'This I feel will loosen me and the class.'

> Also I have helped these boys with their accounting (in class) and have sat in on many of their classes. This has made me less nervous about facing them tomorrow because I know what to expect.

That was the beginning and he soon learned that there were many more subtleties to teaching than he had predicted; but all through his diary his concern is with 'getting to their level' and lessening the distance between the way he and they think. Because of this, Adrian began to overcome his fears more quickly than Angela did.

Joanna, who will be discussed more fully in the next chapter, had moments early on when she felt vulnerable. This extract from her diary illustrates once more how a breakthrough in teaching came to her as a result of close personal contact with a few, rather than a mass of, children:

> Fabulous day!
> Here I am feeling high — largely due to the personal 1 to 1 contact I've had this afternoon in interviews with several 4 P pupils. The inverviews were originally planned to investigate what pupils thought of and about their writing (at school & at home, if any) ... whether ... particular types of writing had changed since their early work in school — thus kids came with any past Engl. work ... they still retained. Comparison of work over the years was interesting. However, most important to me was the time we spent talking fairly directly, honestly, personally ... In the 10-15 mins intervals with each pupil I really came to feel for & know them each as individual

persons far more than I've been able to over the past term & a bit. I also gained some interesting ideas for future classwork ...

Boy! I'm really looking forward to next week's work & wish I may be able to gradually talk personally (like today) with all the others in the class.

In fact, if I were teaching F/T English classes I think I would definitely try to see each pupil individually (or in pairs?) out of class. This would result in more satisfying classroom relations and 'work'.

For Joanna, the way into group participation and learning, both as a student and as a teacher, was found by getting to know people individually or in very small numbers.

Another student, Andy, describes most convincingly his nervousness during his first day at the community school to which he was attached for the year. It happened to be the morning of the weekly school meeting, and he found himself helpless with embarrassment until a teacher shrewdly gave him a purpose for talking to two pupils:

> I remember sitting between two form 2 kids, thinking the reason I'm here is (partly) to learn how to relate to kids and how little I'd talked to people outside my age group before and not knowing really where to begin. As it happened I didn't begin — the meeting did however, and saved me from any further contemplation of the matter ...
>
> After the meeting, I was on my own. What do you do when you are placed suddenly into a new environment consisting of 100 people who know each other and whom you don't know? Why, you go and stand in front of the time table and collect your thoughts while you appear to be reading it ... I wandered along to the kitchen and there was Jack with a group of about ten girls and one boy ... I'm still finding it hard to talk to kids when along came Peggy and Jim — an almost inseparable duo — to Jack with a chemistry problem. Jack is busy and refers them to me — my first teaching assignment. Did I ever take it seriously? Looking back at my diary I took up three pages of careful analysis and evaluation. In any case, I did learn something about teaching, and I did start talking to kids.

Andy, it seemed to us, lived happily ever after, both in that small school and in the much bigger one that he taught in in following years. Although he was extremely quiet and reticent, he had inner strength and a persistent love of making science exciting to his pupils. It could be suggested that it was easier in a community school, for in a small, intimate school it is almost impossible to avoid a close relationship with pupils. But for some students it had its own special challenge in that pupils did not hide their boredom, and it took some students a long time to find out how to translate their own enthusiasms into terms that pupils could and would share. There was no escape into the sort of false anonymity that a big, formal school could provide.

Self-doubts

Students in all kinds of schools — big, small, formal, innovative, supportive, cold, strict, lax — had to come to terms with themselves, and for a minority this was exquisitely painful. For very few was it quite painless. For some, facing up to teaching forced them to recognize fears that they had been barely conscious of previously.

In the following accounts from students' diaries we should note that each student had his own idiosyncratic fears. The means of mastering them were different in each case, and so the problems of school-based teacher education defy easy generalization. The students whose diary extracts have been selected were those whose anguish was extreme and must not be taken as representative; but all of us who are concerned with people in their twenties (whatever their calling) might well be reminded of how vulnerable, insecure and even self-indulgent they can be at that age, and how hard many of them find it to distance themselves from (or, as Hirst would put it, to objectify) their dilemmas — to see themselves as they are and as they might become. Some of the students' desperate attempts to spill out their suffering might make some readers uncomfortable. If so, all I can answer is that the extracts are indeed authentic and that that is the way things really are, at bad moments, at least for some.

Jill, for example, found herself dogged by false pride:

> I wouldn't ask for help in the early part of the year — that stupid independence, maybe even fear of intelligent adults which has plagued me for ages. Fear of being broken, squashed & laughed at — every time you lose this fear with one person, it's a lot easier to get to know others.

And, having observed that, she noted that it had affected her in all sorts of other ways: most particularly, her boyfriend had remarked that she had become more 'discerning' in her 'waffle'.

'Traumas' seems to be the vogue word in the diaries of the most sensitive students. One sometimes wonders about the wisdom of causing so much soul-searching. The beginning of the year is worst, for most, because of their uncertainty about whether or not they will ever find a workable rapport with pupils. The badly designed lesson, the badly run school, the troublesome love-affair, overtiredness — all contribute, but are seen by some students almost exclusively as assaults on their personality, on their incurable inadequacies: 'I kept telling myself it is the school <u>not</u> me,' Martha wrote half-way through first term. 'But I think more and more I am beginning to realize that the problem lies within me.' Everything was combining to make her doubt herself:

> I really could not have written this last night I was so upset. Even more so than my traumas with form 3. Then 4A. John [her supervising teacher] relocated large nos of them & then gave them a talking to. I set them a question & the relevant pages to be read. John went out and <u>bingo.</u> They told me they didn't want me to teach them — they didn't like me etc. etc. I exploded. What makes them think I like them? For the most part they are M.C. [middle class?] with all its prejudices and bigoted attitudes. They are rude, inconsiderate, irresponsible, disrespectful & all the other words I can't think of at present. As far as they are concerned form 4 is a 'mucking around' year and they know they'll be promoted to form 5 come what may ... But when they hit tertiary institutions BOY, OH BOY, they will feel it.

How much of this she actually said and how much she only thought is not clear from the diary. She didn't know whom she hated more — herself or the 'kids'.

At this point one supervisor misguidedly videotaped a lesson. The equipment, let alone anything else, 'threw' her. She summed up some of her reactions:

> I didn't change my class i.e. teaching method at all.
> I did the same thing as I had planned.
> I felt so self-conscious regarding (a) how I stood (b) grammar (c) the clothes I was wearing.
> I felt so nervous I was twisting the cord, playing with my coat — all sorts of odd little movements.
> I talk much too quickly.
> I project a very pompous image over to the kids.

At the week-end she wrote: 'I really don't feel like continuing. It's not the course I have developed an aversion to, but the school & worst of all — kids.' Some weeks later she is still bemused by self-criticism. The problem is 'my whole attitude towards the kids. I guess it's a defence mechanism but I do mean to be sincere — not pompous & dictatorial. Do I really want to teach?'

Martha's difficulties were complex. She had a deeply disturbing family problem; a critically important love-affair that was being destroyed by her anxieties; a sense of being isolated from the student group and threatened by them; a very difficult school; and an arid

61

approach to her subjects, despite a record of the highest academic distinction. To be constructively critical was extremely difficult in that it could so easily become a source of persecution — like the videotape:

> There has been a lot of discussion about feeling threatened in classroom situations. Well I feel threatened by other things as well — supervisors viewing my lessons, video-tape of the lesson is a new and consequently paralysing fear because the full extent of its use is unknown. The UNKNOWN QUANTITY IN A BLACK BOX = Video Man.
>
> It took me all of 5th period to quieten myself down.
>
> My pulse rate slowed back ...
>
> I grumbled about how I felt re the course — sick of the school etc. I could easily have cried. I have become very tearful lately — I think it's because I feel I am a failure as a teacher.
>
> I realize my teaching has loads and loads of faults, & I am trying to correct them. But I hate the thought of anyone seeing that tape. It's like hanging your dirty washing on the line for everyone to see.

The personal difficulties gradually spilled out and that made it easier to tackle the teaching weaknesses. Martha had a muscular, inflexibly sequential approach to subject-matter — all firmly logical and totally unrelated to the pupils' own experiences. I tried planning lessons with her, suggesting starting points for historical topics that began from some sort of shared concern; but by this time she was frozen. The first break occurred when she reprimanded a child for not having done his homework. In the stress of the lesson she asked him to see her after class, when she discovered that the child was in as many difficulties as she was. She was afraid of being duped, then she had second thoughts — his excuse was 'almost feasible — in fact I feel that he was telling me the truth ... I think he is beginning to *trust* me. I could be wrong, but if I have achieved nothing else, I'd like to know that he is a friend and not an enemy.'

Finally we moved her to another school where the classes, we knew, would respect her thoroughness and her supervisor would help her with her presentation. She was amazed to be advised that she needed *more* structure in her lesson planning, whereas she had assumed that the reputation the Course had for radicalism meant that structured planning was disapproved.

Some students had a sentimental idea that if they imposed a structured order in presenting their lessons they would inhibit children's spontaneity and dam up their intellectual energies (for variations of this view, see pp. 45, 88-9). Some of the radicals came to the Course with this conviction; some students thought that their supervisors and/or the Course subscribed to it — to the 'wait and it will happen' school of thought. It is easy to see how students came to interpret our encouragement of initiative and self-reliance as a criticism of structure, although nothing was further from our intentions. Drawing the line between the two was in practice very difficult and Martha was experiencing a crippling conflict over this very point. She was incapable of giving an unstructured lesson, but she seemed to think that she had to abandon structure rather than to structure more imaginatively.

> Well, the 'structured' class ... It was really amazing the difference it made. Because it was organized in terms of the materials available in class, everyone started off on an equal footing. Hence normally quiet kids really blossomed. Instead of 'bright' kids dominating they had to fight to get their say ...
> No one grumped that the work was too hard, or that there was too much ...
> It was quite exciting to use this method as a means of gathering the class together as I had felt that I was losing some of them.

She was learning to teach with children in the forefront of her imagination, and thus to do justice to the content that had previously totally absorbed her. At the end of the year she commented:

> I am very tired, but no longer as nervy or tearful. I think I am beginning to cope with myself and that's the greatest attribute of this course for me. Once you know yourself — then you are in a better position to relate to kids. Keep the old chin up ...
> I guess I still feel isolated to a degree, but I have found that at the second school I have coped far more efficiently and effectively — there is a need to be independent here and I am slowly responding to this. Independence — the ability to think and act — in a teacher is essential.
> This year has been a challenging one; a year of extreme ups-and-downs. Probably its greatest value to me has been in my own personal development. It has illuminated my failings & so now it's up to me to correct them.
> Academically, I doubt that I have done a great deal. In fact, the standard of my written work is well below last year. But prac. experience — teaching and organizing — has improved so much it's hard to believe. And <u>that</u> after all is why I took this course ...
> Thanks Gwyn, Bernie & Rod for a year I'll never forget.

I'm sure she won't, and we shall never forget our own self-doubts. It was Martha, in her worst doldrums, who consoled herself by her close contact with a friend who, after a traditional Dip.Ed., cracked up in her first year's teaching. As Martha said herself, *her* Dip.Ed. would protect her from that. Although it had been touch-and-go whether or not she would survive the year, she was convinced that block teaching rounds would not have revealed her great difficulties, and she felt that it would have been altogether too testing to have discovered them for the first time as a full-time teacher on her own. In fact she has taken a leading part in curriculum revisions in the school she was posted to.

Norma's difficulties with her pupils were rather different from Martha's. Norma reacted by being casual and friendly instead of deceptively frigid and 'pompous'. Early in the first term she recorded:

This has perhaps been the most traumatic day of my progress toward teacher status. (Unfortunately, I am writing this on Sunday when it is a far away event of the past and must lose much of its immediacy & emotion) ...

Final period of the day — 4th form S/S ... Walked in & from the first moment everything went wrong. Disaster!!

My eagerness & naivety in wanting to teach was certainly brought to bear in this class. From the start I had no control. My tack was to be cool, friendly & smiling even though I had been warned that the only thing they understand was authoritarianism. Instinctually I am ag. that approach but obviously the kids can't grasp or appreciate a more intimate friendly approach. Even saying this, however, dismisses the responsibility from me of making a complete mess of even this ideal aspect. I seem to have gone over this so much that it now seems redundant to be talking about <u>what</u> went wrong. I know, however, that I need to analyse & understand the situation as it did have such a traumatic effect on me.

1. Material — I wasn't interested or sufficiently conversant.

2. Class interest & participation — I made it a monologue especially when I realized there was no chalk or duster for pts on the board: I had it in mind to get them writing — this was supposed to quieten them down! ...

Let's say, for the sake of brevity, that I fell into <u>all</u> the pitfalls of first-class experience ...

Even though I've destroyed confidence with that class I'm glad for my own self-respect that a teacher wasn't in the room. My self-respect suffered enough anyway. Another teacher stepped in on the problem, then began a concerned attack on how I shouldn't have been allowed in a classroom unsupervised; young women, women for that matter, can't cope with all-male classes. I still don't agree ... bloody male chauvinists! Concerned as they were, their paternalistic attitudes made me worse, rather than better. At least I didn't break down completely ...

Thursday evening was terrible. After 2 hrs blubbering I emerged a physical wreck. I was totally exhausted physically & mentally.

Friday — I felt and looked terrible on rising. Knowing that I had to face the other Dip. Eds & staff who would have heard versions on the grapevine, I dragged myself to Uni. The concern — it was killing: but I must admit rather nice.

Although she did not see it at the time, there was a good deal of healthy fight-back from Norma even at the worst moments, and she did not turn her bitterness against 'the kids'. Like many new teachers she was often 'lost for words'. The strain of thinking simultaneously about the 'what' in the lesson — the next point I want to develop — while meeting unforeseeable crises in classroom behaviour causes both mental paralysis and a strange feeling of being outside oneself looking in as if watching oneself through a telescope and being caught between the acting and the observing.

Myra, for example, like Martha, was so obsessed with listening to herself that she found herself out of touch with her pupils:

I was too jittery to take in what the kids were doing — too busy listening to my grammar & making sure my voice didn't cut out altogether. It was kind of unreal, seeing one of the rows of kids ignore me almost completely. (I later meandered over & discovered that they had nearly all finished at home the work I was setting for the rest of the class.)

The same thing happened to Jock:

I don't know where to begin. I am still totally lost as soon as I begin talking to them. Even though a discussion did take place about *Kes*, I still couldn't even follow my own plan (I'll have to have the progression of things more clearly sorted out in my own mind before I start next time). I find it hard to concentrate on what the kids are saying even when they're answering questions, because I'm too caught up with what I'm to do after the guy finishes speaking.

When students are acutely self-conscious, our words as supervisors can confuse and confound them still further — can make them uncertain about which way to move. 'Have your plan more clearly worked out', says Jock, probably echoing what his supervisor had suggested. 'I did things as I had planned', says Martha, bearing in mind our advice to depart from one's plan according to how things go.

It was true that Jock needed to plan more carefully, for his natural tendency was to teach inspirationally and he could not yet do that successfully. He lost his place and his lessons fell apart. It was not that he had not prepared enough: he was academically very solid; but his preparation did not take into account (I gather from his diaries) the

65

sequence and the methods by which he would proceed, so that the lessons ran away from him and he had no strategies for calling them back. It was true that Martha 'did things as I had planned' far too unswervingly. She 'pushed on regardless', with dedicated logic that blinded her to what sense, if any, it was all making to the children. Jock and Martha would inevitably make quite different sorts of teachers, and both could be admirably effective in their different ways, but helping them to solve their problems wasn't as simple as that.

Sometimes we gave contradictory, or apparently contradictory, advice to the one student. 'You need to plan more thoroughly', or 'You should have changed your plan then', could both be right suggestions. Words are the very devil for the adviser. Martha, in her moments of greatest difficulty, was paradoxically both too structured and not structured enough in her planning. She had an inexorable sense of where she was going; but early in the year she was so preoccupied with this that she had little sense of how the children saw where *they* were going. It is no accident that her final breakthrough came when she concluded that she needed *more* structure, not less. She could not get to this point spontaneously, by being guided by what children said in reply − or antagonism. She came to it by structuring in a different way. Her supervisor helped her to build up a collection of excellent materials and to plan to use them in such a way that children would acquire a sense of progressive mastery and achievement, and could then contribute to class discussion. Once they responded to the material, what they said fitted her own standards of relevance and logic, thus giving her scope to be flexible in dealing with what they had to say.

Another student, Jocelyn, the year before, had grasped this point almost immediately. She was one of the quietest, shyest, least confident (I thought), least articulate students I ever remember. I was apprehensive when I went to see her teach. I had thought that she would be paralysed. So had she; and what I found was that she had prepared her lessons so imaginatively, with carefully thought out and intensely interesting materials, that the class went on profitably almost without her having to say more than a few sentences. It was superb organization. As soon as a child had completed one task Jocelyn intervened simply to guide the child to do something rather more exacting. I saw her teach several years after that, and she still used the same method basically; but she had become more articulate and utterly confident, and it still worked.

Jock would never make that sort of teacher. Neither would Norma. Neither would Martha, though it helped her most to adopt Jocelyn's methods for the time being. Before doing so, she unintentionally became aloof and apparently pompous, whereas Norma wandered around the classroom seemingly aimlessly, smiling charmingly and pushing the discussion along with encouraging noises like, 'mm' or 'yes' or with repetitions of what the last child said — that at least gave time to think of what to do next.

In going through all this it is scarcely surprising that the dominant question for each student is not only, 'What sort of a teacher can I be if I am to survive?' but also, 'Do I really want to be a teacher?' Late in the year Norma gave a lesson that 'wasn't entirely unsuccessful', but was no great shakes either, yet she found it a 'very rich experience. I became aware of myself as myself, I began to understand things about kids, the teacher's role and classroom dynamics', even though 'I felt as if I was being dragged through a torture chamber it ripped me apart so much at times'. She concluded, 'The 2 most important things are a concern for the kids and responsibility. I can forget my own fears, insecurities etc. and take this responsibility. Forceful words??'

Shortly afterwards we find:

> Stand up another disillusioned student teacher! Just when does one start achieving anything in this damned profession?
> This lesson was not a disaster, yet I feel that it upset me more than any I have taught. The anxiety, the feeling of incompetence and sheer inability to cope with teaching reached a climax after this lesson. Perhaps I am just tired and I know I have a lot of personal pressures worrying me.

A correct analysis, for Norma had really made it — though painfully. A part of the 'hidden curriculum' for students is that part which staff never know about. The personal conflicts and doubts, combined with stresses in learning a profession, led to repeated references in diaries to a tiredness that was almost beyond endurance.

'Can't go into all the gory details as I fall asleep on my floral pillow', Norma wrote on one occasion — and later, 'I feel extremely anxious re my ability to find time to read. All I want to do is go to sleep. It's really bad news.' Or another girl, at the very beginning of the year: 'Now I find that this damn education business is taking up ninety per cent of my speaking time', and the next morning, 'What a day. I'm so tired and hot … I had a hard time trying to comprehend Illich.'

Others found the Course painful in ways that we could not possibly have predicted in detail. Half-way through the year Roger astonished us all when one of us, while visiting his school, found him on the point of throwing it all in. Roger was quiet, a moderately good attender at University classes, and he seemed self-possessed though somewhat reticent. As a teacher he had a 'whizz-bang' reputation. He was thorough in his preparation; his organization of projects was outstanding in both the content and the orderliness with which he managed to get pupils participating in difficult tasks like field studies. He was a 'straight-down-the-line' man, but there was no doubt that his pupils learned a great deal and with considerable satisfaction.

When he came in to discuss giving up the Course, he was some-what astonished by my assuring him that I would in no way try to in-fluence his decision. He knew that I knew his reputation as a teacher, and he feared that I would not be able to accept his doubts. He feared also, I suspect, that I would take any withdrawal from the Course as an implied criticism of it. The story tumbled out without anything like the coherence I have to give it in retelling it.

He had always, he said, wanted to be a teacher. There had never been a moment's doubt in his mind; but now he was convinced that he could never be the sort of teacher he wanted to be. He stood in the classroom, he said, hating himself. Above all, what convinced him of the necessity to get out was that he was in an unrelieved mood of depression — a thing that had never happened in his life before. Under-lying this, in part, was his discovery in himself of the capability of violence that he had never experienced before. He gave as example his totally losing his temper with two boys whose behaviour he thought selfish and defiant. With the first boy he so nearly lost control of his temper that he was terrified, and then with the second boy he grabbed his hair and actually hurt him before he could stop himself. When he saw the boy later in the day, he knew that the child was hurt, both physically and emotionally, and he could do nothing — 'I was simply appalled.'

All of this, and other things too, convinced him that he could never establish a proper relationship with anyone. Since this had happened, his sister had chided him with the challenge, 'So you're going to prove your mother right, are you?' and he realized for the first time that his mother had always said he'd never make a teacher. It was now perfectly clear, he said, that he'd be better suited to a desk job — a town planner or any job that would enable him to be the sort of straight-down-the-line impersonal person he now realized he was. His whole education, he now believed, had been totally misconceived. He had always mastered anything required of him and passed with 'A's, and nothing ever lower than a high B' — yet he had never learned to think critically, let alone with originality: 'I am the product of a sterile education and it's too late to change!'

No doubt the astute reader will see an irony in this account. Roger had internalized many of the values associated with the Course. Critics might even suspect that he had been brainwashed. Yet he was asking himself, for the first time, just how many values he had absorbed un-thinkingly during the course of his life, especially during his education. It would have been paternalistic and sentimental to have protected him from facing up to the possibilities of his own violence. Sooner or later, no matter what course he had done, he would have had to face this as a teacher. However painful, it is something that was better examined early, during his year of training, than brushed aside or cosily rationalized; and in the course of talking about it Roger needed little prompting before it dawned on him that a really cruel person would have given little thought to the hurt to his victim. His anguish could not be taken to denote indifference. He is now a successful teacher.

Keeping at 'arm's length'?

Being sensitive and being able to relate oneself to people, however, are not the same thing. Roger did eventually come to terms with his reticence; but he did not find it easy to do. This was a constant difficulty for a minority of students each year. Myra, for example, was still in conflict late in the year about whether she should be outgoing or distant, formal or informal. Her sensitivity on these issues continued to paralyse her in action:

> I don't know why it should be that I get so cut up over it all, but I've reached the stage now where I know Form I is not learning any science with me teaching them & I'm not 'improving' ... It's mostly my fault — even though this form has a lot of 'difficult' students who have pretty severe behavioural and homelife problems. At the beginning of the year I thought I could reason with these kids and if they called me Myra, so much the better for the production of a friendly atmosphere. But they can't appreciate reasoning unless they respect the teacher, and they certainly don't respect me. They were no doubt as confused as I was by my ambivalent stance on discipline — which I theoretically detest but which must, in the practical situation, be adopted I feel like a traitor with the tripey lessons I serve them ... I'm so depressed by the whole scene that I haven't been able to think of anything else. At the moment I've screamed 'Uncle' until I can summon more mental & moral strength from somewhere.

Fortunately, not all students are as vulnerable as the ones just quoted; but a school-based course must make allowances for all manner of self-doubt, and however hard it might try — and *we* certainly did *not* try — it could not be a soft option, especially for its most sensitive students. For them, the challenges do not have to be artificially induced. Perhaps this is in the nature of teacher *per se*. Certainly the question, Who am I? occurs to most of them, and seldom can it fail to carry some threat.

Ronald, a diffident, but inwardly strong student, a more mature student than many, described in his end-of-year account of his teaching how he had tried himself out in many approaches. At first, he said:

> my need was to develop some sort of assurance that I, as a person who has always been rather slow and hesitant socially, was capable of gaining the respect of students and establishing a good relationship ...
>
> On first beginning with form I, I had gone in accepting and even encouraging noise and at first the results didn't worry me ... But as the sessions went on I began to receive messages ... I suppose I first started getting messages from the kids. They were pushing me to see how far they could go, yet at the same time wanted me to stop them. This was because they liked me and enjoyed the sessions ... The messages from the kids were quite explicit: 'Sir, why don't you control the class? Sir, does it worry you that the class makes so much noise? Sir, did you know that other teachers were watching us today.'
>
> And from the teachers, sympathetic smiles – 'how did it go?' – and stories about the difficulties they had had ... Pretty soon I began to experience grave unease about my image. *Although I didn't really doubt that I could control the class if I wanted to, I didn't want to in the way I knew I could* [my italics]. But ... I cracked down on the really rowdy class, gave them a taste of feigned temper with parade-ground volume and edge. It had the desired effect ...
>
> I did a horrible thing yesterday in that I declined to read a student's work during class, I put him off, he was offended and a few minutes later causing disruption. The point was that he was writing for the teacher ...
>
> The thing that astonishes me about a lot of kids' writing is that sometimes they are capable of determining the possible depths of a problem without teacher direction, sometimes going immediately and instinctively to the fundamental without getting caught up on the superficialities that mar most adults. But when this happens I haven't been exploiting it sufficiently ... I have been using their production to say to other kids, 'Look – they did it – so can you – this is the sort of thing I want.' The aim all the time has been to get them to write rather than getting them to think. I have to rethink myself into their position. To recall, what I seem to have shut out, the preoccupations of my own adolescence. What was I like, what were the foggy areas in my understanding, what insights did I pick up to help me on the way? ... I've got to home in on the preoccupations of the kids.

Ronald was unsure of himself partly because he was influenced by the 'image' he presented, but even more importantly because he was trying to reconcile his image with his principles. He says quite explicitly at one point that in attempting this reconciliation many mistakes were inevitable, and it is clear that he could not push himself to acquire a satisfactory image by distorting his nature and his beliefs. He could satisfy himself of his ability to resort to play-acting, but it is quite clear that he would never finally settle for that resolution of the problem. The 'Who am I?' question is both a personally painful and an ideologically testing one.

Another of our older students, Jim, a man in his mid-twenties, had had a year's abortive experience in teaching. He joined the Course as a final attempt to discover whether teaching could ever be for him. He chose Course B and he chose to work in a community school because he had semi-consciously diagnosed his troubles as coming from an inability to make contact with children. We were disturbed by the way in which he spent his first few months — mostly sitting around in the garden outside the school 'talking to kids'. When we did see him teach during that time he was disorganized and ineffectual. He finally wrote his depth study on a small group of the children he came to know closely:

I am critically concerned with the problems of kids who come from working-class families and to whom school is one long piece of irrelevant boredom. [This had been his experience in that previous year of teaching.] What do you do with kids like that?

In a normal school situation of large classes and teachers seeing discipline as a very necessary ingredient in order to do anything at all with 30 kids, then these kids, formed in their defensive groups, must spend most of their time shuffling between periods of time at the headmaster's study, time in corridors, time in psychologists' rooms drawing circles, and time 'wagging it'. I have spent the last four months talking to these kids of mine every day and although I have at last gained a degree of acceptance by them, it is still only in short moments that I manage to 'allow' them the confidence to drop their role in the group and talk in a way that I regard as important i.e. getting at what they really feel and think about things. The implications of this progress for normal school situations are frighteningly real.

I think that the only hope of doing anything with these kids has to be on a personal level i.e. what Kozol would call 'immersion in the situation of the victim' or Dennison might call 'respecting the culture of the child you are teaching in a personal way' ...

It can be a very despairing project to think of kids being fated by their home environments ... I think I can say, without any claim to melodrama, that at least one of my kids will spend a fair part of his

life in prisons and there may be no way that I can have any effect
upon that ...

Helping a middle-class kid to make a bead head-dress, love
Dryden or weave a tapestry can be a worthwhile activity. It is a lot
harder to help keep one of my kids out of jail and for me it becomes
a matter of priorities with my time ...

An entry in my school diary on the 12th of April is the first entry
that I have about the group:

'There is a group of kids who come from working-class families
and who are anti-intellectual and anti-arty. There are rumours of
police scraps and flick-knife carrying. One ... was involved with a
school trial over some used or stolen goods ...

I would like to get closer to those kids and find out if I can
what they are interested in.'

It is interesting and faintly amusing to look back on this account
which mirrors a certain naive disbelief coupled with a paternalistic
[conceit] that I would find out what these kids wanted to learn
about and by this get them into a class where their moral awakening
would begin, guided by pliant handling.

I think it fair to say that the problem was a little more difficult
than I had thought at that stage.

Jim knew best how to sort himself out, and our main claim to success with him is that we gave him the freedom to do it. It was quite late
in second term when he asked me to come and see him teach. To my
joy, he gave a most original, relaxed and beautifully designed lesson – a
talent that he continued to develop!

There are at least two threads running through these accounts of the
students' search for self. I began the Course believing that real teaching
experiences in a teacher-training year carry their own challenge and
therefore their own discipline, regardless of the push for stringency that
the Course staff might give. Students' diaries have shown that this is
even truer than I had thought. While the personal dilemma remains for
the student, every other problem presented will be pale at least, and at
worst will seem irrelevant to him. It is heartening that theoretical concerns took on added meaning as the year progressed, for that indicates
that personal doubts became less pressing for most students.

It emerges, however, that the personal doubts are always streaked
with ideological questions as both Ronald and Jim make quite clear.
The question, 'How do I establish my authority?' moves imperceptibly
into the questions, 'What is the basis of my authority?' and 'What sort
of authority do I want to have?' The ideological implications of this
shift in preoccupation have only been touched on so far; but it might
be noted that, however preoccupied each student seemed with himself

during his worst 'traumas', part of his anguish was a 'should' question — an ideological and moral question.

Jim's account is specially interesting in that his dilemma was resolved as satisfactorily as it could be for him in the closeness he established with a particularly difficult group of boys. He did not 'save' them, though his subsequent work with them suggests that he helped all but one towards social rehabilitation. The point at the moment is that he convinced himself that true teaching lay in a deeply-meant acceptance of, and an insight into, his pupils. His despair lay in his doubts about whether such a relationship was practicable for the ordinary teacher in the ordinary school, teaching many different classes and thus hundreds of children each week, especially when the pupils happened to be profoundly disturbed and resistant. His answer to this lay in his deciding to teach in a community school, which he has done ever since with considerable success both humanly and as a far more competent and inspired 'classroom' teacher than he was at the beginning of his year with us.

The teaching style for me

What the students have taught me from their diaries and depth studies is that, far more than I ever suspected, every glimmer of hope seemed to come when the student in trouble or doubt felt some closeness with even one child. Jim was pessimistic about the feasibility in a big school of generalizing from his experiences; but we can, and shall, turn to examples of students who learnt some of the lessons Jim learnt, but learnt them in a big school. I think, nevertheless, that Jim was basically right in that large institutions militate against the possibilities of children's or teachers' learning to be 'persons' in the way I have in mind. Without getting on to sociological arguments on this point, I am pretty well sure that the difficult question of discovering 'Who am I?' is most significantly and helpfully faced when there can be frank friendliness. Certainly Course B's experience in trying to run over-large group seminars bears this out. Of course a large lecture or the mass viewing of a film, and other big-scale projects, can be educative, and shouldn't necessarily be eliminated; but what we more often learn about ourselves comes from a more intimate setting. Large classes may be shown by research to be as effective as small ones in teaching easily measured skills such as spelling or computing; but I have yet to hear anyone who teaches in a small community school talking about keeping the children at arm's length until they respect your authority.

The we/they mentality, which is expressed so often in metaphors drawn from combative sports or warfare, is odd, to say the least, when one considers that pupils, teachers and school share — or should share —

the one basic object of furthering learning. Often we have to agree with students that their supervisors' advice to be aloof and stern before they can afford to be relaxed and friendly is expedient; but if the advice betokens an underlying acceptance of hostility it can only be accepted as a necessary evil – a temporary compromise until the sources of conflict are better understood. If that is sentimental, then I have been a sentimental teacher at both the toughest south-east London Modern schools and the most academically elite girls' school in Melbourne.

Big institutions create constraints of their own that have little, if anything, to do with learning. Small community schools, while they may justify all sorts of criticism, can seldom be charged with being impersonal and anti-pupil. It is not surprising that 'progressive' large schools like Countesthorpe in Leicestershire, or Thomastown and Huntingdale in Victoria, have devised ways of dividing the school into smaller administrative and teaching units. Even when this is not done, some teachers will find ways of creating smaller groups that work closely with them.

Successful teachers might, and do, have very different teaching styles. One of the most formal, unrelaxed and seemingly haughty teachers I have ever taught with was one of the most successful. When it came to the crunch, the pupils knew that she was on their side. They were awed by her manner, but they saw beyond it. They knew that if she seemed to be overdemanding with them, it was because she had thought carefully that they could profit from being more demanding of themselves. They also knew that she would always behave justly in any conflict, and that she would befriend them in any trouble. When she became a school principal she could make pupils and staff alike confident of this same justice, even in a staff–student conflict. Both felt that she was on their side – because she *was*. She could achieve this without being devious or slick, simply because she saw their interests as being common ones. It all happened with very few words, but there was never, even by implication, a suggestion that things should be settled out of a sense of personal loyalty, or that successes were counted as *her* successes.

Other teachers might seek friendliness and a personal following, and children will see through this too and withhold their respect because they know that they are not being respected in their own right, but are in some indefinable way being used and underestimated. To take an extreme example, I recall a loving and demonstrative mother who talked, without a shade of embarrassment, let alone self-criticism, of her child as being an extension of herself. And 'loving' teachers can manifest that sort of possessiveness without even the excuse of the umbilical cord.

The notions of formality/informality, distance/closeness, haughtiness/ easiness are ones that show again how devilish words are. There are many formal, distant, haughty teachers who are preferable to informal, close, easy ones (and vice versa). But the Methods lecturer who said to students, 'Ninety per cent of teaching is simply acting', upset them irreparably, and in my view they were right to reject his view. The teacher who said to one of my students that if he was a 'crash hot teacher' he'd give him 10 per cent; if he 'knew something about kids, school and society', he'd give him 100 per cent, was not quite so wrong, but was still very wrong. Belittling the subtle skill of the teacher in stimulating learning damaged that student's effectiveness because it was said at a crucial moment in that student's conflicts about the sort of teacher he wanted to become – the 'Who am I?'

Angela, although a most warm and attractive young woman, had a sense of dedication to learning that made her immediately effective if somewhat formidable. Her lessons were prepared with the greatest care, and in giving them she pressed the children to try to ensure that every one of them would rise to the stimulation her material gave. She was quite taken aback when her supervisor said at the end of the first term that she would become an outstanding teacher when she learned to un-bend. Although she taught in a big, somewhat formal and rigorous school, it was the children who reinforced the supervisor's comment for Angela:

Before I started Dip.ed. this year I didn't believe in love in the class-room. I felt that being a good teacher involved bringing prepared and interesting materials to class, controlling, persuading, and coercing students to work upon it. While I still believe this, I also feel that for a total educational experience there must be some emotional contact between pupils and teacher. I don't mean a dangerous dependency or crush, but ... I now feel that students need to know that a teacher cares for them, believes in their potential and is genuinely happy when they answer the demands a teacher makes.

... It is difficult to communicate to pupils that you are com-mitted to them, that your aim is to tap some of those wonderful resources inside them without appearing stupidly weak or sentimen-tal. There is a very delicate balance that must be established. On one side you say – 'I think you are terrific and do wonderful things' and on the other side you must keep saying, 'You haven't done enough yet, you are capable of much, much more.'

At the moment I feel that I am emotionally, intellectually and socially committed to teaching and pupils. I see my role as enlarging their expectations of themselves. While at the beginning of the year I was on about bringing beautiful things to students, my attitude has changed ... My commitment was to my disciplines, I now feel com-mitted to what those disciplines can offer pupils ...

After my last lesson with the fourth formers they gave me a book of Australian myths and legends. I was so happy and touched that they had enjoyed me and my teaching so much ... I'm sure I'll always remember that class as my first <u>real</u> teaching.

If we turn to Martin, we find him coming to his own conclusions, in a large high school that, although in some respects impersonal and bureaucratic, was beginning to encourage innovations and small-scale pilot schemes. Within this school Martin had the good fortune to work with two teachers with very different teaching styles. One, Lloyd Jones, was jointly appointed to our Course and to the school. The other, Carole Buhaj, was a senior teacher there who had worked with the Course for several years as a supervisor of our students. Martin observed that, different though the approaches of these two were, there was something of overarching importance that enabled them both to succeed as teachers. This is how he interpreted what he saw, after talking to them and taping and filming them at work as part of his chosen depth study.

It is worth quoting Martin at some length because his comparison between these two teachers, his admiration for them both, enabled him to work out just where he stood:

Carole Buhaj says that ... kids know that teachers have real, troublesome lives, that they have problems ... and are secretly not easily shocked. But somehow they expect some sort of saint/wowser when the person becomes a teacher. So it's important to maintain expectation.

Later he described Lloyd's classes, as they appeared to him, as ones in which there was a good deal of movement, informality, and lack of 'hassle' which some 'other teachers wouldn't lolerate'.

Martin then looked for significant comparisons:

Originally I thought that the teachers' activity might be fairly much the same within the classroom no matter what ideology they had. I thought there was a limited scope for ideas and activities in the schoolroom situation. But now I realise that their classes are really different. Still I want to point out some fundamental things that are going on in both Carole's and Lloyd's rooms.

Firstly both situations are artificial to the extent that both classes are really shaped by the personality and expectations of the teacher ... Lloyd's informality is artificial ... It's a special ... convivial atmosphere because there is a benevolent adult running it – not another kid.

Carole's class, more straight, more topic-centred is artificial like most traditional classroom setups are supposed to be. In a significant sense one is no more real than the other.

In the framework of Flemington High, and allowing for the necessary implications of that, <u>that</u> form 2 is <u>Carole's</u> class, <u>that</u> form I is Lloyd's. And they can really use that power.

In both cases something happens that I'm really on about. Kids can make emotional and intellectual demands on the teacher. They can establish themselves as a personality there.

That's fairly obvious in the Form I ... The facility to roam and play is fairly important ... In a more teacher-orientated class kids establish their personality in the ability to answer back, to refuse to volunteer, ... even not to be hassled ... In Lloyd's classroom I am aware of tons of different personalities because they have such a good chance of expressing them.

I find in Carole's classes that the same thing is there but a little harder to identify.

In looking at the very different teaching styles of two teachers whom he admired, Martin had found a common element that helped him to answer the questions, 'What sort of a teacher do I want to be?' 'What sort of a teacher can I be?'

Martin then described a lengthy discussion that he tape-recorded in Carole's class. It was on what could have been a really 'hot' issue – the role of migrant women – because it touched on very deep differences in the children's experiences. It was a class in which feelings could become very heated as the 'old Australians' attacked the migrants for greedily working too hard and the migrants attacked the 'old Australians' for exploiting them and leaving them all the dirty jobs. Martin reported that the discussion lasted for an hour and a half. 'The class was divided, laughing and applauding points as they were made. It had become a really good self-sustaining argument':

O.K. They could establish their personalities in that room. Firstly, although Carole's the boss the atmosphere is always really comfortable. Secondly, she makes efforts to include all sorts in the work. Kids are reinforced in that way. Thirdly her attitudes to behaviour demand a fair amount of integrity from the kids. Much more subtly, there is a sense that she knows about and tries to understand every kid in the class and without that being obvious you can just sense that. Lastly, she doesn't try to intrude beyond a point of 'teacher' or 'supervisor' or 'friend' so that you can be yourself outside her sphere of influence and with her good will. I feel that as much as the kids do and it's really good.

Two styles of teaching are really different. Two teachers have

different parts of themselves to offer. But there is an all important
carefulness in both.

The teachers <u>are</u> different in a way I didn't expect. I noticed that
Carole's class has a greater facility for argument or discussion. They
talk about issues really well ...

I guess what you remember in school are the mad times, or the
times when you are affected personally. I think you assimilate learning; it just becomes part of you. So if I go back to Betty [whom he
described earlier as a pupil who puzzled and worried him] ... she
does know something about Newport power station; she has argued
animatedly. And she is a more interesting person for that knowledge.
People might prefer Lloyd's or Carole's style. But that largely
depends on what they are more comfortable with, themselves. It
would be absurd to ask Carole to become like Lloyd ... or Lloyd to
become like Carole. Lloyd has talked to me about teaching methods
that begin with the kids' discovering, searching out for material
rather than having it brought to them and imposed upon them (and
encountering the risk of alienation and rejection). So [in the lesson
he taped] ... there are plenty of books, a resource in ... the school
nurse [who attended the class] and a generally expansive atmosphere. They were learning in that way.

But one kid said about Lloyd, he was a great teacher. When
pushed she said he was really friendly, he did everything for them
(he took them places etc.) and he made them do no work. In fact,
like Carole's class and Betty she was learning things sneakily, via the
back door, so to speak.

Throughout this examination of two different teaching styles,
Martin was trying to sort himself out. How personal can you allow children to become? What is the source of authority? As he watched Lloyd
and Carole he was searching for the underlying strength in two such
different people – one who was very obviously personally in command,
though in a relaxed and by no means autocratic way: the other who
seemed to give the children their head in their activities, but whose
purposeful organization, while apparently concealed, was no less real.
He concluded that his own style was 'to do with letting the kids call the
tune'. At first that may seem a pretty unsatisfactory conclusion; but
Martin analysed how he had come to it and what he meant by it:

There's a really interesting part of my diary which I have just re-
discovered. I said this (it surprised me that I was so intolerant):
These girls live on what seems to me the same cretinous level
every day. They have petty squabbles and whine <u>sir</u> for me to
arbitrate. They say Do you miss me? in exactly the same tone of
voice.

I talked to some one about it and she suggested a few things.
One was: Ignore them. They were <u>calling the tune</u> till then and
that was bad.

I was really surprised that the phrase turned up then. I can still re-
member my frustration with those girls before I understood them.
And it <u>was</u> bad that they had me at a loss for something to do. So
I'm not talking about that sort of calling the tune.

In this case, when I found out the history of especially one of
those girls, I understood. I became powerful again. She still says Do
you miss me? but I listen and she's a good friend ['she' is probably
the Betty previously referred to]. Similarly as long as my power is
recognised in the classroom I'm happy to play the game of giving
them power in terms of the opportunity <u>to make emotional demands
on me</u>, to oppose me, to criticize me, to laugh at me and each other,
to talk, to punch, to some extent to bring their lives, or as much as
they want of them, into the class-room. As long as there's no put-
down involved, or rather, as long as I can cope with the put-down.

I think that situation is as fanciful as Carole Buhaj's. But both
somehow give the kids a chance to establish an identity within the
classroom and the teacher a chance too (that's really important for
me). Both involve the teacher being aware of every kid.

Martin's resolution – and it *was* a resolution – would not have
suited everyone. He had tested himself and been tested. He had discovered that he could cope with behaviour that could easily have
turned into studied pertness if it had continued to threaten his dignity
and poise. He had acquired some inner power that enabled him to treat
childishness for what it was, without descending to childishness himself or protecting himself by a heavy-handedness that he knew would ill
become him. Just as he saw in Carole's and Lloyd's styles different
kinds of what he called 'artificiality', so, I think, he would say that the
role he discovered for himself also contained that quality. Perhaps
'artificiality' is not quite the right word, for when he amplified it the
point he was making was that the personality of the teacher is the key
factor that turns the classroom into something not quite natural, and
presumably distinguishes it from the playground or the dining-table. I
think his point is that, for a classroom to work, an adult, mature
teacher is necessary. Within that broad and somewhat vague condition,
different sorts of methods can be equally effective in different ways;
but as Carole put it to me, neither she nor Lloyd would 'swear at kids,
tell them lies, cry, etc., or they would feel uncomfortable ... [We agree]
that you have to make honest communications with kids or you can't
work with them.'

Both Carole and Lloyd know that children sense the authority that comes from simply being older and wiser. Both are assured of their own integrity, as Martin learned to be assured of his; but underlying the success of all three was the sacredness of the integrity of the 'kids', and the recognition, as Lloyd put it to Martin, that they can teach the teacher too. As Martin concluded his observations:

> Kids don't turn out the same but their expertise is as valuable in its own right as the next. It's important for them to come into contact with a variety of teachers who can offer a variety of opportunities.
>
> What can I offer? I haven't said much at all about teaching methods. And if I should have bulk learning ideas by the end of the year then fail me.

In coming to this conclusion Martin had been influenced by something Lloyd had said to him earlier in the year – something that came to have growing meaning for him as his own experiences widened and as his thinking deepened:

> Lloyd Jones said something really interesting that I didn't quite understand – that in teaching you have to be your own deviant. I think classrooms should cope with socially acceptable deviants.

By 'being your own deviant', Lloyd, I think, meant that the teacher has a right to his own idiosyncrasies. And by 'socially acceptable' Martin had in mind not only that the 'kids' should be respected, but also that they should become 'more interesting' people for the knowledge they acquired – whether they admitted to it or not. I have quoted Martin at some length since he went a long way towards clarifying the criteria by which successful teaching might be judged while allowing for the necessary diversity entailed in encouraging each teacher to be a different 'me'.

And coming to terms with the 'me' is the first – the most difficult – step. Students may and do press for 'tips for teachers' as an escape from, a palliative in, learning to be a teacher. There is nothing wrong with 'tips' or (a more telling phrase) 'survival techniques' so long as they are seen for what they are. Fear of children is linked with students' uncertainty about the 'Who am I?', and quick remedies to immediate difficulties simply camouflage the problem – a problem that remains evident in the we/they attitude in many schools. When that we/they attitude indicates not a difference in role or maturity or learning but a defensive, indefensible hostility, the safety devices, the 'tips', have become ends in themselves that have no place in a school that truly values its pupils' learning.

Chapter 3

Being at risk

Danger as the challenge

In giving teaching practice the central place in our year of teacher training we knew that we were putting the students at risk. Any teacher training, indeed any teaching, will do this, but it is a question of how far one should go. The students chose our Course knowing, as they put it, that they were being thrown in at the deep end. Their choice of metaphor is significant in that it is drawn from an outdoor, physical pursuit. Any physical education teacher or teacher in charge of school camps knows that while part of the appeal for his pupils lies in the inevitably challenging sense of risk and potential danger, it is irresponsible to ignore safety precautions or to encourage over-ambitious daring. It is easier to know when to risk the literal deep end and how to do it than it is to take risks with people's personalities — yet they must be taken no less in teaching than in life.

There are far too many stodgy, unadventurous teachers whose approach to their work and their classes is humdrum and safely set in dreary routine, ignoring the challenging innovations available to them if they were less timid. Challenges cannot be productive without some uncertainty and a willingness to see when failure will become irretrievable. Each person must learn this for himself — the limitations in the circumstances and his personal limitations. Just as fear of drowning becomes damaging when it turns to panic, so fear of failure in teaching can turn into neurotic anxiety or even the disintegration of the teacher. For this reason, there must be a lifesaver standing ready to jump in should the novice swimmer panic or if a shark should suddenly be sighted. It goes without saying that the instructor must be extremely vigilant and a very good swimmer too. Perhaps this is why so many teacher-training courses are exercises in paddling.

Where human fallibility is concerned, some of the risks are

incalculable. And this we discovered increasingly as our experience grew: staff at University and in schools also very often felt *themselves* at risk. If we revert to Martin, whose self-analysis ended the last chapter, we find that he fairly successfully answered the question 'Who am I?' by the end of the year, and in doing so he was aided, more than they knew, by two very effective teachers whom he studied and who helped him. By the end of the year he had come to terms with how he reacted to being 'put down', as he termed it, by the 'kids'. He had learned to understand 'cheek', and in understanding it he rose above it, laughing at both himself and the pupils. He thus converted cheek to permissible, tolerable fun. The little puss who irrelevantly asked, 'Did you miss me?', could now do so without threatening Martin's dignity because he had understood that underneath the 'put down' she really wanted to be missed, wouldn't admit it sentimentally, but was grateful when it was tacitly understood for what it was. Martin had learned to stand outside the relationship while sharing in it affectionately.

The threat that children present to the novice teacher was one that we expected, and the students rightly saw it as of paramount importance. But the problem was seldom quite so simple as we had thought. The difficulty of warding it off or, even better, mastering it, was no simple matter. Supervising teachers can under- or over-react; the lore of the school can militate against sensible responses; university staff can be touched in unexpectedly vulnerable spots when consulted; fellow-students can compound the victim's sense of inadequacy; and that sense of inadequacy can be largely due to personal, private dilemmas. An insecure love-affair can have a student 'all mixed up' about whether he lacks charm, or humour, or intelligence, or whatall, just at the time when childish capers from pupils, displays of brilliance from fellow-students, and abruptness from staff all serve to underline the uncertainty.

For Sandra, for example, the failure of children at a community school to be attracted to options she offered became entangled with her sense of personal failure; and the arrival of one of us from the University, when she was 'so completely dismal and the children even more so', sent her headlong into overwhelming and destructively self-indulgent depression:

> I fantasized for days on how good I would be if I was just out of that school ... At the moment I would give anything to see more faces lined up before me ... My ideas of failure that keep crowding in seem to overwhelm any other thoughts ... My personal life is also a complete write-off ... Feeling unattractive, uninteresting ... and being disposed of by yet another male has only compounded my misery ... I think that I will try to get out of it by

throwing myself into my work but as soon as I try to do that I just get myself into a worse situation ... All I do is sit around and feel sorry for myself and wish that I could wish myself off the face of this earth ... The trouble at school ... is that the only way you can get anywhere is ... by being charismatic ... I hold no attraction for the kids.

This sort of inter-relatedness of personal, professional and academic events makes nonsense of the hard-nosed theorists who try to divorce pastoral care from academic responsibility, as if for the teacher (at school or at university) the two are separable and should be kept separate — each to his own speciality, the teacher to his academic standards and the social worker, the priest, the counsellor, the parent to his pastoral responsibilities.

Of course, no teacher can be a substitute parent or lover or god. Of course, as university staff, our first responsibility is to try to produce scholarly and skilful teachers; but this we cannot hope to do if we segment the student into a 9–5, Monday to Friday working person, and an evenings or week-end other person. Living just isn't like that and it is idle to pretend that it is. On the other hand, there is an inner privacy that staff or fellow-students invade at their peril. It is the stress created by this apparent paradox that this chapter is largely about.

Pupils as the threat

Martin's search for a teaching style that suited him was, as we know, largely a question of working out the kind of relationship with 'kids' that would enable him to teach comfortably and honestly. He learned how to handle mischief with kindness and dignity. It wasn't easy for him, but it was even harder for some other students.

Norma, for example, whom we also encountered in the last chapter, was having serious difficulties with her actual teaching and class management. She was an engagingly attractive young woman — one whom, in pre-Women's-Lib. days, we should have dared to call extremely feminine. She was placed in a boys' school, with a largely male staff. She learned very quickly that, because the school had many steps, she had to wear jeans not skirts — and not merely because of the boys! Early in the year the boys tested her out. Two or three of them dared a friend, indeed offered him $1.50, to ask Norma if she was a virgin. She was quite unruffled, and merely told him to go away and stop being stupid. She thought the incident funny and told one of the staff about the joke; but he took it very seriously and it became a major issue, the boys eventually being sent to the Principal to be disciplined. It was the action that was taken rather than the incident itself that upset Norma. She saw it for what it was — a childish prank that probably said more about single-sex schools than about Norma. She had far more serious worries, and would not have let the two matters become confused if the school had not led her to take it all more seriously.

Liz, by contrast, was in a big co-educational school where she found herself being tested when she was giving the class a test in biology:

> They asked me the answers to test Q's and read my face for the answer. I'll have to develop some sort of protection against that. One boy, a ringleader, asked me, 'Please, Miss, what's faeces?' I said that he'd come across the word before; what did he think it meant? He insisted and the whole room was listening. So I told him that it was shit, and it was left at that, with no reaction that I could detect. They all just went back to work; no titters or anything. A strange experience.

And that, it seems, was that.

Morag had spent the greater part of the year in a community school and was changed to a more typical school, after discussion with us, to give her wider experience before the year ended. It was a boys' school. In one of her first lessons, she moved over to a group of boys who were interrupting the lesson and she (unwisely) picked up their scribbling to discover 'the scrawly drawing of a curly head with specs'. The drawing was labelled 'Sirly Temple'. 'It was me!' she exclaimed in her diary. 'I wonder if "Sirly" stands for Shirley or Surly?!' It seemed to pass off as it should, but several days later when she was taking a small group for reading, the same boys sat next to her and one of them again drew Shirley Temple — 'To get attention?' she asked herself. She concluded, at the very end of the period at the large boys' school, that the community school produced

> different image conflicts … Here the boys can't work out whether I'm:
> 1. inexperienced student teacher & a chance to give false names, have the new teacher on about school rules
> 2. sex object — well, I wasn't used to propositions, smart remarks, whistles and nude drawings at the community school
> 3. a little Shirley Temple and not to be taken too seriously: perhaps a friendly recipient of animals, tales about family & school and of Shirley Temple drawings.
>
> But of course self-image isn't everything. Just one of these student teacher obsessions! I have seen large classes & become aware of the problems of holding attention of, directing, and interesting a diverse group (PLATITUDE GRATIS).

Morag, despite the flippancy, *was* concerned about her proper role and her dignity. She learned quite quickly that the sort of free-and-easy relationships with pupils at a community school could be, and were, misunderstood in a school where the pupils were not used to them.

Perhaps, for student teachers, single-sex schools intensified sexual skittishness and immaturity, but the problem also arose in co-educational schools. Jacqueline, who taught in a large co-educational high school, noted in her diary at the end of her first month:

> I breezed into sixth-form French, this class really appeals to me even though I feel as if I have a problem with one of the boys. I know that he stares at me during the lesson and that he doesn't concentrate on his work at all. I don't know what to do.

And she really didn't. The problem continued to haunt her for some time until it became the subject of a lengthy and profitable discussion over my dinner-table about a month later — of which more anon.

It was not only women students who had problems about being 'sex objects'. Male Libbers may note that, at the very same school, Antonio had his fans:

> The 3rd Form Special Studies class was quite interesting. The group of girls who sit at the back, and who have acquired a dislike for me [I wonder?] decided to imitate my every move. When I scratched my head they did also etc. This went on for a while, so I went up to them and told them it was amazing what they could do when they tried; whereupon, they asked me if I had been circumcised. I responded that anything I had on me didn't need cutting off. They giggled, and I left them as I thought the conversation wasn't particularly relevant to land use in the Mildura Irrigation District.

Antonio was more bothered than he cared to admit. He discussed the incident in a seminar as well as writing about it in his diary; but his sense of the ridiculous saved him. Although Jock also had a keen sense of humour and, like Antonio, was the butt of pathetically juvenile flirtation, he was severely shaken by the teasing he was subjected to early in the year:

> Felt at a loss as to how to cope with 2 giggling girls in the corner — they seemed to sense my inadequacy — one of them even came up to me later in a real 'pally' way and said 'Gee, I love stirring you, Jocky': I must be pretty transparent, 'cause obviously she could see right through me.

Jock met a different sort of stunt from fifth-form boys about a month later:

The kids put on this dumb act for me and peacefully watched me crumble before their very eyes. They just didn't bother answering any questions, till I got really nervous — the more nervous I got, the more one little shit in particular kept smiling (or sneering), till I almost started throwing up all over them.

A little later, with the same class:

The fifth-form composition course was much better today than it was when I 'crumbled' in front of the kids. This time I felt far more confident and prepared, and the kids sensed this. One of them came up to me at the end of the period and quite seriously told me I should try and get a job on T.V. because I had 'such a fabulous sense of humour' — I'm too much of a cynic to believe that he'd be saying anything to me without tongue-in-cheek, so <u>now</u>, I'm wondering whether I'm too dry and humourless with them!! I have a slight case of paranoia, I think.

We can be left with little doubt about his humour when five days later he gives an account of a third-form lesson:

The game I played with adjectives etc. was quite successful ... The highlight of the lesson was when we were doing plural noun forms and some vile creature farted. The effect it had on the class was quite 'explosive' — half the class was almost blue in the face, trying to withhold the laughter, when I casually said — 'I hope we don't hear the plural form of <u>that</u>!' Then they actually did explode — laughing uncontrollably — so that my battered ego was momentarily mollified.

Even three months later Jock was in conflict:

I had my blackest day ever last Thursday — but I've told so many people about what a fool I made of myself in class, that I couldn't possibly repeat the whole fiasco again in writing. (I guess I should have made this journal my first confidant.) Anyway, to face the little shits on Wednesday is about the last thing on earth I feel like doing. To face ... my supervisor I think must be the 2nd last thing I feel like doing. To be a teacher, I think, must be the 3rd last thing I feel like doing.

By then the teasing had taken a more serious turn having created two-way hostility — there's just so far that a sensitive person can be pushed. '<u>How do I get over the nervousness bit</u>? ... I really don't know', and in that mood he planned a lesson around two records, the 'Grand Canyon Suite' and Brahms's First Piano Concerto. There was a good discussion, but when Jock asked them to write, 'all hell broke loose'. He threatened detentions and then decided instead to 'discuss the whole problem of discipline and punishment':

> As a result I was told that I was 'boring', 'only a student-teacher', 'a hypocrite' and any other number of things. That's what happens when you try to be another H. Kohl and find out 'where the kids are at'. I honestly do <u>not</u> think I am boring or not interesting.

And I can assure you that he is not; but taunting had turned to mutual hostility, and for Jock this became an ideological decision: 'I defy the great "Progressives" like Holt, Kohl or "even" Newsome to work their magic ... I say it's not me but the "system".'

In reality, if one has the audacity to talk about someone else's reality, Jock knew it was both. His downfall lay in his gentleness and extreme sensitivity. His dry humour was essentially adult — the sort of humour that was usually turned against his own inadequacies. This made him a delight in University seminars, but fair game for callous, callow youths. Whereas Martin, Norma, Morag, Jacqueline and Antonio could all, in time, treat teasing or crushes relatively lightly, for Jock they continued as a major symptom of his own doubts about where his authority might lie.

The incidents might have seemed trivial, but underlying them were deeply serious matters of principle, probably the most serious being the question of how dependent or moon-struck one should allow pupils to become, or, on the other side of the coin, how much chiaking it was safe to allow. These questions raised subtle further questions about friendliness *vis-à-vis* aloofness towards children; and all of these considerations turned back on and around the question of how important it was for the teacher to want to be liked — in short on how personally dependent the teacher was on the children.

The over-simple and misleading answer to the kinds of problems just outlined is found in the old cliché that never fails to turn up dozens of times each year when supervisors advise student-teachers to keep the pupils at arm's length until discipline is in fact so well established that it is possible to relax and be friendly. What in fact emerges from chapter 2, I believe, is that students tended to fear children and to be ill at ease in the classroom until they established some close personal relationship that broke the barriers both ways. Carole, as an experienced teacher, preferred to keep the myth of the distance of the teacher as a myth; but Martin's analysis of this was that the myth was obviously understood by Carole and her pupils, and they both tacitly agreed that it was more comfortable to work together this way. The thing revolves around just what one means by 'distance'.

Before looking further at this, let us look more closely at the way in which the problem was most acute for some students — that is, we shall deliberately take an unrepresentative sample. For purposes of analysis, I shall concentrate briefly on several for whom the problem was so acute that it became entangled with a whole lot of other related dilemmas that I am sure could never be disentangled by merely listening to lectures or reading books, for the problem is too personal and too deep seated.

It was so for Jock. As we have seen, he first blamed all the 'progressive' writers and teachers who had initially appealed to him. He could not, he said, get anywhere with the idea that the teacher must start from where 'the kids are at'. By trying to do that he found that they ran roughshod over him. In practice he tried to accept the advice of 'keeping them at arm's length', but that did not work either, for what the advocates of that line overlook is that school children – any children – can be extremely shrewd in seeing through feeble defences to their elders' vulnerabilities. Jock's pupils knew that he found being autocratic distasteful, and, in action, he was constantly paralysed by his own ideological objections to the role he thought he was forced to fill if he were to survive. He did not have to hide his contempt for his pupils from them – he really felt it for 'the little shits' as he swung between trying to move towards them and repelling them. It is significant that he chose as his depth-study topic 'Indoctrination'. He was frightened by children's prejudices, and he was frightened by the power that he felt he had to exert as part of the 'hidden curriculum' – power that ideologically he did not favour. To add to his conflicts, the school itself was schizophrenic over the matter, and Jock did not receive the sort of help that Martin was given. Permissiveness was tolerated at one moment and then suddenly the hand of authority descended, often over quite childish misdemeanours. Some teachers were strong (by which I don't mean autocratic), while others were rudderless. Jock did not know where he stood in all this.

He seized on two interpretations of his problem. One was that he must reject the idea that the teacher should start from where the pupil 'was at', and the other was that he alienated the pupils because he was insistent on academic standards. His idea of academic standards entailed his conviction that he should teach grammar. Regardless of whether teaching formal grammar in junior secondary school helps children to become more grammatical or is justifiable for other reasons, most successful teachers of English know that grammar lessons can be great fun and a great source of satisfaction to children. For Jock they were not, as his account of his lesson on agreement of number (on plurals) testifies. He therefore blamed his failures on his insistence that grammar be taught.

Jock thus convinced himself on two points. Getting familiar with pupils, trying to discover what made them spark, meant, it seemed to him, abandoning both authority and structure. In this conclusion Jock was not very different from many experienced teachers who think that friendliness with pupils equals anarchy and chaos. From this flowed the second point that starting from 'where pupils are at' meant stopping there, and was therefore anti-intellectual and led to soft pedagogics. He hated himself for having to come to these conclusions, for they ran counter to all his deeply-felt liberal and democratic persuasions, but at that time survival was more important than ideology for Jock. He decided that he could work only in a rigid school. I thought that I knew better than he did that he would never make an authoritarian teacher. I was sure that if he found a congenial school he would be a rich experience for pupils; but I feared that temperamentally he might not survive teaching at all.

I knew him very well at the University (though I had not seen him teach), and we often discussed in seminars issues that he raised and conflicts that he was facing. What I had not known was that what he represented as conflict was in fact nothing less than torture. The school and the University staff had let him down. I realized this only when he handed in his diary marked 'confidential to G.M.D.' at the end of the year. It was an invitation to me to discuss all the difficulties raised. We had that talk — and then silence. I often thought of him fearfully during the following year, but I heard nothing.

He had said, when we first talked about his diary and he knew it had upset me to discover how unhappy he had been, 'Don't take the diary as me all the time. It's absolutely true in that it's me when I'm lowest. I used to sort of cry on an anonymous shoulder.'

Quite unexpectedly a year later he rang me. He reminded me that I had said that, though he might try to become autocratic in self-defence, I believed he would not be able to keep it up. I had forgotten I had said that. His comments then went something like this:

Well, you might be interested to know that I have been in the most disgustingly autocratic school one could find. Passes have to be issued to any child who wants to go to the lavatory, for example. You'll be surprised to know that I not only survived but can boast that I've become a thoroughly successful autocrat, and, now that I've proved that, I must get to a school where education and not just discipline occurs. The kids are browbeaten into learning nothing, and I must get out before I get corrupted by succeeding at what's easy.

I'm now ready to come out of hiding and to talk to Course B students and ex-students. I wasn't earlier: I was too preoccupied in sorting myself out. I feel that I now have important things to say and I'd welcome the opportunity to say them — and you are free to use anything you like from my diary.

Thus Jock had at last come through his trials with the dignity that accompanies self-knowledge. Peter was different: he was less vulnerable. Although children teased him as much as they teased Jock — perhaps more — Peter failed to see himself clearly or to be convinced by the hints given him by supervisors. One of his difficulties lay in the pleasure he gained from identifying himself with childish poses and capers:

> I think I must dress too informally or something, for the boys just don't know how to take me. I must look like a pupil ... who's just a little better at maths than the rest ...

And then he looks at the boys:

> I do feel that there are a few thugs in the making ... I think most know what I mean — the shoulder-length blond-haired toughs and the shorter-length dark-haired teddy boys with the brush back. Congregating in insolence, hands casually resting in pockets, they stare at you nose cocked arrogantly, even challengingly in the air. I know what it's like. When I was younger, I used to cultivate it and emulate dozens of 'tougher' classmates we'd all look up to ... to adults it has all the hallmarks of larrikinism and vagrancy. It's simply kids. The boys delight in hanging around in a 'gang' — a select number watching each other drag on cigarettes, and enjoying a certain privileged status on the footpath ... I can appreciate this feeling — to be seen, to be conspicuous in public, because in a way I subscribe to it myself. Since Sub-Intermediate [third form] my laugh, my gait, my manner changed. I became more confident, more raucous. I developed a real swagger, a combination of Roy Rodgers and Sinbad, which I cannot get rid of. You might say there's an awful lot of the little boy in me. It's probably why I like the company of younger boys — is it an opportunity to show off? I don't know.

By September there is more unease than he is prepared to admit even in an apparently frank description:

> I'm getting a little tired of ... politics and tomfoolery. I warned Sam I'd hit him if he didn't toe the line ... John is one of those boys who have what I could only describe as a 'crush' on me. It's even rather embarrassing for me to write down, possibly I'm too typical an Australian to discuss homosexuality in any objective light. But he tends to blow kisses once too often in my direction for me to avoid them. He and the others think it's a great joke, which it is, I hope. He's not a poof. Nor is he going through a homosexual phase, but it seems an instant way of gaining immediate attention, no matter of what nature ... Matthew always has a kind word for me, and sidles up self-consciously, a huge grin across his face. Jamie thoroughly

enjoys trading gossip and the occasional punch ... Brian shows all
broken teeth (football) when hailing me ... as for Donald, well he
takes it as a personal insult if I don't devote every spare minute to
looking, smiling, gesticulating at, or laughing with him. No one else
in the class likes him ... He imitates the way I stand, sit, slouch,
walk, clear my throat even.

At one moment Peter thinks the boys are really fond of him, at the
next he wonders if they are having him on. At one moment he is flattered, and then he seems more worried about over-familiarity than he
fully admits:

This thing of hero-worship and adulation of young teachers is a
point worthy of digression. Several teachers have perceived in my
manner a certain trait of great endearment to the adolescent ...
2 G, they're a group who'll seize your weak spot and play on it —
they knew me as a paper tiger — and were willing to gamble that I
would not dish out the hideous punishments that others could ...
That was a particularly valuable excursion I consider as it broke
the back of the barrier between the classes and myself ... Specific
forms and several boys in particular latch on to me as a result ...
3 F tried to get through to me by christening me Digger ... Digger
stands for my army boots that characterize my stance, my gait and
are trademarks of the non-bikie student-teacher on an excursion.
The trouble is that they gave that nickname cautiously, possibly as
an insult, to sling off at me. I don't know exactly, but I know that I
did not approve of it, and they were told so in no uncertain terms. It
died out, and they grew to dislike me.
Ever since my first exposure to form 4, I have confounded them
all, because I'm unconventional and am not embarrassed about how
I appear, how young (possibly too youthful to teach?) I look, and
how naturally I express myself. In my first observation class, I
laughed ... at something the teacher said, which startled the class,
and shocked the teacher ... Several [of the boys] actually took me
into the ranks, invited me to kick their footy, tried to get me into a
brawl inside [the school] ... Or they'd be walking past the staffroom, and then double back to wave, whistle, call out, to the annoy-
ance or bemusement of many staff, in particular the Senior Master,
the Headmaster occasionally.

The ironies in this account are self evident. Peter's experiences had not
greatly helped him with the 'Who am I?' We must remind ourselves that
Jock and Peter were not typical students, in that their problems, in
their different ways, were unusually acute, but we all partake of these
problems and weaknesses to some extent, even those of us who should

have outgrown them. Perhaps they are exemplified by the blow-up at the beginning of 1974 – our blackest period.

The Course and its staff at risk

The second year of experiments of this kind seemed to be the time of crisis. In the first year there is the excitement shared by staff and students in proving what can be done, and, for us, the first year was the only one when we had a favourable staff-student ratio. In the second year we more than doubled our student intake, and did not know how to avoid large groups without totally fragmenting the group as a whole. We were worn down with constant attack from our critics and from fear of our experimental course not being allowed to continue. We were embattled. We felt insecure, unhappy – and lonely. And further, by un-lucky chance, soon after the year began all university teacher-training institutions were threatened with a strike by school teachers over the payment for supervision. This was unnerving for our students, who were already in their schools (seemingly 'unwanted'), and knew the dependence of our Course on continuous school practice.

Some of the University staff over-reacted to all these anxieties by over-dependence on support from the students, and our large group sessions at University were a howling disaster. A few nervously extro-verted students tried to help by talking 'off the top of their heads', thereby intimidating the shy and diffident ones. If we had deliberately tried to set up a risky, threatening introduction to the year we could not have done better.

As a staff we were so tense that we temporarily lost balance. We knew that we put students at risk; but we had not fully foreseen the extent to which we put ourselves at risk, and the strange ways in which we would react to that. Our reactions were blind in proportion to our conviction that what we were doing had already been proved largely right the previous year, and that, therefore, we must never let the experiment fail because of weaknesses in ourselves. In short, our inten-sity about the Course made us unduly vulnerable, just as the most vul-nerable students were the sensitive ones who cared most when confronted by difficulties with their pupils.

We had organized a camp as a means of getting to know each other informally. The year began early in February. The camp was in late March at a seaside place, Airey's Inlet. One student, Jacqueline, the girl who had already expressed her uncertainty of what she should do about the boy in her sixth-form class who had a crush on her, wrote in her diary that four of them, in preparing for the camp, went to the market:

Bargaining together is a great way of getting to know people.

Arrived at Airey's Inlet in the afternoon and were immediately thrown into Bruner. This session was great!

As I predicted people exploded, things blew up which had been brewing for the term; things came out into the open.

Yet despite the unpleasantness experienced, a great time was had by all and everyone lived happily ever after.

Well, not quite; but she's a generous girl. We were in three private houses, one of them being mine, which with six single beds accommodated about ten students and two staff. Judy Walsh, who shared the history Method with me, also shared the one private bedroom in the house. We had had a barbecue around two camp fires and there had been some very talented singing and playing; but the way students sorted themselves into two groups suggested some significant cleavage, and there was ferocious competition for stardom at the fireside I joined.

Judy and I came home early — exhausted. Judy went to bed and I had a drink. By midnight the others were back and we sat around the table drinking coffee or whatever we chose. And then it started. I was already badly bruised by what had been happening to 'my' Course; but I knew I had to see this session out. It took strange forms, because the issues were not nearly so clear cut as any of us had imagined. By 1 a.m. Judy emerged in a dressing-gown, aroused from a peaceful sleep by realizing that I was alone, embattled. It was a great moment of firm friendship, though not of collaboration.

I was far too deeply involved in the issues and disturbed by the whole crisis to attempt to reconstruct it in retrospect. The next day I asked Betty, one of the students who was at Airey's Inlet, to write up her account of it, which she willingly agreed to do. From Betty's report (which she had shown to each member of the group to ensure that it was accurate), a report from Judy Walsh and the diary of one of the students, Brian, who was there, I can try to reconstruct the evening. It began with a 'j'accuse', in which the students spilled out their criticisms of the Course.

There was 'covert pressure', the students thought, to be extroverted, 'groupy', and conspicuously dedicated. The more reticent students felt already condemned for a failure in personality. As Judy put it, 'they feel that the course is most suited to [extroverts] ... Those who see themselves as quieter ... and not yet ready to be pushed into close relationships' felt that the dice were loaded against them. Brian added 'that the fear resulting from this made many keep silent and hide their discontent'. Betty's report confirmed this fear:

> The feeling that we are being judged on our personality is felt by
> quite a few people ... Are we an enthusiastic, dedicated vital person?

What image are we expected to measure up to? Because of the
feeling that we are being judged on our personalities, students tend
not to act according to their 'real' personalities.

The extroverted nature of some of the staff and their followers made
some students respond with hostility, saying, 'We aren't like that and
never could be and don't want to be.'

It was not surprising that some of the most disaffected students had
chosen my house, for I had seemed to them to commit a different, less
threatening error — I was seen as aloof and cold. This was bad enough.
But the damage done was conveyed by the students' feeling that, while
I was indifferent to them, other members of staff took umbrage when
criticized, and counter-attacked by talking about students' natural feelings of inadequacy at the beginning of the year. What hit me hardest
was not only the feeling of stifled criticism, but also the sudden realization that students thought we were keeping secret records — a point to
be amplified later — and that I, in particular, was guilty of this. The
Course had no hope of carrying out its principles while this sort of suspicion existed. I had given many assurances that no records were secret
unless students asked for confidentiality, but I had been unconvincing.

I sat quietly through most of the early outpourings, which were a
release in themselves to the students, but suddenly I found myself
talking fast, which is what woke Judy and brought her in to my rescue.
That they should think I was keeping secret dossiers so shocked me that
I protested passionately, and, for the first time, so it seems, gave them
some insight into what I believed to be the essence of the Course. I
must really have taken off. Brian noted:

> Gwen's emotional attachment to the course I think most people saw
> for the first time and admired, and I think it helped me to appreciate
> why things were done and to understand them better. If Gwen and
> everyone had been better known to us the rationale of the course
> would have been grasped quicker and in a different light.

Betty wrote in her report, 'we now saw Gwen much more as an
approachable person and sympathized with her role concerning the administration of the course'. How uptight I must have been earlier in the
year!

I realize now, though I could not see it at the time, that being embattled had made me defensive, and when I sensed that students were
pulling against us had made vague and unclear statements about the
requirements of the Course, and the rationale behind them. The conflict
I was in made me afraid to encounter further criticism, which I warded
off by confusing impreciseness. Bernie's reaction was the reverse. As
Brian put it, he

came under fire for his ... deducing that because people don't turn up to class they can't cope. His emphasis upon 'get your personality in order' as an essential to teaching was criticized.

Each to his own idiosyncrasy, and the students said that there was 'reticence in approaching Bernie for fears of being slain by his powers of verbalization — though recognizing that he probably doesn't want to do this'.

The 'j'accuse' had its effect on me and on the students. The immediate crisis was over, and we all saw how much we had hurt each other through our earlier inability to get through to each other. At the back of students' minds, throughout their attack on the Course, was apparently a grim uncertainty about their relationship with their pupils. The discussion then surprisingly turned to this worry. If we, as staff, had made damaging and intolerable personal demands on them, how could they be sure that they would not do the same with their pupils? Having criticized us, with good reason, they more easily suddenly turned the spotlight on themselves, and the best discussion I ever remember with students flowed from our mutual anguish and frankness. Jacqueline, in particular, talked about how distressed she was by the boy who came to her classes moonstruck. How could she cope with this? For him she was the model for blind emulation. What was this doing to him? Do some teachers feel flattered by such crushes and 'play on the kids' liking them'?

We discussed hero-worship, homosexuality, the potential power of the teacher with its possible consequence of sycophancy. The students' criticism of us, as staff, had intensified their powers of observation in school. How dependent should teachers allow themselves to become on pupils' like them? they wondered. One student, Carl, took it as normal and unworrying that pupils got crushes, but other students were quick to warn him of the danger of an undue liking for personal power. It could only have been in this sort of intense conversation that such points could have been driven home and attention directed, for each student, to the difference between being fallibly and immaturely dependent on pupils' liking one, and being genuinely friendly and concerned for them.

They were troubled about the power that teaching can give; but they were also conscious of a gauche sort of 'hail-fellow-well-met' attitude that they saw in school and University staff and in their fellow-students. The distinction between being 'friend' and 'buddy', as Betty put it (a distinction that we have seen Peter fail to make), could manifest itself in many ways. It may be seen in the use of first names and of swearing. One can quickly sense when the use of first names at a school is gimmicky and trendy and when it comes naturally; but to analyse this in words is not so easy. Similarly, in schools that tolerate or ignore swearing or obscene expletives, there's a distinction between the teacher who takes what comes naturally and the one who tries falsely to be 'with it'. As one of our own students commented, when visiting various schools for her depth study (and this girl's diary is itself studded with unselfconscious expletives), she visited one where the teacher 'had great communication with the kids ... dishing out compliments like That's fucking beautiful! or rebukes like Stop shitting around.' Her final scathing comment seemed to hit the mark: 'rather than wandering about with ... "love & Hare Krishna" attitudes they should set about the serious business of helping the kids.'

Not only were University staff under scrutiny, but the students were also closely assessing what they had seen in the schools. Towards the end of the evening at Airey's Inlet (I should say well into morning, for we wound down at 3.30 a.m.), there was a lengthy discussion about the relations between teachers and pupils observed at various schools. Brian noted that 'X school was discussed and the danger of sychophantism of kids before teachers well and truly brought out. This was of great value.' The students at that time, in examining their teaching experiences, were deeply worried about apparently trivial things, like children's teasing, and more serious things like crushes and over-dependence. The students very readily and properly applied to their own problems what they saw of the way University staff treated them and how school teachers behaved with their pupils.

How impossible it is to make convincing generalizations on these subtle questions. Antonio (an example from a different year) weathered children's mimicking him cheekily to attract attention, whereas Peter did not, and, even worse, did not fully realize it. Part of Peter was pleased and part of him knew that there's still 'an awful lot of the little boy in me'. Martin and Antonio coped with flirtatious teasing; in their different ways neither Peter nor Jock could. During the discussion at Airey's Inlet, Jacqueline's concern about a boy's having a crush on her and not concentrating on his work was a pretty good safeguard against her encouraging over-dependence, whereas Carl had seemed rather too fond of adulation.

It is in close group discussions with each other or with staff or with children that home truths can be voiced without destroying the person who is being examined. There was nothing cruel in that Airey's Inlet discussion — not even to me, though I was 'in the hot seat' — but it was painful in that we were all under scrutiny and for some the suggestions were profoundly unsettling since they indicated the need for personal stock-taking, even for revising one's whole attitude to authority. No teacher would get very far by saying to a student, 'Your trouble is that you're immature' (as one supervisor did to Peter, and left him totally in the dark about what this meant or what he should/could do), whereas the message can have some force when it is given in a discussion, without any abstractions, among peers.

The fact that discussions of this kind did occur led to our being charged with running T-groups or sensitivity training, neither of which we had any intention of doing. Our best discussions came when there was, as on that night, a shared problem that could be thrashed out through personal examples rather than with too many abstractions. As Betty concluded her report:

> The discussion that took place appears to have been, for those people, one of the most valuable experiences that took place during the weekend especially insofar as the feelings expressed were open, genuine and fairly free from tension. People said what they really wanted to say and appeared surprised to find that other people's often hitherto unexpressed feelings may be similar to their own.

Group discussion failed when that supportive element was lacking, or attempts were made to force it. It was good that, during that evening, students began to help each other, and it was comforting, too, that they began to understand the staff's predicaments and mistakes.

I have always held that teachers should not expect to be paragons, and that children should learn to be as tolerant of and sympathetic with teachers as teachers are with them. The children I have been closest to as a school teacher were the most difficult ones, educationally speaking – children in a very difficult London area, at a very difficult time shortly after the war. It never ceased to amaze me that they were uncannily perceptive, despite their alleged 'stupidity', at twigging my moods, even to the point once of writing me a round robin apologizing for having upset me one day by setting off an alarm clock during what I thought was a serious discussion. I was ridiculously tense and walked out on them to take to my bed for a few days. Their letter was disarmingly shrewd: 'We should of known,' they wrote, 'it was the wrong time of the month in which to play a joke.' And they were absolutely right. The students at Airey's that night, likewise, began to see what made me tick.

It is not surprising, then, that staff, like students, had their own idiosyncratic ways of reacting, and, in retrospect, it is not surprising that, while in our first year we had been closely allied in launching the experiment, the pressures on us became so great that differences temporarily threatened to separate us under stress. The confusion that we consequently created for the students had surfaced at the Airey's Inlet weekend, and that was a good thing.

Jenny, however, who was at a different house where apparently the same things were discussed, interpreted students' criticisms differently.

The students, she thought, were afraid of the amount of freedom they were offered. If this discontent had been felt at the University, why hadn't students said so instead of acting 'like a piece of blotting paper'? If they felt 'group pressures' they should have given a reason for 'why it doesn't gel with them':

> I do not feel that there is any pressure to have the same interests for the same things as the staff ... The staff obviously find education a consuming interest and that if we are to be 'good'? teachers then we should also make moves to foster this interest ... I rather take [the staff's intensity] as a generating point for my own enthusiasms however weak or baseless or unformulated they may be. I may find one word in what Gwen or Bernie or any may say. It sets me thinking. That is enthusiasm, not a set of guidelines on how to approach things ... There is a line between enthusiasm and dictatorship.

Nevertheless, it was true that Bernie and Rod and I, the core staff, were edgy. We were tied in knots with our own anxieties but we had always drawn comfort from the support we gained from our students. Now we had antagonized some of our students, and they in turn threatened each other (especially when seminar groups were too large), and that turned into further suspicion of us. Momentarily we projected our own uncertainties on to the students in diametrically opposite and confusing ways — by becoming aloof and impersonal, or by making too many personal demands that some students rebelled against. We did come to grips with the problem in time, but that is another story.

A few consoling things emerge from this account. One of the platitudes that education lecturers are given to uttering is that education is 'caught not taught' and that we 'learn from example not precept'. We all know about lecturers who hold forth about individualized learning to lecture groups of more than a hundred, or who advocate democratic procedures in the classroom while adopting the most autocratic procedures themselves. Students are quick to pick up such hypocrisies; but we wondered if they ever noticed it when our behaviour exemplified our theories — good or bad.

What interests me, in retrospect, about the early months of 1974 is that students were learning from our mistakes far more than we realized, and indeed they were transferring their own anxieties about their relations with us quite directly to questions about their relations with their classes. Perhaps conflict is a better teacher than harmony; but it took time for us to see possible value in our difficulties. Some of the University and school staff had been guilty of a 'cult of the personality': some of the students rebelled; still others witnessed all this happening and took stock. Our mistakes, and the causes and consequences of those mistakes, were seen to apply closely to them in their new role; but it was easier for them to try to gain an understanding of staff's anxieties than to interpret their own behaviour with their pupils, which was much closer to the bone.

Thus there were some positive gains; but diaries reveal that a few students continued to be unable to reconcile themselves to some elements in the Course. Even when they noted that they found value in some of the things we provided, their critical mood prevailed and seemed to blot out their memory of the positively good things that happened. For a few there was a persistent feeling of antagonism and this might well have influenced their reaction to teaching itself. This is at least one possible interpretation of the results of questionnaires as reported in the Evaluation.[1] The Report (ch. IV, pp. 17-18) reads:

Questionnaire responses to two of the items suggested that a greater proportion of 1975 students feel prepared to teach:

'I am looking forward to teaching next year'

	1974 (n = 40)	1975 (n = 48)
Strongly agree	9	25
Agree	14	16
Uncertain	8	5
Disagree	6	1
Strongly disagree	3	1

'Participation in this program has increased my commitment to teaching'

Strongly agree	9	18
Agree	10	13
Uncertain	10	11
Disagree	10	4
Strongly disagree	1	2

Our difficulties in 1974 might in part have arisen because that year's intake of students contained a group who were predisposed towards criticism and dissatisfaction. I think there is some truth in that; but taking the questionnaire and diaries together, one cannot doubt that we ran the Course much better in 1975 than in 1974, and there is good reason to suspect that students' attitudes were adversely affected not only towards us but also towards teaching.

Evaluation as a threat

One 1974 student, Jenny, thought the students' criticisms of the Course belied a weakness in them that was greater than the faults in the Course.

Writing of the outburst of criticism at Airey's Inlet, she concluded that the freedom we were (however ineptly) offering was suspect because it was unfamiliar. We talked about self-direction and self-assessment, but we kept records. There must be a catch in that. Jenny saw the proffered freedom as something that students could cope with less well than the straight-out judgmental mark they were used to receiving. With Jenny, the question of self-determination and participatory curriculum planning in schools was of absorbing interest throughout the year. She taught in a small community school, and, by the end of year, had firmly turned against 'autonomy' as a workable principle in schools. As a wry comment it might be worth mentioning that she applied only for 'non-progressive' schools in the following year but was posted to an 'experimental, progressive' school. The best laid plans ... A reluctant conscript, she survived with great success, and was teaching there with some real satisfaction years later.

The fear of hidden assessment in the Course seemed to be widespread. The fact that Torrey Orton had just been appointed as a full-time lecturer to make an independent evaluation of the Course was one reason for staff's untoward jumpiness; but why should it worry the students? We were the ones being judged, we thought. Not them. They didn't see it this way, however, and Torrey was no more successful at getting his message across than I had been. Brian wrote in his diary about the Airey's week-end:

> The course invaded people's privacy in other ways too, e.g. there was no escaping it as it took up so much time; Torrey's and Gwen's records just by existing without the person concerned modifying them could mean a person was being judged wrongly.

This was just bad communication on my part. Students at all times had access to their total files; but this was so radical that, in a mood of distrust, they did not believe it. Torrey's files were confidential; but he was assessing the Course, not the students. That was a difficult thing for them to understand, and he, too, had not communicated it too well.

In Betty's report she noted that students found it mortifying to feel that they were being judged on their personalities, even though they knew 'it is not being done for marks'. She dwelt on the students' uneasiness about the records that were being kept. Suspicion of Torrey flowed over into a suspicion of me. It was simply not believed that I would not use records 'against' the students, or that my records were open to any student at any time. As Betty put it:

> Are there files kept on us as students? Established that there were —
> What were the files like? Who kept them? Why were they kept?
> What 'right' does the staff have to keep them?

Patricia's strong feeling against files -- <u>not</u> that she doubted the way the staff would use the files, but objections to the principle that they were there, and was it fair that what was recorded may be entirely false? Tony also objected to the files being kept.

Another student, Bob, voiced his suspicions somewhat facetiously, but underlying them was the nagging doubt about why the Course should have an evaluator and whether this amounted to a sort of CIA enquiry into students:

> Week 5 – to reader of this diary:
> What has
>   REALITY
>   done for
>   YOU
>   lately?
> Go read a comic book ... climb a matchbox ... comb the palm of your hand ... kiss a tarantula.
>   The traffic lights didn't really need to change – I didn't expect them to. I have sat there waiting ... WORRY about course; worry about camp ... I can no longer worry.
>   At the moment, today, I do not want Torrey to read this diary ... why should he?
>   Why should I
>   Why should the staff   } be subject to his assessment?
>   Why should the course

In week 6, he added:

> The course is progressive – 2 years out of date – we'll change it. Although Torrey is going to report 'heat' & 'clashes' etc. it must be done. Oh yes, T., students are getting uptight about your scribbles.

That was in early April. On 24 October he added an afterthought:

> I don't mind Torrey reading any of my work now. I clearly at the beginning of the course didn't understand sufficiently his role; I was also tired of assessing and being assessed – now I don't know how you assess in a real sense.

Had Bob but known it, one of Torrey's big scribbling days had been at a seminar when students were discussing their educational autobiographies – perhaps the most disastrous session we ever had in those black days early in 1974. Afterwards Torrey mentioned in a staff meeting that of twenty-four contributions to the discussion, staff had made sixteen! Rod Fawns and I had been the guilty ones, and it was a measure of our nervousness, for it was most uncharacteristic of the way either of us taught. I know why I did it, and my guess is that Rod's reasons were the same. We had badly misfired in allowing such a session to occur. The group was too big; there were already defensive and aggressive reactions to the students who hogged the discussion; the students threatened each other and did not know each other or the staff well enough for frank personal discussions. Rod and I sat there while some students rambled on about how successful or unsuccessful they had been at school, and we felt embarrassed for them because we knew the impression they were making on their fellows. We both desperately tried to turn the discussion away from personal reminiscences and on to more general matters of educational practice. In averting one disaster we created another.

The lesson to be drawn from this is *not* that educational autobiographies are a bad idea, but that in using them one must exercise the greatest tact, and wait for, as well as set up, the right occasion. Once one gets caught in a vortex, for a while everything seems to add to its force. This is what happened early in 1974, and we seemed unable to tame it until it began to blow itself out at the Airey's Inlet week-end. We never made quite the same mistakes again, and we never made such serious mistakes at any time. They seemed worth analysing, since they illustrate the risks we ran and the students experienced. Those risks were always manageable at worst and a great driving force at best. That one time when they threatened to get out of hand was when we, as staff, had become over-anxious because of outside pressures that unnerved us.

The threat that fellow-students offer

But that is by no means a full account of how students were made to feel at risk in their dealings with pupils and with staff: they also threatened each other both in seminars and socially. Some moved easily and quickly into group work, and they also pushed for gregariousness that seemed to the more diffident to produce 'an unnaturally buddy-buddy atmosphere'. But some students encouraged this, and would not have described the sociability so pejoratively. One student, David, for example wrote (about the 1974 camp):

> It was really Great.
> [In the Bruner workshop] most groups drew up a time line of the ten most important events of their lifetime — past and future, but our group decided to restrict it to all the things we could remember between the ages of 0 and 11 and we really had some fun in doing it ...

The barbecues on Friday and Saturday nights were an ideal means of getting people to mix in ... On the Sunday night we feasted on a roast and bulk claret and then the fun began.

But, by contrast, we might turn to Joanna, in another year, who found the self-exposure and gregariousness of an early Bruner workshop, with its concentration on one's own life history, something that she preferred to do alone. She was no loner, but she was also no *bon viveur*, unlike the Davids, and she sought privacy:

Guy asked whether I'd like to do montage with him but as I ... had a fairly strong feeling of wanting to do something by myself ... I refused. Enjoyed doing the montage and found ... I was really making connections between the feelings and thoughts about loving eg sharing physical loving and sexual satisfaction, emotional satisfaction, <u>fun</u>, freedom, freshness ... Parents and children, animal families, customs (eg ring, wedding service), unity eg in circle and triangle shapes etc. ...
... Joined group at Albion: felt turned off by pub at times and out of group. Guy aggravated my feelings, commenting that he'd never seen me so 'moody'.
Walking back ... improved my mood, perhaps because the conversation was less personal and threatening. Somehow Guy at times seems to present a threat — because he seems to push for a greater degree of activity and involvement than I feel comfortable in giving.

David's and Joanna's priorities could not be more dissimilar, and they show the impossibility of setting up one plan, let alone one structure, that will suit all alike. One structure will not even work equally well with the same person all the time, since everyone, like Joanna, is subject to 'moods', which make a group that is congenial on one day irritating on another. There is no way, for example, of allowing for the 'Guys'. Joanna's reactions were concerned less with the structure that staff thought they were setting up than with the 'groupiness' students themselves tried to evolve.

Neither Joanna nor David was irked by the introduction to the Bruner course that started students off with a contemplation of their own development — the beginnings of their own 'life cycle'. But David thrived on the group enquiry into significant recollections. Joanna wanted hers to be private, and the things she dredged up are the things that she was most preoccupied with at the time — 'sharing' and 'freedom' in love — personal concerns that she tried to put into some general framework.

Joanna, preferring small to large groups both for work and recreation, was at home in seminars. They succeeded with her and she succeeded

103

in making valuable contributions to them. This was not so for Roger, whom we met in the last chapter. When Roger talked about giving up the Course, he was concerned about his relations with pupils. His conviction that he was incapable of making contact with children was intensified by his aversion from seminars and group discussions as a means of learning. He 'confessed' that he could not enter into conversation in class or learn from what other people talked about. His mind went blank. Yet we could see that he had a gift for knowing what would interest children and for organizing their work in such a way that they felt comfortable and would work productively. This, of course, though it escaped him, was an indirect and most effective way of 'relating'. There seemed no point in pushing Roger to face up to what left him intellectually unmoved, and distressed him personally. It had not occurred to him that other ways were open to him. In fact, for the second half of the year, he undertook an ambitious reading course for his history Method instead of attending seminars, and that helped him far more than any of us could to clarify his thinking on how best to teach history. For Roger it was a very private matter that had to be tackled privately.

There were other reasons why students threatened each other. The mixture of students with very different academic preparation can be enlightening and enlivening; but it can also be 'traumatic' for those without a literary 'artsy' background. There is an inescapable slant in educational debate towards the humanities and social sciences, and some scientists or mathematicians, even geographers and economists, find this daunting. All Dip. Ed. courses are bedevilled, and yet strengthened, by this difficult mix of students; but as Rod Foster, who now directs Course B, put it in thinking about his first reactions when he joined its staff, 'I suppose the main memory I carry is that there was not the same level of silent misery ... Anxiety, yes, but at least there were people to talk to about problems, and there wasn't that kind of evasion that accompanies intellectual territorial disputes.' And so we were all conscious of the need to find a common language and a shared approach from which discussion could proceed. For some students, who were not used to discursive and literary intellectual explorations, the strain was great, whereas others thrived on the new experience.

Writing about the first fortnight of the Course, Wanda wrote:

> Discussions in Course B have been mostly interesting and lively so far, which is a real change from the dead uni tutes etc that I've been used to. Because the group is always together, I'm getting chummier with more people too. I'm also starting to form opinions about some of the other students and find some of their attitudes difficult to believe.

About the same time of the same year Maureen was having similar reflections:

It looks as though this year is going to be really fantastic. I've already met more people ... than in my whole three years of uni. – well almost. Anyway it's just terrific being in a course which is so small. They talk about authority making you impotent. I'm much more certain it's related to the size of the institution ... I'm really going to get into the swing of things this year – participate. The course instructors seem great. Gwen appears to be rather more distant and austere than the rest. It's beaut to be able to get with people and to actually discuss what we are doing for a change. I suppose this is because we can't get away from the fact that we'll be teachers next year. I'm sure by the end of the year Jack and Barbara will be pains in the arse. That's the trouble with all our discussions in groups of thirty. It's those two who are the only ones with the bravado to twaddle on ... And Barbara – I don't think she's actually said anything [sensible] yet. I think the most useful discussions have probably come from the small friendly chats over coffee. Despite the conducive nature of the course for discussions it seems as though it will be hard for me to find many people doing the course who are ideologically the same. Coming across someone like Peggy is a shock. I wonder what attracted her to this course.

At the very time when Maureen was complaining of the way Barbara twaddled on about nothing, Barbara showed that she had no idea of the impression she was creating. In fact her cool poise, indeed her superciliousness that was so thinly disguised, while it irritated Maureen, terrified less confident students. Barbara's account of what went on might indicate why:

I entered this course ... with one aim in mind. I needed my Dip. Ed. in order to [obtain] ... a scholarship ... So ... I hold an inquisitive interest in observing how an alternative course such as Course B was to operate. I had little interest, initially, in the problems facing secondary teachers. Rather self-oriented and unconvinced in what I would find, I began the year ... extremely cynical and wary ...

With the initial call to arms being one of 'Hail Fellow, well met' and 'getting to know one another' by working in groups and generally creating a common purpose I was left feeling this was a kindergarten session – not fourth year University.

One year [of Asian education had] nearly destroyed me, emotionally, that is. The remoteness, the segregation, the coldness, the fierce competition and isolated positions adopted by both 'academic' staff and students has to be seen to be believed. But here I was at the other end of the spectrum. I could not make the connection.

Let me say that Term I simply left me cold. I just felt I could not relate to anyone except on the most superficial terms ...

I shall later relate changes that she felt occurred during the year, largely as a result of finding herself somewhat baffled by teaching; but meanwhile, she was the one who dominated, indeed created, the superficial conversation that Maureen found off-putting – and threatening.

To Maureen, Peggy presented a different kind of ideological shock (though I doubt that Maureen realized that Barbara's 'ideology' was largely a pose). Peggy considered, with hindsight at the end of the year, that we really should abandon Curriculum Studies:

I found the introductory weeks at the beginning of the year interesting in themselves, especially the reading. However, I was always at a loss to find how that reading was relevant to me in my future situation as I foresaw it. To be specific, much of what I read dealt with either primary schools, small group work or extraordinary school situations, whereas I could see my future as being a high school teacher in an average suburban government run high school. So my first weeks were spent in a semi-confused state, knowing that soon I would be standing in front of 30 children in a traditionally run high school and be expected to teach, while at university I was reading and discussing subjects that would not help my immediate crisis situation.

There is every chance that Peggy has ended up just where she expected, making a solid, competent and pretty savage teacher. No doubt, too, she will never see the irony of the sad antithesis she finally asked us to accept – an antithesis that is contrary to the very nature of the Course in its attempts to relate theory and practice throughout:

I think the staff and those in power over Dip. Ed. Course B should think deeply about the basic aim of the course, is it to train secondary teachers or to produce educational academics?

What Barbara found reminiscent of kindergarten, Peggy found too academic. How were we to please both? 'Talking Jack' whose 'twaddle' also annoyed Maureen we shall return to later.

On reflexion, the same stresses acted as both spurs and irritants, or as inhibitors, to the Curriculum Studies groups. Especially early in the year there was the strain of thinking aloud in front of strangers, some of whom nervously hogged the conversation while making others clam up; but without these conversations there could not have been the undoubted advantage that many refer to of talking intensely about shared educational problems with people of vastly differing ideologies and backgrounds, both social and academic.

106

Certainly, in first term, staff sometimes failed to recognize when some students were getting out of their depth. By second term this problem had begun to diminish. This had something to do with a greater shared background and, with the students' choice of option for special study, they had defined a common interest. It had a great deal to do with the fact that the students had faced their first teaching ordeals. But there was more to it than that: there was the smallness of the groups and the more tightly-knit planning of the staff. Some, or all, of these elements are revealed in students' comments. Hear our old friend Peggy:

> The area of the Course known as 'Curriculum Studies' was the least satisfactory to me personally. First term seemed mostly irrelevant and the groups were so large that discussion tended to be dominated by a few 'loud' or outspoken students. Second term curriculum studies was extremely interesting and enjoyable in itself but on the surface its relationship to Dip. Ed. was difficult to see, except perhaps the fine example of enthusiastic teaching given us.

Wanda also shows uncertainty about where we were going in first term, whereas her major complaint about second-term options was that she could not go to more of them:

> 1st Term Curriculum Studies — I didn't get much out of these (some were interesting) ... There didn't seem to be any theme or any cohesive element in them ... I don't know though, I reckon large groups like that are preferable to small groups initially, as long as they keep people together ...
> 2nd Term Options — Gwen's 'Equality in Education'. I really enjoyed these sessions — found them really thought-provoking and interesting. I would have liked to know what the other groups were doing tho.

In a year that is fraught with risks, it is of tremendous importance that students support each other. It was difficult, probably impossible, to structure the Course so that this could succeed early in the year; but it was good that so many students right from the start found themselves in congenial discussion groups at the schools, in the 'caf', or in pubs. Certainly the less gregarious ones needed to feel that their privacy was respected just as much as was others' 'clubbability'. But there was a further way in which some students unwittingly threatened others by the very disparity of their educational experiences which made some students feel inarticulate and poorly read, as some indeed were.

Lesley, a very shy scientist, complained after the first month or six weeks of the Course:

107

I've spent the weekend trying to fulfil a few of my methods requirements. I'll have to watch I don't get too involved at school and
hence find myself overworked. I've discovered a major problem in
trying to keep up with the reading – I really have to force myself to
keep awake. It's not that I don't find the books interesting but the
language does become a little advanced at times and I tend to get
rather 'lost'. I'm sure I'm intelligent enough to understand what the
authors are saying, but it takes a while to get used to reading this
type of book (probably after a Science Course!).

Would that all educationists wrote with Lesley's directness. Later on
she listed some of the books she had read during the year – some thirty
that ranged from A. S. Neill to Dewey or Vygotsky or Erikson. For five
years she had not been required to write sustained prose of any kind,
read a collection of books, or engage in an ideological debate. Suddenly
she was in the midst of many fellow-students who were adept at such
things – whether the result was waffly bluff or really hard thinking is
beside the point at the moment.

Or is it? For another student, not so:

One thing that puts me off this seminar group at the moment is the
way a few of the kids must labour on and waffle about hyperthetical
issues (related or not) and bring in great philosephical issues that I
know nothing about. Maybe that is what should go on in such a
group and my psych. and maths background has molded me not to
search into such areas as these kids continually do. I'll be interested
to see how I feel about this later in the year but at the moment I
don't think we're all on the same wavelength.

Towards the end of the year this student had won an award to carry
out some community work, and he found himself having to write
reports as well as to give public addresses. He was tortured with embarrassment at his inarticulateness and his spelling when writing reports.
He blamed his high school and university courses for the specialization
that led him to neglect abilities he now urgently needed; as far as he
could remember he had been asked to write only one essay in five years;
and he expressed the wish that he could have had two years, not one, in
an education course; but that is not to say that our way of doing things
came near to solving the problem – least of all the problem of what to
do about different 'wavelengths'.

Roy, who had completed a Ph.D. in science, was somewhat less
tongue-tied; but at the end of the year he still felt ambivalent about
exploratory writing:

This is not a diary ... I ... decided not to keep a running record of
my ideas, thoughts, plans etc. ... In fact, for me this has been a very

odd year and in some ways a very fruitful one. The amount of written work in the form of assignments, lesson notes, seminars and general records has been quite small ... This is quite easy to explain — I don't like putting myself on paper — it requires one to commit oneself to certain ideas, make a lot of value judgements —especially where education is concerned — and compose a string of words that get the message across without other meanings being taken. In short, minus data/facts which can be formulated into hypotheses, I prefer to reserve judgement — the ideal scientist, of a 'sort'.

Few science graduates were as good as Roy at trying to analyse what the scientific mode of thinking was. Some, instead of being tentative, would counter-balance their hesitations with rash and simplistic generalizations; others would press for hard data as a basis for logical reasoning where it was quite inappropriate. Many scientists would disagree with Roy that scientific enquiry is value-free, or, rather, discourages speculation about values; but Roy certainly found it to be so:

I had better back track a little ... Several years ago I enrolled for a Ph.D. ... However, I wasn't at all happy with what I was doing. The more I did, the longer it went on the less and less I felt I was doing anything for myself or society, both of which I feel have to be considered.

... Having spent six years ... doing a lot of learning and storing of facts, the change to thinking about ways of teaching other people, in particular adolescent kids, requires a lot of time. I guess I basically had the idea that some people have a flair for teaching and some haven't. I don't think that is true any more.

For Roy, the year in Education opened up the possibility of delving into the historical development of institutions and the role of the school system. He saw schools as alienating most youngsters from their society. He welcomed the discussions that baffled some of the other scientists, and he expressed his determination to seize on these opportunities for reading and talk that he felt he had been denied. He delighted in the new challenge. Risk, for him, was invigorating.

Libby, who describes herself as unreservedly a Course B success story, was another scientist who eventually revelled in the 'waffle', though at first terrified by it. In trying to come to terms with what to her was a new approach to learning and thinking, she, unlike Roy, turns to reflexion on what is wrong with a scientific education:

A scientific education has led me to believe that I must never state a point of view without hard evidence to back it. I find it hard now — to write subjectively. To talk about issues on which I feel strongly ... through 'casual' observation, informal thinking, following inclinations and intuitions. And yet surely there is a place for intuition in science? For feeling? My education made me suspicious of hunches ... I have real trouble sharing thoughts that are still in the process of formulation ... I admire the ability of the English people [that is, students of English] to waffle on — although much is peripheral waffle. But just as I use this journal to shape my thinking as I write — I can see that they are using their talking this way. And not having the criteria of objective proofs constantly pushed at them seems to have left them with more confidence in their early thinking. I think the lesson is to stop worrying about being right and to concern myself more with sharing the benefits of group thinking — (took a while to get that one out of my system!)

In a letter that Libby wrote me at the end of the year, she amplified this. She began by recalling the difference between primary and secondary schooling:

There was more spoon-feeding. There were twice as many notes on the board and now there were more exams, presumably to keep pace with our increased consumption of knowledge ... But the thing was that exams. tested your rote memory and I become very good at memory tricks ... They do not result in significant or retained learning ...

The power of personal interpretation and relevance, of doubt and critical thinking, did not become apparent to me until well into University ... The problem was compunded by my choice of the sciences in fifth and sixth forms. Science was taught as a discipline of ultimate truth and objectivity, beyond which there was no appeal; as something which cannot, of itself, be mistaken, although some of its applications may be dangerous. But we were never presented with 'science gone wrong' or 'science influenced by subjectivity' (or 'by politics' or 'by economics') and our evaluative abilities, when seldom summoned into play, were subsumed to tools such as statistics.

From what I can gather from my humanities oriented friends, the situation there was not much better ... The shades of grey, the dialectics that riddle all fields of human understanding, were just simply left out.

Yet it was clear from Libby's diary that she envied the ability of non-scientists to engage in speculative conversation (though she was not aware of how much better a writer she was than were many of her fellow-students who had graduated in English):

Talking in groups I find threatening ... I don't often talk in ... seminars — unless someone says something outrageous which I cannot allow to pass. I have great admiration for people who can think aloud – to say something which is only half-formulated and then think in conjunction with others on it.

Obviously I've got a problem – I've set myself the task of observing the dynamics of conversation; the nature of talk. I'm trying experimental pieces of creative writing – something I haven't done for a time. I think I'll push myself to talk more ... I guess my ideas are no more half-baked than anyone else's. Something happened in the last five years of my education.

Libby concluded her letter to me:

I felt throughout the year, that my mind was making gigantic leaps forward. The limits that I had once perceived now seem many miles away ... It is thanks to Course B that I now have this intellectual confidence. And it is because all that I experienced and theorized over was so relevant to me that I feel the need to practice my ideologies ... I have a newly won confidence in my ability to comprehend academic works and I now read, with avid pleasure, works that would formerly have passed by as too hard for me.

A toast to the ongoing process that is 'the getting of wisdom' and many thanks.

It wasn't just the scientists and mathematicians who found the flighty talk unfamiliar. One student, Aileen – a graduate in geography and economics – noted in her diary:

Curriculum Studies. A.S. Neill Summerhill. Really good to hear others' points of view and criticize a pretty persuasive book. The discussion was good in that no one dominated it and everyone (or nearly) participated. Lots of questions arose which have to be answered and weren't. Paul, John and I went to Caf and talked for another 1½ hours. More on Summerhill, and philosophies of Ed. school. It was really good. It's the first time I've ever followed up a session at Uni and gone to the Caf and talked it out.

With her, as with Libby, 'open-ended', speculative conversation was a new, stimulating and refreshing experience. It had thrown Libby into torment, but she overcame it. With some others the threat was at times too great. Pam, a first-class honours graduate in geography, clammed up early in the year:

Hist/S.S. seminar. Jan [a student] gave a paper which meant nothing to me. It was a lot of words. I am not sure I followed any of the seminar. In fact all I gathered was what Diana Heath [a member of staff] said early – is sociology a discipline? I don't think it is.

Jan's paper certainly was very abstruse, and that is one of the inevitable risks of seminars (or indeed of lectures). Many students had felt lost, and we agreed that this must not be passed by — that we must all be prepared to say when a paper or discussion was incomprehensible. Pam was disarmingly frank, and she took this agreement seriously; but she was thrown totally off balance by having grave difficulties with her teaching at this time. Her sense of insuperable failure at school became entangled with her feeling of inadequacy in seminars:

> I feel engulfed by (a) highbrow nature of some aspects of the course
>   — discussions especially
>   (b) expectations of me by Course B staff, and also
>   at school
>
> So I have honours in geography. That doesn't mean my honours have provided me with the capacity of a Jan and Peter for talking, logical argument etc, etc. ...
>
> I am tired — so very tired of pressure. Five years is too long — I wish someone would take the weight off my shoulders before I go under for the last time.
>
> Please give me the strength to pull through this course. I can see that this course is valuable in that it is preparing us for next year in a way not generally done in Dip. Ed. But I feel out of phase with the course ...

Pam felt as if everything was collapsing at the one time. Unlike many of the students who found abstract talk difficult, Pam had the courage to interject and say so; but even this she felt went against her:

> There has been a lot of talk about feeling threatened. I feel this when I attend seminars (and now with the Skinner paper to give) and am continually afraid of not coming up to scratch. I know it's always Pam who doesn't understand and it's a bit of a giggle because she is a bit slow. <u>But</u> it hurts me, and I'm tired of not u'standing and tired of asking all the time to have things explained to me.

In fact, Pam misread the impression she made. Her interjections were invaluable in bringing the Jans and Peters down to earth. Pam's was always a plea for less abstraction, less abstruseness — one that was needed and won the group's respect for her honesty. Some of the big talkers insensitively used a form of shorthand before some members of the group had become acquainted with the longhand; and as other students indicated in the diaries quoted, it often came from English graduates, especially if they had dabbled in philosophy.

The fresh frankness that Pam introduced had an effect, and at least some of the offenders were chastened by being teased by their fellow-students for being too long-winded and seemingly highbrow. The Peter whom Pam complained of, for example, took himself seriously to task and discovered that a lot of what he lightly tossed off in pretty 'high-falutin'' language was indeed hot air rather than really 'highbrow', as Pam had generously described it. I noticed him restraining himself in seminars, and he talked quite openly about doing so. In his diary he wrote:

> I discovered something about how I can contribute best in a seminar. I decided to say nothing but was soon jumping up and down almost bursting but none the less I stayed shut up. What happened was that my brain kept feverishly ticking over about what I wanted to say and eventually got it into a clear and concise form. Eventually I could contain myself no longer, and leapt in. However by this time I knew just what it was I wanted to say and the words to say it in. The result was that I spoke briefly but very effectively, largely, I think, changing the course of the seminar. This happened again; but then I got caught up and started speaking out as soon as I thought of things, almost off the top of my head. Immediately I started getting verbose and incoherent. Moral: shut up till I've got clear in my head exactly what I want to say; then say it and <u>only</u> it. In all other cases shut up and stay SHUT UP.

Libby was right about the value of exploratory talk; but it had its weaknesses not only for those who were made nervous by it but also for those who were not made nervous enough, as Peter testifies. It was hard for the staff to check the big talkers at the beginning of the year; but it became increasingly easy for the group to do it as they got to know each other well. One of our best achievements was with the biggest talker ('Talking Jack' referred to earlier by Maureen). He devastated his listeners by name-dropping all the authors he had recently been reading (and the number *was* impressive). And so we asked him to conduct a seminar playing the part of Stenhouse's neutral chairman. Stenhouse's rules were that the neutral chairman should not advance his own opinions but should prompt his students to informed argument by feeding in material that provoked heated discussion and that corrected biases or convictions that were being expressed. Jack studied Stenhouse, did a vast amount of work in selecting and preparing materials for the argument, and he carried out the task irreproachably, much to the amusement of us all — including himself. Nevertheless, there were difficulties inherent in the seminar system.

In an article written by a Course B student, Suzanne Spunner, published in *Farrago* (the newspaper of the Students' Representative Council) late in 1973, the first year of the Course, she saw the problem this way:

> Our 'close' relationship has inevitably thrown up certain problems but I think it significant that they don't usually appear in the typical

mass learning situation, not because they don't exist there but because they are either not discovered or aired ... I am thinking of the enormous difficulties we have found in talking to one another — the endeavour to find a common language that is both rigorous and fully expressive after years of specialised, isolated disciplines with their own 'forms of life'. It is not merely a question of jargon and emphasis, but often one of antagonistic ways of thinking. At the simplest and most distressing level the science students quite simply accuse the English students of dominating discussions and complain they've never had to read so many books, much less talk about them. Attempts to remedy this vary from formal procedures such as: provision for both theoretical papers and research investigations in areas where substantial work is expected, meetings with the people giving the papers and those (usually) science students who want to talk it over before the 'heavies' arrive, to more informal gripe sessions in faculty corridors, people's houses and pubs with Rod and Bernie doing their bit as counsellor-advocates for the warring factions.

Survival

It is not within the power of education faculties, even if it were their wish, to influence other faculties' practices and policies. Nor have I quoted from diaries to show that different branches of study can and do provide different kinds of lopsidedness in their graduates. If that fact emerges, it does so incidentally, and will be considered more fully in chapter 4. The point at issue is that students come into postgraduate education courses with different sorts of immaturity, with different ways of looking at things, with different sorts of vulnerability. But vulnerable they nearly all are. I have probably always tacitly believed that sensitivity and its accompanying vulnerability are necessary qualities in good teaching. In this chapter I have perhaps emphasized the anguish that the most troubled students experienced, and, to come back to an earlier point, I am aware that with a few people like Pam we ran a danger of exposing them to risk — a risk that produced reactions dangerously close to terror. She needed help and was given it. She said herself that, had she had a more protected Dip. Ed., she believes she would have gone under in her first year out as a teacher. But that is untestable conjecture. As it is she is a most effective and imaginative teacher. What had not fully occurred to me was how many of the most distressed students have become highly successful teachers. I have forborne throughout from underlining this, since it could look like a puff for our 'experiment'. Yet there is some indication that those who have become more pedestrian teachers were seldom worrying students; we hear and heard little about them.

I look at the picture-gallery of the first year of students — the twenty-three in 1973 — because I knew them all and have a fair idea of what has become of most of them. The two most deeply distressed students are extremely successful teachers. Two of the shyest (both science-maths students) have acquired quiet poise and great competence. The 'heavies' have taught happily enough but with an eye to higher degrees and probably eventual academic work. One over-sensitive but imaginative and talented teacher even as a student in her Dip. Ed. year 'went under' in the first year out because she was placed at a school that was too brutal, and no amount of advice from us could persuade her that teaching could ever be for her. But she is now back teaching again. There are a few that I'm a bit hazy about; but the only one I know nothing about was the most dogmatic of them all — and he is probably surviving very well, because he was less dogmatic with pupils than with fellow-students, and teaching increased his poise.

This is a most impressionistic sort of analysis. It hides such things as the suitability of the placements students obtained as well as my own criteria for judging successful teaching — though possibly something of that is emerging anyway. What is sure is that student-teaching puts students at risk whether one devises a structure that is a buffer or not. In planning the Course, it was never our calculation that it should be a brutal testing ground; but we did explicitly intend that it should provide means by which students would face the consequences of their own actions. In this I have now no doubt we were right.

After four years of experience with Course B, and especially when reflecting on the students I have quoted because they expressed the greatest self-doubt when at risk, I am led to conclude that the most vulnerable students seldom failed as teachers — indeed, among them are some of the most successful teachers from the Course. This is not to say that the untroubled ones, the ones who appeared to glide through the Course and seldom had recourse to their diaries for a release from anxieties, are not also often successful. Some of them are highly successful; but the pedestrian, plodding teachers are more likely to come from this group than from the other. Extreme sensitivity, when it is not merely egocentricity, seems to be a valuable ingredient for imaginative teaching.

A course of teacher training, whether it is aware of it or not, puts the novice teacher at risk; but the more it bases the learning on experiences and the more responsibility it throws on to its students for learning in action, the greater the risk. Risk may be regarded as a necessary component not only in learning to be a teacher but also in the act of effective teaching itself. Given that understanding, it would be foolhardy not also to ensure that there are safeguards. The painful story told in parts of this chapter about early 1974 would possibly not be worth recounting if it were not to illustrate how easy it is for a staff to put its students and its course in serious danger because the staff itself is suffering intolerable anxiety. School, too, put students at risk, and, ironically, students threaten each other; but, by the same token, it was the support that school and University staff gave the students, perhaps even more importantly the support that students gave each other, that prevented dangerous risks from being disastrous, and that provided a year of experience which in my personal (not too biased, I trust) view helped to provide the schools with uncommonly effective educators, many of whom have turned out to be adventurous and imaginative to boot.

Chapter 4

Methods: where the 'what' and the 'how' most readily meet

Having something to teach

I have dwelt so far on the inherent difficulties of introducing students to educational practice and theory, to both of which they are relatively speaking newcomers. It is time, now, to look at the strengths a post-graduate Education year already has, although much of what will be said later in this chapter is as relevant to concurrent courses as to postgraduate ones. Courses that have a graduate intake have a ready-made initial asset that can be exploited. One of the guiding principles underlying the planning of Course B was expressed in my submission for funding:

> that teachers' scholarship is a necessary condition for pupils' effective learning, and that specialization should be concentrated on continuing the mastery of subjects studied in undergraduate years while examining the relation of such subjects to curriculum as a whole.

With this in mind we apportioned more time to Methods seminars than to any other University component in Course B. It is customary for Australian graduates to have undertaken a combined course as undergraduates, and therefore it is assumed that they will have two teaching subjects. Most of our students took two Methods, each of which ran for about fifteen sessions in the year. The weekly seminar in each Method usually lasted for two to three hours, and most Methods included excursions or field work, which, of course, took more time. Thus one could say that students spent the equivalent of a full day a week in Methods seminars, and that the core staff had been appointed with their interest and competence in at least one Method in mind. In Australian terms this was giving unusual emphasis to the importance of this component of the Course.

Our reasons for this were two-fold. It gave us the opportunity to be rigorous by taking the obvious step of building on students' existing

117

strengths instead of concentrating too much on their weakness – their ignorance of educational theory. We knew that, with many students, the Education year had a reputation for being superficial and insufficiently challenging, and this same charge is discussed widely in European and American writing on teacher training. We saw that one way to rectify this was to deepen students' existing knowledge by encouraging them to reflect on and analyse it in terms of its teachability to pupils. At the same time, by concentrating attention on teachability, we were broadening their studies to include such considerations as how children learn, why they don't learn, whether what we had to teach was valuable and justifiable, and whether it could be taught without being distorted if it were integrated into programmes that were thematic or problem-centred. In this way, and by offering Curriculum Studies separately for groups with mixed academic preparation, we tried to offset any tendency towards intensifying subject-mindedness and narrow specialization. Whether or not the combinations of subjects and the kinds of specialization that universities encourage are well suited to future teachers is a pertinent question, but one that (except in passing reference) is somewhat beyond the province of this book; but the danger of fostering myopic specialization is one that we shall have to return to.

Our second, and allied, reason for concentrating on Methods was our belief that good teaching entailed scholarly teaching, and that to be scholarly one needs not merely a scattering of information but experience of the sort of intensive effort that alerts one to the phoney – that makes one what one of my students called a 'crap-detector'. Whether or not all subjects do this equally well is a moot point; but any one subject or topic done reasonably well is more likely to achieve this result than is a large number done superficially.

Given that statement of faith, Course B would agree in thought and action with Professor R. S. Peters's plea in a recent book:[1]

> If anything is to be regarded as a specific preparation for teaching, priority must be given to a thorough grounding in something to teach ... This mastery of content is more than ever necessary nowadays in the light of various attempts to develop a topic-centred curriculum in some junior and comprehensive schools. For my impression is that if such experiments are to prove more than a new set of gimmicks, they will require a *more* thorough grasp of the forms of thinking that are to be so integrated than the more traditional subject-centred curriculum.

There is no doubt that, as Professor Peters says, it is easier to mug up (my term, not his) material for a lecture than for a discussion, and it is easier to teach a subject than a cross-disciplinary or interdisciplinary course. It is not quite clear how he would prepare students for this, for he seems (p. 152) to be asking for the teacher to be able to give all sorts of 'informative answers' at one point whereas, at another, as the quotation shows, he seeks a grasp of 'forms of thinking'. And there's the rub. I feel sure he would not seek to produce 'quiz-kids', nor would he be satisfied with the teacher whose speciality was, say, the ablative absolute in Latin. The problem of mastery of balanced content in those who are to teach is within the hands of colleges and universities that are responsible for the total post-secondary education of their students, but for the postgraduate teaching year, we must work from what the student brings with him, and that tends to be highly specialized — more so in England than in Australia and far more so than in America.

Yet the best practices I have seen in teacher education in England, America or Australia have been in Methods work in some English postgraduate courses. This may have less to do with the students' previous specialization — with its advantages and handicaps — than with the quality of the staff and with their emphasis on relating academic/educational studies to school practice. This first occurred to me when I visited schools in London, Leicestershire and indeed some other counties, where I found the school teachers were working closely with Methods staff from the universities. Then, looked at from the other end, I attended university seminars where the staff were knowledgeable in their own subject, the pedagogical implications of teaching it, and the educational context within which teaching and learning took place.

Yet even in England the high status given to Methods in teacher education is by no means universal, and in universities there seems a detectable trend towards building up the Education subjects at the expense of Methods. In many primary and secondary colleges in both England and Australia, where the whole of a teacher's post-secondary education and training takes place, there is a sharp split in curriculum, in staffing and in administration between the 'professional' and the 'academic', which is often a source of bitter conflict.

It is as if what one teaches is at war with how one teaches, instead of the two being in harmony, and further as if the 'what' and the 'how' were both separable from an understanding of the educational context in which learning is allegedly made available to the young. Hence I can be told by students in an M.Ed. seminar in London, as I recently have been: 'That's not a curriculum question: it's a pedagogical one. It's got nothing to do with what you teach but with how you teach it.' Yet two minutes earlier the same students were talking about the 'hidden *curriculum*' — by which I take them to mean *what* you informally (and probably inexplicitly) teach, by what you and the school do and how you do it — that is, how the teacher behaves and the values implicit in

119

his behaviour: how the school is organized and the values implicit in that organization.

Examples are obvious if one considers content that is concerned with moral attitudes. One may take Lawrence Stenhouse's approach – that conflicting views should be confronted and informed by evidence and rational means in discussion under a neutral chairman – or one may consider Peter McPhail's insistence on experience and 'living' the situation, not just talking about it, as being the way to foster learning about values and to change attitudes. Broadly, the content may be identical –racism, sexism, poverty, to name a few possibilities – but what happens to its development depends on the very different methods adopted. No doubt the content of some studies may seem to be little concerned with values, social attitudes or morals – though far more than some holders of 'the scientific view' would maintain – yet all are concerned with attitudes to learning and with methods of teaching. Witness the early leaver who said to an interviewer:[2]

> You went into Maths. class for instance ... these numerals x = y,
> algebra and diagrams, I couldn't see the point of it. I still can't ...
> We've all got adding machines and calculators at work and I did most
> of the accounts [for a big furniture company] on my own at the age
> of sixteen, but I couldn't do the Maths. at school!

What content, one may properly ask, was there for this pupil at school except perhaps in his teachers' minds? Or one may take the example offered by one of the M.Ed. students in the London group referred to. 'You want to teach children the effects of alkalis and acids on litmus paper. This is the content. You may do it by demonstration, or by having the children doing it. That is the method, the pedagogy. The content is the same, the methods differ.' But is that so? At the lowest level of being convinced that litmus paper will do this or that, he may be right; but the content might change if the methods differ in that children might ask, 'Why should I want to know? What practical problems will using this technique help me to solve? What would happen if I put litmus paper in my mouth or stomach?' As soon as one moves from the memorized fact, without any context, the methods and the content will change, and looked at the other way round, the methods used in establishing the bare fact will lead to different sorts of questions and content – or to no questions at all, and therefore to minimally valuable content. In making this point, I am not suggesting that there is never a place for memorization or even drill, only that such mastery needs to be undertaken with an understood context – for example, having some sense of the pattern of a language before engaging in specific language exercises.

Knowledge, whether it be the knowledge of each child individually or the knowledge at the frontiers of research, is acquired by interaction, not by the mere absorption of a fixed content or the employment of stereotyped skills. Michael Paffard, writing from the University of Keele, expressed this view very convincingly in arguing that in Education courses the 'how' and the 'what' interacted most meaningfully in Methods work:[3]

> 'Methods' must become the core of the post-graduates' course in Education and, given adequate time, such courses will not be merely 'practical' in a pejorative sense. Emergency tips for tyros has, too often, been all we have had time for and it is little wonder if such courses are held in low academic esteem. Given adequate space, methods can be a most intellectually challenging and integrative study.
>
> ... After all, would not a really thoughtful consideration of *one* lesson ... in fact raise with urgent reality most of the questions about which educational sociologists, psychologists and philosophers have worthwhile things to say?

Paffard keeps good company, in my view, when a little earlier he reminds us of Whitehead's maxim, 'Do not teach too many subjects: What you teach, teach thoroughly'; and he repeats I. A. Richards's warning against trying to do too much in too little time, thus producing 'a tangle of semi-systematic mutual misunderstanding practised professionally'. Paffard reminds us that postgraduate students have had three years (or more) of scholarly study, and they want to 'use knowledge and develop skills creatively'.

This chapter will show how being a teacher in Methods has led me to suspect that much of the scholarly learning during undergraduate years could be much more scholarly if students had not been so exclusively 'bookish' or 'theoretical' or tied to routine 'lab' work. Graduates can be extraordinarily lacking in what Peters calls 'the forms of thinking' that characterize their own speciality. If this is so, it would seem to follow that those colleges which have three or four years of the total education *and* professional training of their students in their own hands could become more (not less, as they fear) rigorous by constantly asking students to examine the ways in which teaching a subject or a topic can, indeed should, focus attention on what is essential in the matter in hand — that is, in the content as revealed by the way in which children understand and master it.

Children's learning can be shaped and coherent in the long run, although it may be erratic and unpredictable at any one moment. An irrelevancy may be the most generative learning exploration for a particular child. Tuning out may be a sign of the gestation of ideas, and that is very different from never tuning in; but effective learning must

121

be generative in that one thing leads to others which are grasped in their increasing complexity. While teachers cannot play God with any child's psyche, they at least need some conscious and reflective understanding of their own patterning of meaning, and that requires such a deeply-felt understanding of 'forms of thinking' that it will enable them to recognize when a child's deviation might 'better the instruction'. A superficially 'educated' teacher could never do that. To me it is shockingly arrogant and anti-intellectual for highly esteemed academics to dismiss the possibility that they could ever learn anything from a student. It suggests that knowledge is 'out there' and pre-ordained, that the teacher has the most direct telephone communication to God, and that there is only one way of structuring our experiences that can lead us there.

To suggest this is to imply that there is one immutable road to the truth for all people. That assumption is surely vexatiously arrogant. What is equally anti-educational is the opposite assumption – that each person's route is as good as everyone else's, and therefore we need no structure, no passing on of the structures that others have made or discovered: that we can leave it all to spontaneity born of individual experience. Such an assumption is vexatiously stupid. There are abundant examples of both heresies. The first is authoritarian, the second is sentimentally permissive and likely to end either in confusion or a tyranny of ignorant individualism.

One of the problems in concentrating on Methods is that different branches of knowledge employ different kinds of theory, and students will not be master of them all equally. Thus, for example, the scientific law has a status different from the statutory law, the historical generalization or the grammatical rule, each of which will lend itself best to a different method of teaching. Again, a scientific empirical judgment requires a different response from an aesthetic one, though both may be 'theoretical' – 'she has measles' and 'that is chocolate-box art' both imply theorizing, and it is in that broad sense that I use 'theory' or 'theoretical' throughout this book. Different branches of knowledge also develop different kinds of expression and of awareness. The Methods lecturer needs to be thoroughly steeped in the appropriate methods of enquiry and interpretation that characterize the acquisition of his kind of knowledge, and he needs to understand their limitations.

If this sounds unduly academic, we should consider the kind of thing that can happen in practice if one is not. I recently read of a science class on the mechanics of flight that began with two lines extracted from Hopkins's poem 'The Windhover'. There is no reason why 'The Windhover' should not be read in conjunction with a scientific study of flight. Science can be made much more wonderful than it often is; but please let us have 'The Windhover' in its fullness and its own right as a mystical reflexion inspired by the beauty of nature; otherwise it is a pointless gimmick to dismember the poem merely to introduce a scientific explanation.

It is a very different matter when Rod Fawns has his Course B science class studying and producing Brecht's *Galileo*, because in doing so he respected the play on the writer's terms, in its own right. That made it more, not less, relevant to science — and history, we might add. It would be rigid indeed to suggest that only a graduate in English should do this, for proper integrated studies require us often to be prepared to master tough and unfamiliar new areas of scholarship. Rod's respect for his own speciality prevented him from belittling another — that is, from treating literature as a 'tool' — as the following extract from his handout to his class indicates:

> We will explore Brecht's purposes in writing the play ... and examine the relationship between Brecht, Galileo and us. We will do the play in a way that Brecht would have approved — as a workshop reading ... The first half of each session will be spent in small group rehearsal, reading aloud and discussing. In this way we will understand the content, structure and vocabulary of the play, and by coming to grips with Brecht's language and purpose be able in the end to understand and control the performance.

Literature can enrich almost any study, but teachers of English often rightly object to debasing their subject by 'bending it' to subserve a theme that it might illustrate, thus destroying the integrity of the literary example that is taken out of context. This is not to say that extracts from large works should not be used, but that the selection of extracts must be based on consideration for their intrinsic worth as well as for their relevance to something else, and they should be taught with the respect that is their due.

Language as well as literature is also often treated as a tool study. There is nothing wrong with the fashionable idea of 'teaching language across the curriculum', but one reason why it is so controversial is that so few specialists have thought about the role of language in their own studies. If one thinks of language in home economics, in mathematics, in physics, in physical education, in geography, in history, in anything, it is clear that language study must be an integral part of all substantive scholarship: otherwise it is seen as a content-free skill, which it can never be.

This brings to mind a conference with a team of teachers who wanted to introduce a programme of language development across the curriculum. Some of the teachers could think only of how to teach the jargon of their subject. They could not be blamed, for nothing in their tertiary education had caused them to think about language as part of the essence of their knowledge. When the early leaver previously quoted dismissed his maths teaching as worthless, it was a criticism not of maths but of the language of maths. Before children can learn, except by rote, how to manipulate shorthand symbols such as 'x' and 'y' — the language of algebra — they need to understand the longhand, the ideas in words. Some maths graduates before graduation have learned masses of formulas, have spent all their swotting in applying those formulas to problems that they try to foresee from earlier exam papers, and as graduates have no idea of how the formulas were derived, let alone of their applicability to unpredictable problems.

Two great masters of language teaching in recent years, in my opinion, have been Father Milani and Paulo Freire, the first working among poor Italian peasant children at the School of Barbiana and the second working with adult illiterates in South America. Both knew that language was no mechanical skill divorced from content. Both knew that social grievances were paramount in their pupils' eyes. And both knew that language, far from being some disembodied parroted learning, was the articulated 'me' — the spring to a sense of personal worth and power. 'Every word that you don't know', Father Milani said to his pupils, 'is an added humiliation in your life.' This led him to direct pupils into intensive research into educational and social inequalities. And these peasant boys mastered the language of social research and learnt to distinguish between how to present statistical generalizations, how to argue from them and when to be appropriately rhetorical. Rather than accept language deficiency as a 'given' to which teachers must adapt their own middle-class reverence for language, Milani said: 'He who knows how to fly must not throw away his wings for solidarity with pedestrians, but must instead teach everyone to fly', and his teenage pupils produced a brilliant social document which is also superbly well written — *Letter to a Teacher*.

Compare this with a mother's account of what happened to her son when history was 'used' to teach language. Mrs Gillian Taylor's letter (*The Times Educational Supplement*, 14 October 1977) records her conversation with her son of thirteen:

> 'For history, we've got to be a reporter and inverview Voltaire.'
> 'Goodness, I thought you were doing the slave trade.'
> 'No, that was yesterday. Voltaire done the French Revolution.'
> 'Have you got to be a modern reporter? — We could look at an interview in the paper and see how it's done. Or an eighteenth century paper? Newspapers were different then, you know, and Voltaire would have to be careful how he answered.'
> 'Didn't say — doesn't matter.'
> 'Have you got any notes?'
> 'Mm ... encyclopaedia in the library ... look, he wrote Candide

with a mentor and he wanted the government to be very infamous like England was and he thought the church should have The Tolerance.'

'The what?'

'The Tolerance. We done it last year. If you didn't pray right the Catholics burnt you to death and cut off your ears.'

'Er ... perhaps we should find another book before you write this up?'

'Oh no – he said two sides so this'll be O.K.'

1066 and All That! Of course, Mrs Taylor, your son would really know when to use 'did' and 'done', and would not have many children's problem of unlearning a habit; but what would really worry us both is the sloppiness of thought and therefore of language that could lead a child to talk about anyone 'doing' a revolution, not to mention the total misinterpretation by your boy's teacher of how a child's historical imagination might be stirred to produce historical writing.

I recall a student in a University history Method seminar bringing in old purses or wallets that young secondary school pupils had picked up in junk shops. Each container was made to belong to an imaginary figure at a chosen time in the past and the child who possessed it filled it with goods and documents that the imaginary owner might have put in it – coins, diaries, knick-knacks, mail, newspaper cuttings. This the children did as their home assignment over several months, and what they produced was historically accurate – if they could not find samples of what they wanted, they made them. Each wallet was of absorbing interest even to adults, and much imaginative writing had been done by the children. No spurious Voltaire or The Tolerance here.

None of these examples is to suggest that I see knowledge as being divided into clearly distinct compartments – rather I see it as forming a spectrum. The point to be made is that the teacher should be alert to what is phoney and to when he is out of his depth. Nor is it being suggested that his approach to teaching should be highly academic, but rather that he should see the difference between simplifying and being simple-minded. Concentration on Methods seems to be the best way to emphasize such principles, for the students' background in a particular branch of scholarship can be developed into an understanding of its nature as well as of its teachability.

Sometimes it became obvious to us and to the students that it was not until they came to think about how they would teach particular topics to children of this or that age that they began to think for the first time about the *nature* of the knowledge they were concerned with. Many had sailed through their undergraduate studies with but the

125

barest notion of what being a scientist, an historian, a mathematician, a geographer, an economist entailed.

In my original submission, I had said on this point:

> It is possible that the traditional approach to 'Methods' which at its worst descends to tips about the tricks of the trade, could be replaced by an analysis of the students' undergraduate specialities, somewhat along the lines of theory and methods courses in honours work ... Detailed subject analysis would raise questions of what concepts and methods of enquiry are distinctive to a particular study, and whether these are teachable to children in secondary schools. Thus the vexed question of interdisciplinary study *vis-à-vis* subject specialization would be examined.

I still stand by the gist of that, but experience and other Methods lecturers have taught me to be rather less pompous in approach. Students came to reflect upon and to analyse their subjects not by our starting with a philosophical enquiry but by their trying to plan a series of lessons that were teachable and respectable. If one started with a philosophically theoretical approach, the response was either, 'Oh, we've *had* that', or one of sheer nervousness. Starting where students were academically strongest did not mean starting esoterically, but starting with the practical, with the action.

Methods courses

If we take 1975 as a sample year, we shall see that the eight Method lecturers in Course B stamped their own priorities on the course they ran. That year we offered English, science, mathematics, social studies, modern languages, history, geography, economics. In all but mathematics and modern languages an attempt was made in first term to examine the nature of the subject and its potential contribution to children's education and to culture. Certainly in modern languages the culture of the country whose language was being studied was examined, but this is a somewhat different point. In geography and history we began by drawing on students' memories of their own education. It may be significant that Doug Robb (the geographer) and I in history were both concerned with what Whitehead calls the 'inert ideas' that had passed for history or geography in so many students' undergraduate studies. Hence Doug focused on this by asking students to recall what was lively and what was counter-productive in their own studies of geography. Also, with this in students' minds, he made a class available to them at his school so that they could talk with the pupils and discover what *they* thought of their own geography classes. Each student interviewed two or three pupils, looked at the resources that were being used, and eventually discussed geography with the class as a whole.

The students found this enlightening in the extreme. As one student put it (and others would agree):

> This was absolutely fascinating and rewarding. I learned of their feelings with respect to their course, their peers and their aspirations. The overall impression from all these exposures to different sorts of kids confirmed and enforced the belief that a teacher's continued contact with kids is fundamental to any sort of successful educational experience. The teacher must know his pupils, they must believe that he cares, is on their side and represents a model. It also confirmed the belief that organization of a course is essential. Haphazard, stop-gap presentation is NOT ON!

During the first term Doug strengthened this first impression by presenting students with structured and unstructured lessons, showing the effect of each on class management. Class management was seen not as a product of disciplinary or controlling techniques, but rather as the response to sound planning. He ended the term with a study of the structure of geography, its concepts and the skills it required, from which he went on to a consideration of difficulties entailed in teaching geographical concepts.

In history I asked students to bring in the work that had given them most satisfaction during their undergraduate years and that they would most like to use as a basis for teaching. A small group read all these and selected ones that would lend themselves to school work. Our early seminars were concerned with the teachability of each unit of work and the values that could be derived from it by secondary school pupils. We looked, in particular, at the sources students had used and whether they were suitable or could be made suitable for junior- middle- or senior-form pupils. It came as a shock to many students to discover that they had never gone beyond second-hand accounts and interpretations even in their most searching essays, and (understandably) the books they had used, unlike so much primary material, were quite unsuitable for school children.

It so happened that in our first year of trying this we were lucky in having a splendid final-year honours essay that we were able to study very closely. In summing up the kinds of skills and values that it revealed (it was a study of the 1851 bush fires in Victoria and the effects on various people's lives), Judy Walsh, who took the history Method with me, listed the following points that gave us a framework for our seminars that year and in subsequent ones. The work demonstrated the importance of historical imagination — 'What it would have been like' to be in a particular happening, to have to make a crucial political decision, to

127

hold particular beliefs (for example, about 'the wrath of God'); the recognition of different frames of reference such as modern and inappropriate reactions to how people behaved at the time; the place of hindsight and the interaction between subjectivity and objectivity; hypothesis formation (the questions that data raise); hypothesis testing (selection and use of evidence). A good deal of this was possible because of the richness of contemporary documents.

Roger Kennedy in economics was also concerned with the students' somewhat stereotyped approach to their subject. A recognition of this was elicited by asking students early in the year each to prepare a lesson on 'scarcity'. He then demonstrated a more flexible, less 'inert' approach by using the group as his class and himself giving them a lesson on 'scarcity' as he would prefer to tackle it. After that each student in turn took the group to teach a different concept. Roger's emphasis throughout was on the development of economic concepts, and this was in part dictated by the fact that economics is begun in the senior school (fifth form) and entails the introduction of unfamiliar, complex ideas and methodology.

In social studies, which included students with most varied academic preparation, Rory Barnes concentrated in first term on value formation, providing the content by studying material from Stenhouse's Humanities Research project, and examining Bantock's attacks on discovery learning. Both social studies and history groups dealt at some length with the question of indoctrination.

Rod Fawns in science adopted a very similar approach, examining the values implicit in old and new science programmes, the controversy over the nature of science (Kuhn, Popper and Schwab), and the use of exclusive, mystifying language in science. Rod, like Rory, also examined enquiry and discovery methods in science and the place of process or methodological skills as a valid aim in science teaching.

Bernie Newsome, like Doug, Roger and me, was concerned with the rigidities in undergraduate teaching in English, mainly in the preoccupation with sophisticated skills in literary criticism to the neglect of the study of language development. His emphasis was very much on the relationship between language and thought — why children write or don't write compared with how they talk, and the kinds of writing and reading they do in school. He and they would go back over what it is like to write in certain ways on demand simply by doing it.

It perhaps has something to say about the subjects themselves that modern languages and mathematics were the two Methods where there was little introspection on the nature of the subject but a far greater concentration throughout on teaching techniques related to different kinds of materials. Certainly in both there was concern for an historical consideration of how teaching, and the underlying ideas, had changed over a period of time, and in modern languages the place of introducing pupils to a foreign culture was examined. One gets the impression that the maths students were more on the defensive than those in modern languages, partly perhaps because foreign language study in many schools is commonly taken voluntarily by pupils; but the maths students were in a constant sweat about whether or not compulsory maths (as presently taught) could be justified. In another, earlier, year one student suddenly exclaimed in his diary: 'At last X has given us his philosophy of maths teaching!' And in a different year again (there were constant changes in the maths Methods staff), the students invited their lecturer to dinner so that they could informally press him to answer 'Why maths?' In the other Methods groups those who were critical tended to ask, 'Why so much of the "Why"?'

In all Methods, however, there was considerable time given to resources, to analysing the syllabuses and examinations in sixth form, to visiting schools, to looking at children's work, to assessment and reporting. In all, also, there was a study of learning theory and the influence that learning theorists like Bloom, Piaget, Bruner, Vygotsky and others had had or might have on syllabuses and course construction. Each Methods lecturer set his own requirements and his own assignments. There was none who did not ask the students to prepare a unit of work, to justify it, to show how it was to be presented and the materials to be used, and to evaluate it. We tried, as far as it was practicable, to have students base this on a series of lessons actually given. We all, I think, had students give an actual lesson to the Methods group itself, using it as an imaginary class. Roger Kennedy and I probably used this approach most extensively. And in one way or another we nearly all had each student undertaking one piece of sustained theoretical work, either in preparing and giving a seminar paper or through a written assignment.

Nearly every lecturer, in one way or another, was concerned with the interplay of a number of inseparable, interacting elements. To use the word 'element' is itself misleading, but will do for the present purpose of simplifying the analysis. First of all, some consideration was given to the nature of each subject – its syntax, its concepts, its sources (not merely related narrowly to the resources to be used in schools, but also to the sources on which the development of knowledge depends), its contribution to knowledge, its aesthetic qualities, and various forms of expressing its meaning. Some lecturers covered many of these characteristics: all covered some.

Second, although this may not be quite so obvious, every Method was concerned to some extent with each student's personal development of a sense of meaning. Becoming conscious of the values and abilities they had gained from their own scholarship helped to sustain them

129

when they were unnerved by having to teach unfamiliar material in their subject and became aware of (previously unworrying) gaps in their knowledge. They needed to be able to say to themselves, if they had to read up American history, Greek peasant culture or solar energy for the first time, 'I am a good enough historian, or sociologist, or scientist to do this' – or, 'I know that I can't.'

Third, every Methods seminar group considered how (and if) children of different ages, in different kinds of schools, with different kinds of backgrounds and experiences could be helped to share what the students had gained.

Half-way through 1974 Bernie Newsome reflected on the theoretical/ practical problems facing our fifty students. He noted for our discussion:

> We strive, I believe, to see the student, who is in a practical situation, confronting himself with
>   (i) himself as an authority on his subject
>   (ii) how to be open to the demands and intelligence of kids in large groups
>   (iii) how (i) and (ii) dovetail
>   (iv) how teaching could generate renewed/new excitement in the possibilities of learning
>   (v) coming to grips with what are possibly new areas of thought to him.

He noted that conscientious students were involved with all five issues at once – a formidable task.

The Centre for the Study of Higher Education, as part of its evaluation of the Course, sat in on several Methods, and conducted a questionnaire at the end of first term in 1975. Out of fifty-three students forty-three sent in answers. (It must be remembered that this response can be related only to first term, during which a few students had done almost no teaching in at least one of their Methods.) Cleo Macmillan, who reported on the results of the questionnaire, came to the following conclusions:

> In all groups there is evidence that what might be broadly called 'theoretical' questions have been seen as personally significant for some students. [Questions] relating to ... values and aims in teaching their subject ... come through most directly and strongly from the science group (all but one) and clearly from the history and English groups [where] about two-thirds of the respondents ... give some indication of linking the questions ... with the conduct and preparation of lessons, this being in some cases 'thinking about' rather than immediate practical impact.

> It should be noted, of course, that many of the other Methods did

not attempt to deal with the more 'theoretical' questions until after first term; but what is significant is that it can be done with some success even early in the year if the approach is not esoteric. In some of the Methods, even as early as first term, students were asking for some direct discussion of the justification for teaching their particular subject.

History is the one that I can say most about. Taking Paulo Freire's point that, without a sense of history one was lacking a sense of identity – that is, one could not see oneself as a part of the stream of past events or as having any influence on, stake in, the future – we asked how we could teach history to restore that meaning to it for children. This, we thought, was most obviously demonstrated by tracing family histories in the first instance, though ultimately it was true of all history, however ancient. Some students offered to write biographies of their own family, and some worked on family biographies with pupils at school as well.

This led to a good deal of work on oral history, the use of contemporary documents, diaries and ballads. One group of students in their final honours year had interviewed survivors of HMAS *Perth* (sunk in 1942). We discussed their tapes and written reports, and this gave a good basis for discovering the richness of historical memory that surrounds us and some of the dangers – both diplomatically and historically – of oral histories. We also compared various accounts of a particular past incident – for example, ballads on frame-breaking as expressions of popular views, and Byron's speech to the House of Lords on Luddites. Above all, several students wrote brilliantly illuminating family histories – the memories of a Lutheran clergyman in Holland during the Nazi occupation and his personal recollections of helping members of the underground; a middle-class grandmother's vivid anecdotes about pre-war inflation in Germany; a Jewish family's escape from a Russian pogrom and subsequent migratory life; (from a mature student) a father's upbringing in a Catholic orphanage and later 'career', during the Depression, as a swaggie (the Australian term for a man who wanders around the countryside carrying all his possessions on his back in a bundle – or 'swag' or 'Matilda', as in the song 'Waltzing Matilda'), to name but a few.

The translation of one's own specialized learning into teaching – that is, someone else's learning – is the major pursuit of those running either concurrent education courses or postgraduate ones. Bernie summed up the problem for a graduate of English in these terms:[4]

> To study the teachability of one's own discipline is to engage in
> theoretical discourse about the content and processes germane to
> that discipline, which in turn leads to a discussion about the priorities
> individuals decide on within it. In each and every case, the discussions

must engage the student in how he values his disciplines for himself
... They must also be discussions in which the student investigates
his actual teaching concerns, and explores the gaps in his understanding and knowledge ...

Within such deliberations, the classroom confrontation is central.
Consider, for example, the teacher of English when he first enters
the classroom. He will have had three to four years' experience [at
University] of reading Literature, which he has discussed and
written about at length, mostly in a highly discursive [way] aimed at
examiners. He may have studied theoretical linguistics, although that
is less likely. It is even rarer that he would have considered explicitly
the roles that language has played in his learning, nor will he have
seriously considered what distinctions should be drawn between
writing and speech, either as modes of language through which one
learns or as means of communication.

He is almost certain to have no notion of what a pupil will write
during a week in English lessons, during a week of schooling, or
during the year as a whole. In so far as he has such notions, they
would depend upon his memories of past experience, which, in
relation to the school population, would be certain to be exceptional.
In reviewing the work done by the class, he is likely to see wrong
spelling, punctuation, incoherence, a good deal which is composed
according to the recipe 'write anything at all in any way you like
about anything you like to nobody in particular', and is almost
certain to perceive the pupils' spectrum which ranges from those
who like writing and can, to those who can't write and won't.

... He could be forgiven for feeling ... that he is on Mars for the
first time.

To come right back to Professor Peters's plea, it is clear that, although
most of our students would have had a 'thorough grasp of the forms of
thinking' they were to be teaching, having actually to teach showed
that it was not thorough enough. I am not concerned with encyclo-
paedic knowledge, nor I think is he. No lecturer, let alone student,
would know all his subject – all English, all history, all biology, all anything; but when students came to look at programmed material, at
examination syllabuses, at children's work, at their own plans of lessons,
as they all did in Methods, they could detect conceptual and methodological flaws even in unfamiliar content – 'that evidence won't *do*',
'that's "lifted" and imperfectly understood', 'that's contradictory',
'that mistake comes from applying the wrong rule'. Of course many
things might have escaped us all, as they will with most examiners; but
there was a certain shared ground of common understanding.

Yet the value of Methods was that it highlighted the students' deficiencies, as learning to teach will do if it is treated with respect. In the Arts subjects many of the students had manipulated their subjects but without gaining personal insight in the process. Many history graduates could play with the language of analysis; they could interpret and 'place' in the right historical school of thought the historians they knew; they could amass evidence, evaluate it shrewdly and present it convincingly. But this understanding often does not show them what school of thought they are unconsciously representing in their own statements; its relevance to how they might *teach* history does not occur to them; and when it comes to preparing lessons or evaluating children's efforts their own criteria are often confused or blinkered. There is a parallel with English graduates' familiarity with 'Lit. Crit.', for some of whom it has become a sort of disembodied form of gamesmanship that bears little relation to their own reading, writing, or teaching. By contrast some of the Arts students who show the most perceptive and imaginative grasp of how English or history can enlighten their classes are most reluctant to talk about 'Lit. Crit.' or 'historical method'. Ability (or willingness) to verbalize analytically is obviously not necessarily synonymous with the ability to theorize in action – in this case, in teaching. Heady talk can be mindless. A student can dupe himself and his lecturers with his great powers of verbalization, although we must recognize that it may be more than a superficial show, indeed it may be an expression of the ever-present attempt to explore meaning.

The science and maths graduates, by contrast, were often self-consciously apologetic about what they took to be the poverty of their education, not only when introduced to unfamiliar educational issues but also when considering the nature of science or maths themselves: many had been so preoccupied with 'demonstrations', with the dogged learning of given theories or formulas only superficially applied to closely related new examples or problems that they tended to have little verbalized or intuitive grasp of the nature of their disciplines. Certainly few of them had ever thought about the language of their disciplines either in terms of its conceptualization or as a means of wider communication.

A critique of our concentration on Methods

The evidence adduced by the Centre for the Study of Higher Education in evaluating the Course suggests that we were right in the importance we attached to Methods. A few students criticized a whole Methods programme; all students criticized some parts (though often the criticism was contradictory in that one topic was regarded as extremely valuable to some present in the sessions but missed the target with others); but

133

for students in general our Methods work was among the most important things we offered at the University.

Lloyd Jones, looking at our total programme with the eyes of a new member of staff closely connected with school practice and with Curriculum Studies which he took at his own school — Flemington (see p. 7), gave some interesting and provocative warnings about how students tended to cling to their Methods groups. Lloyd's doubts in no way take issue with the kind of argument that I have been using in advocating our concentration on Methods: rather they tend to be sociological. The openness of the Course, with the consequent scope it gave for initiative and diversity could, he suggested, unless deliberately counterbalanced, lead students into isolated groups: the tie with a Methods group at the University led some students to find a corporate group or a particular mentor at the University rather than in the school. Lloyd continued:

> The [attitude] of 'you're largely on your own' — first year out and forever after — is one of the most negative factors in teaching. It contributes to misguided notions about what is possible, leads to neuroses of many kinds, and kills the spirit of most young teachers. I think it very important that as part of teacher preparation, a course should spend lots of time ... engaging the participants in shared responsibility, and in understanding how to initiate it in a school. Interdisciplinary activities ... seem the most logical channel for opening up such possibilities ...
>
> The way in which Method lectures are organized (subject disciplines) and students are allotted to supervisors tends to contradict, even deny, such possibilities.
>
> I admit there is encouragement to cross these barriers but largely it seems fortuitous ... At the university base I think there should be more prescription, more demonstration, more commitment to this aspect of the course: i.e., equipping the prospective teacher to be flexible outside his own speciality, beyond his own personal approach — to be confident about his own thing yet also highly responsive to other possibilities. I feel that 'too much' liberalism can lead to a retreat further and further into one's own delights and in a teacher I think this produces inward rather than outward behaviour, self-interest rather than group interest, and encourages interest in particular kids and minimal interest in *all* types of children.

I would take issue with Lloyd here — I doubt if any but a very few Methods would have intensified individualism. One must allow that, although each different undergraduate study might have put its special stamp on its graduates, within each subject a wide range of warring factions could be found — some historians, for example, prided themselves on being scientific while others saw their subject as essentially a literary one. Moreover, Curriculum Studies set out to bring interdisciplinary groups together to see broad issues by sharing diverse kinds of knowledge.

While agreeing that Methods probably did have a valuable place, Lloyd was worried that they seemed 'to promote not only division of students but also division of staff ... Staff set themselves tasks such as seeing every student in their own Method group'. Certainly, Methods lecturers were torn in their responsibilities: Methods seminars benefited if the lecturer had worked with his students in the school, and, if a student of a Methods group was in serious trouble in his teaching, the lecturer felt compelled to try to help. In fact, as chapter 7 will show, we gave first priority to attaching each member of staff to a particular school so that he could be closely related to the students and staff there, no matter what the range of Methods. We tried to make the most, by way of compromise, out of this policy decision by trying to match the schools and the lecturers − I, for example, would be attached to a school that had a preponderance of history, English and social studies students, and Rod Fawns to a school with a preponderance of science and maths students, though this often proved difficult to arrange.

Lloyd also pointed out that the supportive, corporate framework that was needed required commitment from the University staff in the schools, but even more important from the schools themselves. As he rightly observed, this was much easier to achieve in the small, flexible community schools than it was in large schools with all their administrative complexities.

It would be unrealistic and it would seem like undue interference with the autonomy of schools to suggest that they should examine their structures and practices in order to give better teaching practice to student-teachers, although it is surely quite proper to suggest that their planning should take some account of this responsibility along with all others. There are some faults in many schools that, if rectified, would benefit pupils, staff and student-teachers alike. It seems ludicrous, for example, that any one teacher should be expected to teach hundreds of children each week. This dehumanizes the role of the teacher and as a by-product makes it impossible for him to be as helpful as he otherwise might be to any student he supervises, and it demeans the pupil by making him little more than a unit of instruction. Again, structures that rigidly divide teachers in some schools (especially large ones) into subject groups militate against consideration of the total programme of individual pupils or groups of pupils and divide their school day into unrelated, fragmented bits of learning, to the point where, as one child put it, 'School is the place where you're frequently told to stop doing something that you're really interested in and to start something else that you haven't the time to begin to get anything out of.' Teachers develop territorial groups and vie with each other; and the well-being of the pupils becomes of secondary importance. These are just two examples of ways in which schools might re-examine how they are organized, and in the process better ways could be found, not only for pupils and student-teachers, but also for setting up more supportive and less lonely sub-communities in the school for the teacher in his first full-time year in a school, when many claim to feel lost and lonely.

If the widespread complaints about the divorce of teacher training from schools and school teachers are to be heeded, the indication is that there will be a move in the direction of more school-based courses. Schools, education authorities and teacher-training institutions will have to work together to solve the problems that Lloyd describes.

Recently the National Association of Schoolmasters/Union of Women Teachers has called for greater influence of teachers on teacher training (see p. 198). Seven years earlier the National Union of Teachers in *Teacher Eucation: the Way Ahead*[5] pointed to the need for student-teachers 'to come to terms with the realities of a teacher's duties, to gain familiarity with routine tasks, to experience teaching as a continuous process'. These sentiments are echoed in Australia where, in 1975, in a survey of 130 Victorian high schools conducted by the High Schools Principals' Association, the need for students to gain a closer knowledge of school practices and lesson planning was widely commented on, and twenty-four schools referred to the 'conflict of practice (realism) and theory (idealism)'. They concluded that 'practising teachers should be given a greater role in the structure of courses of teacher training.' The OECD report, *New Patterns of Teacher Education and Tasks*,[6] summed it up in these words: 'There was considerable emphasis on the need for practising teachers to participate actively in decisions on the development of teacher training and retraining. Indeed, such participation by teachers and by students was seen to be a central feature of the new forces of professional training.' The implications of such demands are amplified in chapter 7.

The Course B Methods lecturer's close relationship with the students in his Methods group did cut across his attachment to one particular school and tempt him to run flying in as many directions as there were schools to which his students were attached. There is the further point, made by Colin Lacey (*The Socialization of Teachers*[7]) that students tend to form themselves into 'sub-cultures' according to their subject. This may be more pronounced in the English system, where graduates tend to have read one subject, than in Australia and America.

In Victoria, there is a long tradition of staffing secondary schools with a graduate profession, and control of entry is carefully policed. This being so, we should heed the warnings of people like Lloyd who saw something clannish in our emphasis on Methods. It has always amused me that colleagues who are not involved in Course B assume that it is an interdisciplinary Dip. Ed., although our use of teaching Method as a central pivot makes us more discipline-centred than the traditional course. We seldom teach philosophy, sociology, psychology or history as separate subjects, but Education faculties oddly enough tend to regard these subjects as being disciplinary, while the teaching subjects are given lower status in their academic hierarchy.

Crossing subject boundaries

Team-teaching

I have given considerable thought to the question of whether students in Course B do tend to club together according to their teaching subjects, and to form fairly close 'sub-cultures' within the year, as Lacey suggests they do in England. Lloyd's impression is obviously that they do; my impression is that they tend to, but not to the extent that Lacey finds it to be so in England. On this we have no hard evidence; but if we are to persist with our present emphasis on Methods, and to retain the benefits that I have suggested are derived from it, it becomes more than ever important that we deliberately break across subject barriers and find ways by which students with different academic backgrounds can profitably talk to and learn from each other. This must be done both at the practice schools and at the University. In 1977, in response to Lloyd's suggestions, staff and students explicitly demonstrated at weekly University sessions how subject boundaries could be crossed by team-teaching.

In addition to the organizational changes already suggested, many more schools might well foster more collaborative planning and teaching, so that groups of teachers can identify themselves with a group that shares educational tasks and some real, not just token, political responsibility. Fortunately, the practice of extending consultation and decision-making in staff meetings is growing; but this is just a small part of the sort of participation by staff – and pupils – that we hope to see fostered.

Without abandoning our belief in the importance of Methods, it is true that emphasis on Methods needed to be counterbalanced by a deliberate attempt to break down the isolation of students, teachers and subjects in the schools. It was undoubtedly with this in mind that Lloyd, in his second year, 1977, as co-ordinator of teaching practice and the lecturer in Curriculum Studies at Flemington, was working towards an interdisciplinary curriculum project at Flemington High School.

There is no doubt that when students planned an interdisciplinary unit of work in their schools, and taught it by team-teaching, they benefited greatly in broadening their understanding and in learning from each other.

In some years we took joint sessions with groups from the various Methods. Each mixed group prepared a term's unit on an interdisciplinary topic which they might plan to teach as a team in school. By late second term they were able to plan with a rationale to guide them; they had thought enough about their own Methods to be on guard against making a travesty of them in the interests of an overarching theme: and they were well able to elicit the principles underlying each other group's detailed plan and to evaluate it. This was a good, though lengthy, project, usually taking half a day or a full day. It was also one further way of coming to terms with Lloyd's worries about the danger that Methods work might isolate students and make them inward looking. The staff also produced a possible interdisciplinary course for the students' analysis and evaluation, and this proved to be an important thing to do. When we were asking students to undertake fairly personal work, as in writing autobiographies, family histories or scrutinizing some of their undergraduate work for its teachability in schools, it was always important that the members of staff concerned undertook the same work themselves, for it tended to reduce any sense of threat that the students might feel in displaying their own work. It also showed that we took the task seriously.

Language across the curriculum

Language study actively promoted cross-disciplinary activities. In 1976, for example, Professor R. D. Wright, Emeritus Professor of Physiology at Melbourne, offered a course in the Language of Science which attracted mathematicians, scientists — and humanities students. I understand that he examined ways of verbalizing and making concrete some of the seemingly mystifying non-verbal symbols in which mathematical and scientific concepts are usually expressed, and that he drew analogies between many 'scientific' generalizations and everyday ones, showing the logical or conceptual similarities. This was both science for the layman and language for the scientist. It made a proper excursion into language across the curriculum, and, if we had had more time to organize it properly, he would have been willing to work with students and maths or science teachers in a school to conduct a pilot scheme along the lines described. It gave him, he said somewhat sardonically, 'the opportunity to see an "unemployable" generation giving of their best in an idealistic endeavour to learn better how to do their job of education.'

Bernie and Rod repeatedly took science and English groups together in a study of language and thought. This was done both in Methods and in Curriculum Studies, and it made an excellent meeting place for work undertaken by humanities and science graduates.

Drama workshops

Friday afternoons were always free for students to organize recreational or extra-curricular activities. They varied from year to year, but the one that caught on and persisted was the drama workshop. Rod Fawns, as a scientist with an intense interest in drama (as we have seen), was aware of the dramatic talents and experience of some students as well as of the need for expressive activities for some of the less articulate students. It was our good fortune in our first year to have Richard Tulloch as a student. He did a great deal of work with drama in his school, and, with Rod's help, organized a drama workshop for primary school children living in a near-by high-rise area. In the following two years these two began to move outwards with performances that entailed audience participation, and thus began to take their plays on visits to schools.

So far as the plays were scripted, they were usually designed to present dilemmas or unpredictable situations that gave scope for impromptu acting and audience participation. Rod insists that theatrical polish and professionalism are not needed, but rather that the play must contain genuine dilemmas, the structure must be sound and the performance must be sensitive to children's responses. Unexpected reactions from the children, as audience and yet participants, could change the planned direction of the play, even if only momentarily, and required the cast to adapt their moves to the new direction.

In 1973 the students worked with primary children in a high-rise area on a space travel odyssey in which they visited a new mystery planet each week. Rituals for take-off and landing were the binding threads under the control of a captain and his mate. Children were given scope not so much in responding to a dilemma in this instance as in working out a fantasy. One student, who had had trouble making contact with her pupils at a community school, noted in her diary that these children really 'got through' to her:

Terrifying to speculate on the sort of home environments and play opportunities they ordinarily have ... They don't talk very much of themselves and when you try to get them going they tend to respond in monosyllables. And yet as violent and socially uncommunicative as some of the really fierce boys are, fantasy still gets at them and

139

they are as vehement in upholding each other as they are at most times in bashing each other up ...

The 1975 drama group wrote a historical script, 'The 1890 Shearers' Strike' — the confrontation between strikers and strike-breakers and the influence of this episode on the formation of the Australian Labor Party. The first scene introduced pupils to the background of unemployment and industrial troubles, and then they became involved in the action, some of them getting employment, others being laid off, meeting union organizers, picketing and the like. In the final scene the strike-breakers and the police faced the advancing strikers across the classroom floor — a combination of students and pupils.

'The Box' in 1976 was based on a machine which modified behaviour under the direction of 'Feelgood', who tried to mesmerize everyone into 'being cool'. 'Feelgood', one of our students, recorded the impact of the play on him as the chief actor:

> The mindless or thoughtless responses of the kids when they were TOLD to 'groove' or to destroy the 'box' was eye-opening to say the least. There was no thinking process involved — just DO IT — like 'KILL, KILL, KILL!' Most of the kids who experienced the play had probably never been to a rock show ... To see the kids at times standing dumbstruck with mouths gaping wide open at what was occurring on stage, worried about and anxious to know what was happening to some of their friends ... was something which had to be seen by a detached person to be believed.

Another member of the cast wrote:

> The power of Feelgood was stunning, but the pupils' resentment of such power was far more exciting. Feelgood always had to fight and mystify the kids in order to dominate them, and it was a strange sight to witness a 'teacher' living out such a colourful fantastic role.

These were just some of the examples, either as part of Curriculum Studies or in addition to it, of how students were drawn together regardless of their Methods. The drama workshop consisted of students from a great variety of Methods. It should not be thought that drama workshops are cited as a form of interdisciplinary work, but rather that the appeal of theatre attracts students from vastly different backgrounds, as music, crafts and many other pursuits might do equally well.

Methods seen at the school end

As the next chapter will explain, students and supervisors were asked to write joint reports on each student's teaching. Sometimes teachers asked the students to write their own reports and then added comments. I am selecting extracts from a few teaching reports to show the sorts of experiences students had in schools in thinking about their subjects and ways of teaching them.

We have already heard a good deal from Libby (pp. 109-11) and her reflexions about what studying science had done for and to her. It is interesting that her first concern when she started her teaching practice at a community school was to get the measure of 'kids' (first and second form) before she could start thinking about how to present her subjects. She wrote a lengthy report on herself at the end of the first term. It began:

Aims

Primarily to get to know what kids are thinking. To take advantage of position as 'learner-teacher' to spend a lot of time with kids — listening to them, questioning them.

To experiment with different teaching methods for different topics, in an attempt to find most appropriate methods for different areas. How much can I ask of kids and expect them to co-operate? What sorts of levels are they operating on? What are the best ways of extending these levels? ...

Subjects taught (each a series of 4 lessons, each an hour and a quarter)

(i) 'Illusions' — a fairly teacher-dominated course on the physics of light and colour; a little on the psychology of perception and an introduction to some common illusions. 'Things are not always what they seem! You can't always rely on your eyes!'

(ii) 'Just What is Women's Liberation All About?' — an informal series of discussions centred upon feminism. An attempt to get the kids relating personally (negatively and positively) to the various issues.

(iii) 'Can We Make a Radio Programme?' — an attempt at team-teaching with Jo. Exploring the possibilities and limitations of this medium. Broken up into small interest-groups — some writing and performing scripts; some doing interviews; some exploring sound effects ...

Achievement: Self and Kids

I feel that I am learning what goes on in kids' heads which is my primary aim this year. I am happy with the way the various units have run. The kids enjoyed 'Illusions' and asked questions which showed that they were thinking about the concepts. The radio unit is producing some good tapes. I am particularly happy with the feminism unit — a number of the group are contributing sensibly and they want to extend it ...

One supervisor wrote in a lengthy comment on Libby:

> I know that students have been interested in your units and, during
> the moments in which I observed the progress of 'Illusions', that you
> were very well prepared with the materials which you presented.
> Kids were subjecting me to illusions for days! None succeeded in dis-
> appearing however. I also observed self-motivated work for the
> 'Radio Programme' class occurring outside of the classroom which is
> a good sign of abilities to 'motivate' students in a task.

Another supervisor observed:

> I read with interest your self-analysis and thought if only all teachers
> could and would stop from time to time and do just this, the teaching
> profession would benefit in many ways.

Libby, we can see, took no narrow, specialized view of teaching
science; but at the same school another science graduate gave voice to
the self-doubt of many scientists:

> I have been having doubts as to whether it is science I want to teach,
> being a product of our specialist society ... My specialization in
> science has made me abysmally ignorant in most other fields of
> knowledge ... It has probably affected quite considerably my per-
> formance during the latter part of the term ...
>   One of the problems I am having is not having a full-time super-
> visor. I find it very difficult to think of things to do which seem
> worth doing. One of the things that annoyed me intensely about my
> own education was the amount of time spent doing seemingly irrel-
> evant, abstruse and boring things. Science, especially for younger
> kids ... needs to seem relevant to life (largely because it obviously
> is). I have been finding it difficult to find suitable teaching material.

This was a student Rod Fawns spent much time with later in the
year, even though she was not at 'his' school. He also worked with her
on her depth study getting her to do a critique of a wide range of
science materials.

Regular reports from students and supervisors helped us to evaluate
the extent to which ideas in Methods seminars were of practical use in
the students' teaching. Alongside this, until the end of 1975, the Centre
for the Study of Higher Education was conducting its independent
evaluation, derived from questionnaires and from many visits to schools.
From these sources Methods staff were given valuable feedback. One
report from the Centre's notes on an interview with a science student
gives an example of thought in action:

When X did Physics at school he had found it rather boring — particularly parts going into the history of discoveries and how they were made — wanted to focus on the theories as now developed. Now thought that perhaps what they were trying to do was important because Science shouldn't be taught as a dogma but as the results of a process of human striving that was still going on. But somehow this was not conveyed in the way he was taught.

I asked him if he had developed this point of view recently or had it happened during his undergraduate Science? He stopped and said he would have to think ... He said it had begun this year when ... he had to begin teaching Physics and it had crystallized only last week when he started writing his Science assignment on the value of Science in the Secondary Curriculum. I asked, 'And the discussion in Science Methods contributed to this?' Answer — 'Yes' — and by the way he reacted and was pleased ... this was a really nice example of the sort of learning that Course B aimed for.

The Centre found many students taking stock like this. One student who was interviewed late in the year recalled that half-way through second term she had had a 'mini-crisis' about whether being a teacher of English was right for her. Classroom experience made her realize that she was living from day to day and suddenly the force of working to a whole plan, with continuity, came through to her:

> It was mentioned in Methods earlier but the impact didn't strike me then. Getting a class with Jane [another student] ... was the big thing that happened — trying to work out the total programme, its aims and ultimate goals ... Looking back on Methods notes makes sense now ... I asked myself 'Why do I want to teach?' You do it abstractly in essays but it's different in practice ... This year is full of learning more than University ever was — practice to reinforce and change your ideas.

In English, Bernie seemed to sense when he was needed for day-to-day crises in schools, and this was where a good deal of Methods work was tested in practice — where seminar work was reinforced. He walked into a school when Jane was half-way through a lesson for fifth form on two poems — Dugan's 'To a Trainee Accountant' and Yeats's 'The Scholars'. She had not, she said in her diary, been at all clear about how she would conduct the lesson, and that came out in the way she taught it:

> Bernie talked with me for nearly an hour afterwards about trying to concentrate on a few particular subtleties of method, e.g., arranging furniture for discussion, using 'silences' and developing them,

method of questioning, means of 'extending' kids' answers, really becoming familiar with the work beforehand and planning a direction which may or may not be followed ... It was very useful — and I'm going to try to put it into action.

Naturally we could not always be there when we were wanted, just at the critical time, and this made it all the more important that the continuous supervision of the teacher in the school should be constructive and that we could work through him. An uncritically glowing response did not hurt the student; but neither did it help much.

James, for example, was a student who was given enthusiastic reports by his supervisor:

> Lesson planning and preparation — always most adequate, especially for sixth-form English ... He made a valiant effort to generate interest and response ... any lack of success and his resultant exasperation I would attribute to this particular class's apathy, rather than to any fault in his approach.
>
> His initiative and independence is most evident in his teaching of ... junior classes. He seems to need very little guidance in planning lessons, and his approach is always varied, interesting and novel.

James's own report was not so sure:

> I feel that this report is far too flattering ... I still have an awful lot to learn, particularly with regard to class management and syllabus planning. The thing I find most difficult is timing, particularly in junior classes ... My supervisor has given me support and reassurance at all times.

However, he felt that there were such great weaknesses in the school that observing classes did not help him to improve his teaching. He noted:

> Children are laboriously ploughing through set novels which sometimes take as long as two terms to cover [in junior school]. Grammar is being taught without thought for its function or practical application ... Children are encouraged to do a lot of drawing and beautiful headings, but unfortunately I do not feel that this is a policy dictated by any real conviction on the part of teachers that drawing is a valuable form of expression. It is used as a stop gap. Higher up in the school this activity tends to be discarded in favour of more 'worthwhile' assignments ...
>
> At no time have I observed any real teaching going on in sixth-form. Students are assigned various tasks and expected to perform them with very little help or guidance. If they fail they are chastised

144

and told their chances are slim at the end of the year. Morale is consequently very low.

It seems clear that James was providing ideas and techniques for the staff at his school and not the other way round.

He was so distressed at all this that he turned to his Methods seminars for constructive thinking. Later in the year, Doris Cosopodiotis, the English Methods lecturer, took the opportunity at another school, where a senior teacher had resigned and the school was unable to replace her quickly, to take over some senior English classes with James and some of the other students.

Another student, Phyl, influenced perhaps by original accounts that we had used as sources in Methods seminars, decided to try out teaching history in this way with first and second forms at a little community school. She planned a series of lessons on 'migration to Australia', and this with children many of whom were migrants and had great problems with reading and writing. She recorded in her diary:

> I began this lesson by asking how someone would find out about what it had been like to live in Melbourne one hundred years ago. Leroy told me simply 'read a book'. — 'Written by someone who knows what life was like then?' I asked. He nodded ... I then told them I was going to give everyone a copy of a letter written 186 years ago by a convict to tell his family what it was like in Australia ... The letter itself went quite well. I asked written questions which required brief answers involving either straightforward comprehension or a little reading between the lines ... I received a good range of responses and many puzzled-out answers.

Her problem was Pete, whom she was taking individually for remedial English:

> Pete answered the first question through what might appear as a casual piece of copying and then put a dollop of brown poster paint in the centre of his page ... I did not know what I ought to do. I was reluctant to drop the use of documents because ... it looked promising, but I did not know how to accommodate Pete (who was ... proud and intelligent). When correcting his paper I copied out some answers on to a spare question sheet and wrote his name across the top and handed this back to him when I returned everyone's work. He accepted it quietly, I suspect partly as a face-saving device ... It kept him within reach and allowed him to take part in the general discussions which he enjoys ... I do not pretend this is any real solution but it was all I could think of at the time.

This was good junior history teaching, and, though unorthodox, a compassionate and sensitive attempt to encourage a child's written and oral expression.

The following account of Bronwyn's discussion with second-formers at a small community school shows a historian's attempts to lead children to consider testimony and evidence. It occurred spontaneously when the class had been listening to a tape on the Eureka uprising (in Victoria in 1854) in which the narrator referred to the expectation that 4,000 men would rise up in protest against mining licences. One boy scoffed at this — there couldn't have been 4,000. The discussion was as follows — the T refers to the teachers, the P to various pupils and the D to Danny (who could barely read or write):

T: Why don't you believe there were 4,000?
P: They did it to confuse us. They lied.
T: Why?
P: To put it over us.
T: But we can prove it happened — for example from newspaper reports.
P: But you know newspapers are all bullshit.
T: But a lot of people said it happened.
P: They made it up.
T: There was a court case. There would be records.
P: They could have made that up.
T: If you died today, Danny, how would we prove to a new girl tomorrow that you had existed?
D: My room upstairs. [There is a small room in the school with Danny's collection of things, and it is known as Danny's room.] My books. Others would say I was here. It's well known.
T: Why should we believe all that?
D: Because it's true.
T: We could have made it all up. What about your birth certificate?
P: Your mother could lie.
Other pupils: No!!! Your <u>mother</u> wouldn't lie.
T: Imagine a tram accident — a child thrown into the air, ten, fifteen, twenty feet depending on different people's reports. Which is true?
P: Ten or fifteen feet is all the same.
T: Then why isn't 2,000 or 4,000 all the same at Eureka?
P: Because there are ways of counting — for example a man counts cars with a meter [the children had recently been counting the traffic in their road] ...

Despite the somewhat childish language, the verbalization is promising. Despite the occasionally naive assertion, the children were thinking big. What were they raising in this unexpected turn in the lesson?

They were concerned about testimony. We can infer that they suspected that a group of rioters might try to exaggerate their strength,
therefore their testimony is questionable — but their mother's is
absolutely reliable! The children were concerned about what is historical truth, what evidence is trustworthy and what is uncertain or
untrustworthy. They conclude with considerable shrewdness (even
though examiners might find it irrelevant) that using meters to count
cars is more reliable than spectators' impressions or memories, and
that if we want the truth we want some better way of counting than
relying on the impressions or believing the accounts of those with a
vested interest.[8]

Sometimes the students did bring ideas to their schools that teachers
found stimulating and imaginative. Lou, early in his experience in
teaching fifth-form history, was so dismayed with the class's written
work, some of which was gobbledygook and the best was painfully
culled from the texts and presented logically but soullessly, that he
tried out the idea of personal histories to see if he could arouse in the
class some feeling for history. In this he was greatly influenced by
having read Freire in his Methods seminar — not that Freire discusses
family history, but, as Lou put it, 'I hope to stimulate them to an
appreciation of their own historical background and from that I hope
to kick off into a study of the particular events which interest them.' I
happened to be at the school throughout this project, and Lou quickly
learned that he had to be less vague and to give the class some specific
guidelines. A fortnight later he wrote:

The personal history presentation was a mixture of results. Some
were quite interesting, whilst others were disappointing. I was
amazed to find one student who was able to date his family back to
1690 in a small village in Sweden. He had a fantastic set of documents.

This project bore fruit in many ways, in that he did an outstanding
depth study on his own family history, and this was published in a
scholarly context (see p. 35). He also gave the Methods group a most
interesting seminar using the pupils' work and showing throughout
how this sort of historical work was inspired by Freire's ideas, which
he examined in some detail. His supervisor wrote that Lou had seemed
quite at home and in command while teaching the French Revolution
and the Napoleonic Wars; but then.

he spent two weeks introducing the class to the techniques of com-
piling family histories. This was a novel activity in our History
Department. Mr Soccio managed to explain his plan very expertly.
The outcome surpassed our expectations, and the final reports (either

written or taped) contained a surprising amount of historical information. The latter was supplemented by a number of historical
documents (photographs, newspaper cuttings, passports, etc.). I feel
that the undertaking achieved its objective of making students aware
of the practical problems arising from the historian's task and encountered during the search for historical facts. It further illustrated
how conclusions can be made only on the basis of such hard-won
facts.

That was an open-minded supervisor. At the beginning he had been
sceptical and worried about whether one was justified in sacrificing the
set syllabus for a class that had to sit for external examinations the
following year. I don't know how Lou felt, but I was certainly nervous
lest the results were disastrous. It was not an easy class, and the pupils
were poorly motivated, lacking any great self-respect. The migrant children's enthusiasm was more easily kindled than that of the long-time
Australians, who tended to be defeatist about it, saying, 'What interest
could there be in *our* families' lives?' Although the migrants did tend to
produce more fascinating material, and it was a migrant child who
found a First World War veteran and brought him to the school to talk
to the class, the project aroused the interest of all in twentieth-century
Australian history.

Cleo Macmillan's summary of an end-of-year survey in 1975 showed
that students had profited from the early concentration in the Methods
seminar on history as personal exploration. In summing up their reactions, she noted that they favoured the emphasis on history as 'relevant
and significant' in 'creating self-awareness'. Personal histories and the
study of Freire were appreciated for this reason, and the concentration
on original documents, though sometimes regarded as almost a fetish,
came to be practically useful — 'Gwyn has been on about resources all
the year, something I could not understand until the end of term 2',
one student wrote, while another rightly advised me to 'come down to
tin-tacks' and tell her 'How do I present this class with this lesson involving preparation and all?'

One student commented on the usefulness of doubting 'that historical documents and events can be studied objectively'. She added:

The seminars have demonstrated that the subjective approach,
that which relates back all the time to me and the kids as part
of their history, can be profitably exploited ... How can I teach
... 5th century Athens with the same richness of personal memory
as modern histories? ... They have restored my faith in history
... As a consequence I can approach the kids in a more relaxed
way.

I feel sure that must be the student who gave a series of lessons to third- and fourth-formers on women in Athenian society. It was based entirely on translations of Greek literature and documents. Two other students prepared and gave to their own classes (and to the seminar group) a series of lessons on 'Andrew Jackson and Myths in History' which grew out of a study of the sentiments and assumptions in the ballads 'The Hunters of Kentucky' and 'The Battle of New Orleans', which they recorded on tape, sung by a friend who was a splendid ballad-singer. The sentiments and beliefs in the ballads were then examined beside some of the realities, and the project ended with an exploration of some Australian myths.

At another (community) school, a student concocted a drama about a pupil in the school being judged on a trumped-up charge – a charge involving the reputation of the school. The class acted out what might have happened and how they would have responded. This was then used as an analogy for studying the Dreyfus case and the moral dilemmas involved in it. She and another student then made a detailed analysis of Richard Jones's *Fantasy and Feeling in Education*, with its criticism of the over-emphasis in Bruner on cognitive development and cerebration. The success of the classes on the Dreyfus case led them to think more searchingly about involving children emotionally and stirring them personally in their study of history. Jones's exploration of the power of 'fantasy' and 'feeling' in children's learning prompted them to undertake a more ambitious project that would encourage pupils to try to 'live' imaginatively within a different culture, at a different historical period, through almost unimaginable but true events. Thus they alternated between action and theory throughout.

They were no doubt also influenced by Alex Haley's personal history, which we had heard in a rebroadcast of a BBC programme (and has subsequently become famous through his book, *Roots*), when they took a class through a series of incidents in a Zulu tribe from 1790 to the present. They established the context by a map and by preparing slides of the country, the village, the clothes and the work of the tribe. They taped African tribal music. They then gave each child an identity in the tribe, a name and a role. They had them enact a Zulu wedding and various other events. Each pupil was told that he was expected to 'show real talent and skill in portraying his role', to 'create behaviour' and 'demonstrate feelings suitable for the role beyond what was described in the briefing'. The assessments were discussed with the children. The *pupils* then assessed the project – they were young secondary pupils. It was pleasing to see our students drawing on pupils' reflexions and evaluations, just as we, as University staff, drew on our studnets'. Among the comments were the following, which are quoted without any alterations:

I thought this method of Teaching was really good. It allowed the students themselves really <u>particapate</u> in the lesson. Putting the students in a Zulus place gave the student a chance to sought've experience a Zululife. Peg and June had a good idea in actually making costumes. Getting records and tapes was good to. I don't think there is much more to write except that this method of Teaching would work just as well in other classes.

I really liked doing the classes. Especially the way they were run in a fast, continuous manner, so they didn't get boring. Taking the role of an individual Zulu was good but I didn't find myself fully understanding the reactions of each Zulu which made the last class a bit sort of beyond me. It was really good having people there who knew a lot on the subject so questions could be answered. I think it would be good to have more of these type classes, especially in primary school and also especially to teach that Africans, Indians etc. aren't always like the way they're shown in movies.

I was very impressed, by the amount of work Peg and June put into the classes. I think everyone worked a bit harder because of their example. The two lessons that I think worked best were: the one where Pedro dressed up as a slave ship captain and we were all bundled into the place under the stairs and: the one where we were sold to slave owners. The second one in particular worked very well.

I thought it was a very successful class in that it got nearer to what it was like for the Africans then. Not that we got a fantastic idea of the way it felt but at least we touched on it. I think that I possibly learnt more than I would of otherwise.

Naturally I have more detailed evidence of how the work in history Methods seminars influenced students' teaching than I have in other Methods, and so we might take the testimony from students' answers to the Centre's questionnaires. Cleo classified them into 'most favourable' and 'most unfavourable', though in some Methods, notably economics and modern languages, there were no unfavourably critical responses. The questions students found most valuable were:

Should geography be taught as a body of knowledge? Should concepts be made relevant by content or content used to introduce concepts? Reason for geography.

The importance of one's competence in the foreign language and one's knowledge of the culture and history. Motivating children — and the difficulty. Variety in lessons — very pleased and of great benefit.

It is possible to teach the Higher School Certificate [the external sixth-form examination] ... with imagination. [Seminars] have helped in understanding of the learning process in economics. How important a part should teaching of social responsibility play? Questioning methods very important.

Idea of individual learning in maths good — I'm following this up in spare time ... I wonder if there is a time in a child's development when repetition and rote learning are advantages.

To what extent have I the right to expose and/or impose my values and beliefs about society on kids? ... What is learning? Education? ... Is Integrated Studies possible? ... Seminars ... have raised important questions, e.g., spiral curriculum and discovery learning ...

The value of science is relevant transferable knowledge. The complexity of science. The complexity of education ... Mainly the theory behind the practice we are attempting to develop, and means of correlating the two.

It is a valuable opportunity to swap ideas and raise questions on the actual work we are doing [in English] in school. I find this group analysis of the problems and the offering of theoretical basis of problem solving ... most relevant.

The criticisms were nearly all of the one kind — the request for greater help with lesson planning, and showing how resources could be found and used for individual lessons. Many of us sampled students' lesson planning and examined it in seminars; but it would take a universal genius to help each student individually with each of the eighty-odd lessons he gave during the year. Indeed, the students' expectations were quite unrealistic. They did, however, indicate the need for Methods lecturers to be in the schools as much as possible, for some supervisors to give more detailed help in lesson planning, for better resources centres, and for students to help each other by sharing their expertise. The felt need of the students for greater help in lesson planning shows that this was the point at which the 'how' and the 'what' were inseparable. Most students at some time or another were gravelled for material and frustrated in attempts to get appropriate resources, while at other times they amassed their resources well enough but lacked the experience and imagination to use them most profitably. This was a year in which they had to try to make the two gel.

If we were right in the importance we attached to Methods, as I think we were, it was because this was where we could be rigorous by seizing on the practical to reinforce the theoretical; it was because Methods enabled us to assume in action the importance of being well-grounded in the knowledge to be taught; and it was because (as staff and the Centre could often see better than the students saw at the time) we had direct evidence of our influencing the quality of students' teaching. But to avoid perpetuating the sharp divisions existing in many schools between teachers (because the curriculum is usually organized into subjects), it was necessary for us to encourage students to undertake team-teaching, for us to have powerful cross-disciplinary programmes at University, for us to spend considerable time in the schools, for us to be able to employ staff who were strong in Methods, and for schools to co-operate with us in what we were trying to do. Naturally, not all of these things could be completely realized: not all of these things were under our immediate control.

Chapter 5

Assessing oneself?

Self-direction

The most radical feature of the Course was our abandonment of competitive assessment (ranking of students), replacing it by consultative and open assessment, as well as our promise that students would collaborate in day-to-day decision-making about the nature of the Course. In my application for funds to run Course B as a pilot scheme, I had argued in 1972 (with some misreading of the political future):

> We might expect in future to feel more urgently than we have so far the effects of student unrest. So far, the universities' response to student demands has been to extend their representation on policy-making bodies. This, desirable though it may be, is a cumbersome and indirect way of involving students in decision-making. It would be more direct and more immediate, as well as more challenging, if they became active agents in their own education — planning their own work, learning to ask the right questions instead of merely giving the right answers, and having to evaluate themselves. Our [i.e. Education] students are all graduates and, as such, should have the maturity and educational background to enable them to see the responsibilities that are a concomitant of freedom.
>
> In addition, it is most important that education students should have first-hand experience of autonomy in their work since they will face the problem of pupil participation in the schools to which they will go after leaving the university ... Students need the opportunity to discover how much they can manipulate the school environment for given ends (in our case maximizing pupils' learning) and how much there are irremovable limitations on their powers.

It should be noted that, in part, the Course was a deliberate attempt to respond to changes that had recently occurred in Victoria's educational

153

system. From being a highly centralized system, geared to (mostly) external examinations at the end of fourth, fifth and sixth forms, the secondary system had recently been freed by the abolition first of the fourth-form ('Intermediate') examination and then the fifth-form 'Leaving Certificate'. Only the sixth-form Higher School Certificate remained. Accompanying these changes, the State Education Department had expressly invited each school to reconsider its curriculum and school organization in an attempt to take advantage of the newly-won freedom. Many schools had already abandoned ability grouping or 'streaming', and many more now did so; some schools replaced external examinations with internal ones, while some changed to continuous and participatory assessment of pupils; the Department's and the examining body's suggested syllabuses lost their importance and disappeared from many schools; and many would no longer allow Departmental Inspectors to visit them to give guidance in school policy and practices. A new professionalism was won by teachers which many of them relished but many found bewildering. In the schools there was a new stirring which often led to bitter conflict over educational policies and practices. Teacher-training institutions, always a handy scapegoat (and often deservedly so), came increasingly under scrutiny for their being divorced from schools and their failure to equip students to meet the new and pressing demands.

Two things seemed clear: there *had* to be (whereas there always ought to have been) a strong partnership between schools and training bodies; and training bodies had to respond to the new autonomy of schools by exploring the notion of autonomy themselves. Despite the proud tradition of autonomy that is so prized by universities, their successes — that is, their graduates — often were severely discomposed by a course that offered it to them. And as staff we found ourselves tyros in trying to put democracy into practice.

The least troublesome part of this, oddly enough, was student participation in student assessment. I say 'oddly' because our critics and even our friends thought that this would be our downfall. Despite our bravery in denying the validity of well-worn clichés, deep down we were haunted by them. What if we found that students won't work except for marks? What if that nebulous thing called 'standards' did decline in our Course? What if students turned up in schools at any old time as the whim took them, long-haired, bare-footed, ill-kempt and smoking pot? What if they decided that we, as staff, had nothing to offer them and they totally rejected us, using our promise of autonomy to exclude us from their deliberations?

By a fey sort of logic any of these consequences could have been possible, and it was true that for staff to have any 'authority' they had to command it, not demand it. This was very testing for staff, as I believe it should be. Our worst errors, I think in retrospect (with the help of students' diaries) were when staff occasionally felt so insecure or beleaguered that implicitly they gave the students the impression of expecting some kind of personal loyalty, which the students described (rightly I think) as 'covert pressure'. Fortunately this was rare.

For all of us there was the constant reminder that children compulsorily at school have, if they but knew it, absolute power over their teachers. It helps our peace of mind that they tend to exercise this by inconspicuous withdrawal — a personal and sometimes total rejection of what is offered them at school. Because this is a secret act we, as teachers, can ignore it in a way that we cannot ignore overt and organized rebellion, but it is none the less real. If we look at it this way, students always have the final power, and millions of them exercise it unbeknown to the teacher every day. They simply tune out.

All should pass?

It can be, and has been, said that staff had the final resort to artificial incentives in that we explicitly reserved the right to fail a student. This is correct, and must be seen as qualifying any claims we made for offering students autonomy. It is a qualification, however, that I never found to be a 'compromise' of the basic principle. Only a naive fool would believe that anyone, even Robinson Crusoe, can have absolute autonomy. To examine realistically the fulfilment of the principle of autonomy one must examine the constraints and limitations that are inevitable, the ones that are desirable, and the ways in which they can be acceptably influential.

To be allowed to exist under the aegis of the University, to be tolerated by the schools, the State Department and the unions, and to do justice to children and their parents, it was essential that the qualification we gave (the Diploma) be respected. It could be argued that better means of certifying teachers should be found, and I should be willing to consider seriously other ways of doing this. But to wait for this change would be to accept inaction and to refuse to change what can be changed within present constraints. Our task, as I saw it, was to offer as much autonomy as we reasonably could under the circumstances, and I suspect that, in the process, we came as close to the ideal as was possible.

First of all, we consulted students about our every move. Admittedly, we made no great song about the fact that we had the final decision about their passing. Rather, we said emphatically that everyone was assumed to be academically capable of meeting our requirements, which would be worked out with them, but they had yet to discover whether or not they could succeed as teachers. They could all assume that they would pass unless they heard to the contrary. This was a sort of 'all innocent until proved guilty'.

Although it was agreed that there would be no competitive assessment, we attached great importance to constant assessment that was to be educative rather than classificatory. This was a point that I had made in my application for funds — that assessment could not be adequately justified unless the student learnt from it. Once this purpose was genuinely accepted, it meant that there could be no private or arbitrary judgments made, and so it followed that no secret records were to be kept.

These procedures were, I would maintain, radical in the extreme. As we have seen, they were so strange to students that we were sometimes not believed.

Assessment of teaching practice

But what is important is what this led to in action. Let us first take teaching practice. The Faculty had set up a 'Schools Committee' to be responsible for school practice. This consisted of Course B staff, other Faculty staff, representatives from each of the schools that worked with us, the people who were independently evaluating the Course, and students' representatives, though any other students who wished could also attend. This Committee agreed with Course B staff that no supervising teacher should write a report on a student without showing it to the student before it was sent to us. Ideally, the Committee agreed, the report ought to be written by the teacher and student conjointly, in consultation.

The common practice, not only at my University but I think generally, is for supervisors to receive some sort of a standard form, often a questionnaire, to be filled in after a teaching round and sent in as a confidential document to the university. Many times have I sat behind a desk with the confidential report in front of me while the student has given an account of what she thought had happened during the teaching round that bore little or no resemblance to what her supervisor had thought. I found this uncomfortable, to say the least. Sometimes it simply meant that supervisor and student hadn't effectively communicated with each other, if they had talked together at all. Sometimes it meant that the teacher's 'tact' with the student so camouflaged his true opinion that what was said to the student and what was written to us were dissimilar or straight-out contradictory, and the students naturally felt aggrieved. Above all it seemed to me to demean the student. I came to regard the practice as unhelpful and unethical.

Teachers connected with Course B readily complied with the new policy, and most, I should say, agree with it in principle. What in practice happens can vary widely: some write a report and have the student sign it; some write a report with the student; some ask the student to write the report which they then sign or add a few remarks to amplify. Sometimes students asked their pupils to write reports. In all cases the report, while filed with us, is freely available to student and teacher.

For this procedure to work as well as possible, a really close understanding between University and school staff is essential; but, as our student numbers increased and so we had students in upwards of thirteen schools, this was not always possible. We tried to meet this with end-of-year and beginning-of-year meetings with all supervising teachers in each school, but this was often beyond our resources, and the staffing policy in Victorian schools, which results in massive transfers of staff, militated against the informal understanding that comes from familiarity. Teachers new to the Course often asked us for guidelines. Occasionally when we moved a student to a new school for just a few weeks we sent the standard form. Once, when we did this, one teacher answered the question about the student's appearance in the classroom: 'Her lipstick and nail-polish don't match. Come orf it!', and this summed up pretty well the reaction to the standard form. But we were diffident about putting other guidelines on paper, partly because we did not want to lay down specific criteria and partly because we could not. After two years we wrote a discussion paper on supervision, discussed first with the Faculty's Schools Committee and then to be discussed with teachers in each school. Sometimes this resulted in valuable conversation, but more often it suffered the fate of circulars and correspondence to schools — it sat in the Principal's office, was stuck on a notice-board and not read, or it lay around on the staff table until it was eventually thrown away in a clean-up.

Our undertaking with students was that no one could fail unexpectedly. No one would fail on teaching without full consultation with school staff, and in practice we were very reluctant indeed to fail anyone whom supervisors thought should pass. We retained the right to fail a student who disagreed with our judgment, but we hoped that that would never happen. In four years, with 170–180 students, it did not happen. Several students withdrew; but this is not a real option for many, since those who hold Departmental studentships, as most of them have done in the past, would have to refund to the Department a large sum that had been invested in subsidising their university education in return for their undertaking to teach in Departmental schools.

Risking failure

We believed that we subjected the students to a much more testing and

157

risky apprenticeship than was usual. This made us incline towards giving them the benefit of the doubt, if there were one, but not before we had availed ourselves of the opportunities we had, because of our close knowledge of students and schools, to transfer students to where they could obtain the kind of help they needed. While we knowingly subjected students to risks, even at times to great anxieties, during the Course, we tried to be very careful that we should not add the fear of our failing them. Learning to teach, like all real learning, entails successes and failures all along the way — swings between satisfaction and frustration, even dismay. In this sense, true learning (or proper education, if you like) contains its own inbuilt discipline.

External threats of, say, failure or low 'ranking' may do considerable harm. The threat of being failed, and certainly the experience of having been failed, can erode a student's energies. What we can do as teachers is to eliminate, or at least to minimize, the demoralizing effects of comparative ranking that is embodied in the ritual of class lists. Our view in Course B is that the personal ordeal of learning to teach, and the necessary academic challenges entailed in gaining professional mastery, themselves provided sufficient discipline. The trend in many schools to abolish class lists and to adopt more constructive forms of reporting on pupils' learning is an extension of our point of view.

It is romantic nonsense, on the other hand, to talk loosely about eliminating all failure from education. The possibility of successful learning entails the possibility of failure. It is in the nature of learning that the child, or for that matter the adult, must be constantly grappling with intellectual problems and with difficulties (failures) in expressing ideas. ('What *is* the word I want?' 'Why can't you see what I'm trying to get at?', we see him asking himself.) This period of frustrating gestation may be momentary or protracted, simple or complex. Inherent in it is a temporary sense of failure. Permanent and total failure is a very different matter, and can be only destructive.

What we can do as teachers is to find ways of inducing the sort of unease that challenges students or pupils to grapple with problems, to give expression to their ideas in speech and writing, and this is what I mean by pushing pupils to persevere rather than taking the permissive and pessimistic view that some 'progressive' teachers take in allowing pupils to abandon anything they find difficult. The easiest way out of proper teaching is to be permissive. It shields the teacher from the responsibility of seeking ways of encouraging pupils to tackle problems anew and of giving them the will to go on trying. This is very different from 'instant success', with its romantic faith in 'content-free' inspiration. And it is very different from irreversible failure too.

What we too often tend to do is to play God by demanding that pupils acquire insight and the words in which to express new meanings

at our bidding, as we do in examinations. The moments of enlightenment cannot be contrived or predicted. This is true of our humdrum
little discoveries that relieve us from teasing frustration just as it is true
of major creative acts of discovery. Michael Polanyi, who is among the
great thinkers on the acquisition of 'personal knowledge', uses Poincaré
as an example of the process (*Science, Faith and Society*, p. 34):

> He noted that discovery does not usually occur at the culmination of
> mental effort — the way you reach the peak of a mountain by
> putting in your last ounce of strength — but more often comes in a
> flash after a period of rest or distraction. Our labours are spent as it
> were in an unsuccessful scramble among the rocks and in the gullies
> on the flanks of the hill and then when we would give up for the
> moment and settle down to tea we suddenly find ourselves trans-
> ported to the top.

Libby's description (pp. 109–11) of the way group discussions un-
settled her profitably illustrates the way in which exploratory talks,
sometimes apparent waffle, came to be seen by her as 'an unsuccessful
scramble among the rocks', in which students help each other to assemble
all the ideas that might bear on a complex question yet come to no
answer in the process. Repeatedly students express their irritation at
the inconclusiveness of seminars; but that very irritation can be (though
it may not necessarily be) the prelude to enlightenment — a new meaning that opens the way to more complex, more subtle exploration of
further meanings.

A practical problem, like learning to teach, entails the interplay of
innumerable variables — at the centre of which for most beginning
teachers is their sense of their own identity. Often supervisors can relieve
the students' strain by helping them to 'decentre' their analysis. Once
we can help them to see the thing whole, as the complexity that it is,
their diagnosis is likely to be less cripplingly self-centred. It is no accident that, for many students, the breakthrough came when they first
made genuine contact with one child or a group of children. When that
happened, they suddenly saw a different complexity because they saw
it with the eyes of the child. The libretto changed from one which
depended entirely on 'my' singing, to seeing how other people in the
cast were integral to the whole performance and were also affected by
the shape of the stage and the interpretation given by the producer.

This enlargement of vision, the move towards objectifying one's
vision, is likely to be obstructed by an intensification of the fear of
personal failure, which, if it becomes obsessive, will be regressive,
whether it produces paralysing stage fright or a charismatic prima
donna.

159

I have tried to illustrate why, paradoxically, we saw risk as potentially constructive but the external threat of failure as destructive. The discipline lay in the value attached to the quality of the performance.

Our gamble lay in our hope that, by the end of the year, each student would have some sort of clarity in seeing himself objectively, if necessary to the extent of recognizing that teaching was not for him. We were put to the test in two memorable instances. In one, the student made no contact with children throughout the whole year, even though he was in a community school where relations with pupils were informal and, if not necessarily easy, at least more easily fostered than in a school that depended on large, formal classes. In case the emphasis on 'groupiness' (as the students put it when they found it bothersome) was an undue strain on him, we made available teaching at a more formal school, and that didn't work either. What further worried us was that neither his fellow-students nor his supervisors (including University staff) could 'get through' to him. Bernie and I were extremely apprehensive when it came to the final interview in which we had decided that we must tell him that we could not pass him and why. This came as no surprise to him, for he knew how much time we had all spent with him in trying to help him to face up to teaching. At first he was aggressive and argued that we had no reason for singling him out. We had to explain that we could not allow him to be placed in a school when we had no evidence that he would or could make contact with children, and that, apart from our responsibility to schools and pupils, we believed that the strain on him would be insufferable. Why, we asked him, try to undertake work that by its very nature demanded personal give and take when he clearly withdrew from that and could do other work that was more solitary? Was there any shame in not liking or not being suited to teaching? At this point he cracked and admitted that, since the end of first term, he had wanted to give up, but he had concealed this because he could not afford to pay back his studentship. Fortunately, that was handled more easily by failing him than by passing him, and so the poor young man shed at least one load that must have seemed heavier week by week for two terms.

Len, our other memorable problem, was also on a studentship. He was a bikie, who seemed to have more tenderness towards his bike than towards human beings, but he did keep in touch with us, though knowing that he only intermittently gave us grounds for thinking that he could teach. He was torn between a passion for maths in which he wanted to take a higher degree (a hope he had made difficult by always having a 'crisis' before his examinations), and a hunch that he really might like to teach maths. Nearly always when I visited him at school I would find him secreted in a cubby-hole doing advanced maths problems; but he did do some teaching and he clicked with 'kids that liked maths', though he found those who were 'maths blind' a bore. The consequences were obvious to all, including Len. He was, moreover, unreliable about turning up, either because he was so elusive that he could not be told what he was expected to do, or because his bike broke down or he had an accident. He seemed to be accident prone, literally and metaphorically. He was equally erratic in his work for University sessions. His fellow-students at the school tried to involve him by getting him to teach *them* higher mathematics, and as a group we challenged him to give us all a session to demonstrate to those of us who were mathematically deficient or 'shy' why he found maths so engaging — so all-absorbing. This he did, as the result of fiendishly difficult thinking and preparation, and it was a brilliant exposition. His speech was usually careless, halting and crude, but when he 'took fire' he became miraculously articulate.

Despite glimpses of this ability at the school, Len's supervisors thought he should fail. They didn't doubt his teaching ability so much as his reliability. He could undoubtedly have been an academic asset in any school; but would he be? We had three options: we could fail him, but an outright failure would be wrong; we could pass him, but that was chancy and might be wrong; we could defer his pass, which would mean re-examining him during first term of the following year, and this seemed to be the best solution. It so happened that the Principal of the school he was to be placed in was an old friend, and a member of our Schools Committee. I rang him and discussed the question at some length. Fortunately he was a wise man. His first reaction was to agree to deferring the result, and then he speculated that, no matter what we decided, he was still left with the same responsibility towards Len and the school, and so, he concluded, by deferring the result we would merely be 'passing the buck'.

Bernie and I faced the interview with grave trepidation. We explained to Len our dilemma, very much as I have described it here. We told him that he had put us in the position where, whatever we decided, we could not be right. He replied that he was no longer in conflict about whether he wanted to do research or teach; he had decided that, before he went on to research, he ought to teach, and that that decision was not merely the solution to an acute financial difficulty. Perhaps he was rationalizing, but I had come to know him well, and I believed him to be frank and honest. He was convinced, he said, that part of his difficulty had been in teaching to other teachers' syllabuses and being observed. Given responsibility for his own planning and teaching, he would meet it, even to the point of working with 'kids who don't understand how beautiful mathematics is'.

Finally, in desperation and indecision, I asked him to put himself in my position and tell me honestly what he would do if he were me. He started to go over the same ground about how different it would be if/ when ... I stopped him, and suggested that, instead of being irrelevant, he should answer my question. There was what seemed like a ten-minute silence. We waited. Then it came: 'Gwen, I would pass me and feel unethical.' When Bernie and I had stopped laughing, we seized Len's answer with relief.

When I next met him the following year, and he was already establishing himself as a teacher, he did have the grace to tell me that he had deliberately chosen to take first-form mathematics and had formed a junior maths club. He became as fanatical about teaching as he was about his bike, or about solving abstruse mathematical problems. His reliability in meeting his commitments was exemplary, for he became committed. But we could have been wrong, terribly wrong. As it is, we have added to the teaching force an uncomfortable eccentric, and the full implications of that I am in no position to explore further.

The threat of being failed by someone else, as distinct from being convinced oneself that one would fail as a teacher, we removed as far as we possibly could, and the best measure we have of how radical this was comes from our difficulty in convincing students that we really meant what we said. In chapter 3 we saw, certainly at a time of intense anxiety for students (largely a spin-off from our own anxieties), that they still feared that secret records were kept. They realized that having no marks or grades made it all the more important to keep detailed records so that they were not disadvantaged if it came, for example, to writing testimonials for them, yet some still resented the records.

Educating, not labelling

But there was more to it than that. Eliminating competitive assessment, refusing to give marks, preferring not to give examinations — none of these meant that there was no assessment. If anything, there was more assessment than the students were used to, but its character was different. It was always engaged in as an educative device and never as a labelling procedure; therefore it had to be participatory. It was always approached as a way of seeing how things could be improved, never as a superior passing judgment on an inferior. Even if there came the final crunch, as in the cases mentioned, it was never our wish to damage the ego of the student. Only sadistic examiners would wish to do that, but the power of an examination, like the power of a jury and a judge, is frightening to contemplate, particularly because it is easier for staff to be impersonal and remote, thus withdrawing from the human consequences of what we are doing, and shutting out our own imagination.

Students, we found, were so conditioned to the possibility of being

162

sentenced that it was hard for us to convince them otherwise. We were least successful at explaining our view, I suspect, when our own fears were uppermost – our fears that they would 'run away' from us, play us for suckers, push us into a corner, or prove to our critics that what we were trying would not work. Some of them did push us by questioning the validity of any sort of assessment that was suggested. This never, as far as I can remember, extended to their questioning the desirability of guidance and assessment of their teaching. In fact, paradoxically enough, those who questioned most persistently our attempts to agree on academic requirements often turned out to be the very ones who thought we should use more extensively our right to fail students for faulty attitudes, especially for authoritarianism.

It would be totally misleading to suggest that the testing point of our assessment programme lay solely in the question of whether or not a student should pass the year. That was merely the culmination of all that went on during the year, and for nearly all students was never in doubt. What is far more important is the question of whether students might work poorly unless they had the incentive of a mark or of competing to do better than the next chap – as so many of the Black Paper writers aver.

This was not our experience. If anything, most of what has already been reported adds up to the fact that we were far more often worried about students' overworking than about their slacking. If we were to need vindication of our belief that students *will* do their best without competitive assessment, we need only refer to the number of students (some already mentioned) who had writing published, and we could refer to many more whose work was kept in the Faculty's Resources Centre because of its likely value to future students. But that is not to say that our approach was without difficulties. The greatest difficulty lay in the conflict students constantly felt about whether they should put their effort into this rather than that – whether, for example, it should go into Wednesday's lessons or the history assignment due at the end of the term. Avoiding unbalanced efforts required constant vigilance all round, most especially from the students themselves. But constant staff meetings were followed by questions here and prods there. We tried to keep a constant tally.

Necessarily, not all work was of an even standard. Each student had his own priorities and, within limits, a right to them. It was the year's work as a whole that had to be looked at, and undue lopsidedness to be averted; but students were good at abiding by their undertakings provided that they saw the point of them (as they presumably did do since they had helped to formulate them), and particularly if they saw the value in them for their colleagues. I cannot recall a seminar ever being let down by a student's failure to give a serious paper, if that task had been accepted. I can recall endless trouble in getting written work in on time if other people were not depending on it – and that was only a bloody inconvenience to staff.

Occasionally students made token gestures. The best example I can think of is Paul. He was one of the most outstandingly successful students, academically speaking, that we ever had – right through his schooling to his final honours results. He wrote in his autobiography at the beginning of the year some sort of an account of his education (omitting modestly any reference to his results), which he concluded with the remark that at the end of it all he came to the frightening realization that he had been effectively educated only 'from the neck up'.

At the end of first term, not a minute late, he handed in a history assignment describing a series of lessons actually planned for or given to one of his classes. All members of the group agreed to do this, as soon as they had taught enough. The description was expected to show the methods used, and the account was to include a justification and evaluation of the course given. Paul's lessons were based on one book which contained some good extracts from documents relating to early Australian history. It was very much a 'chores-to-be-done' exercise which failed to exploit the richness of the documents being used or to build imaginative work around them. It was stolid and pedestrian, leaving, I felt sure, Paul (let alone his class) quite unmoved. In keeping with our principles of assessment of students' work, I gave it no mark but I wrote a detailed comment on it and made many suggestions about how it could be enlivened. In discussing it with Paul, I expressed surprise that someone with so distinguished a record in history could approach it so lifelessly, and I took it as an indication of the difficulties he was having in teaching history. I refrained from saying that I read it as a diligent and fairly meaningless token gesture to fulfil an agreed-upon requirement. Although I didn't say this in so many words, apparently Paul sensed my reaction. About three months later he stayed behind after a history seminar and said that he was going to do a totally new history assignment because the earlier one was unworthy of him. He was planning a series of lessons on China and he would write it up fully as a basis for discussion with the Methods group later. As he was about to leave he turned around and smiled, saying, 'It is taking me quite a lot of unlearning to get used to doing things well without expecting a mark.'

For Paul the Course demanded a radical change in his attitude to work. His difficulties lay, not only in his being deprived of the incentive of marks, but also in the fact that he was unwittingly teaching only 'from the neck up'. He knew what he wanted to do but he had trouble doing it or seeing how what we were doing in seminars might help. Of

Curriculum Studies he said in his diary that he switched off when discussion became too abstract:

> It isn't a matter of being intellectually lazy — just my experience has made me see the wisdom of being practical and realistic. For me the most important thing arising out of Bruner's work is that for effective learning to take place, the emotions as well as the intellect must be engaged ... Heretical?

Yet this is how he wrote up a history lesson that he gave to a sixth form:

> I started talking about the economic consequences of gold, but since nobody had done the work, there was not much point in discussion. I wasn't prepared to lecture on the subject, so I talked about the problems of history, questions of evidence, historical judgment etc — they were dumbfounded. I probably aimed too high.

Imagine. He found some of the University graduate classes too abstract, but in teaching in school he got himself out of a hole — or tried to — by discussing historical method itself in the *abstract*, without reference to the pupils' work or to other historical writing.

His diary contains many searching questions about his teaching and his own learning. Was his trouble lack of defined aims? Was it that what he was given to teach couldn't interest him? Later in the year he concluded:

> The doubts I have as to the worth of the work stem from my own deeply ingrained attachment to external assessment. When I was at school a good mark and praise made me feel on top of the world whereas a poor mark and criticism was akin to catastrophe. I learnt to value myself according to external standards, a pernicious habit which our education system which embodies competition actually perpetuates! Standards are necessary, yes, but when their importance is elevated so that they become the central aim of education — Anyway, I am developing an attitude of not looking to the results of my work, but rather trying to find reward in the work itself. It is important to take satisfaction in performing a task to the best of one's ability.

From memory, this was about the time when he had told me that he was going to submit another history assignment.

Few of our students handed in shoddy work brazenly (not that Paul's could be described as shoddy), and, when they did, it was returned with the suggestion that it be done anew and differently. This was seldom a matter of argument. Most often unsatisfactory work revealed that the students really needed guidance and did not see where their weaknesses lay, though no doubt there were some who bluffed us, and we still don't know the truth. And there were a few unmitigated villains; but it is interesting to note that they were never the ones who bothered to argue with us or question us about the principle of assessment.

When I said earlier that the problem of assessment turned out to be far less bothersome than had been predicted, I had in mind that students came easily to see us as partners in their task of becoming professionally competent. Our possible contribution was seen and sought — it was unquestionably 'relevant' so long as we were credible. So long as our criticisms of work done were well grounded and seen to be just, students mostly appreciated our suggestions and sought to attain a standard of work that satisfied both them and us.

Participatory planning

Where the major difficulty arose was in the participatory planning of course work in its early stages, before students could see what academic work was integral to professional competence. Some of them were continuously torn between their commitments to the school and to the University. Some of them always gave top priority to preparing adequately for their teaching, even if their study of educational issues suffered in consequence and, indirectly, their teaching suffered, too. We, as staff, were often torn on this question ourselves. Who was to say that academic rigour in preparing for their school classes was less important than that required for our University classes? But there still remained educational questions that we were sure students should meet and examine if they were to become professionally competent.

In coming to grips with this we faced the intractable problem that confronts all teachers, anywhere, who try to encourage self-directed learning. How can any student make free choices before he has some knowledge of what there is to choose from? In time, a course that lets the approach to theory be guided by what the practice reveals is bound to confront the major ideological and pedagogical issues in education; but they become pressing for different people at different times, and there is but a year in which to make sure that they have not merely arisen but when they arise are seen in their full complexity and not dismissed with deceptive simplicity.

Our attempts in the first two weeks of the year to give students a preview of the major questions, to sensitize them as it were, in advance, met with mixed success, as I have already indicated. In 1973, our first year, this worked with considerable, though not unqualified, success. In 1974, with our numbers doubled, it met with considerable, though not unqualified, failure — a failure that could not be attributed to this issue alone.

166

In 1973 we had genuinely worked out with students just what form of assessment we would use. The idea of keeping diaries came from the students. We had outlined our problems of evaluating the Course, both for its betterment and for external evaluators. Although the conclusions the students reached were ones that we hoped they would, this could not be called mock-democracy or veiled manipulation. We all had a problem to be solved, there was a strenuous and high-powered discussion of possible ways of solving it (and, after all, the students were well initiated into and experienced in assessment). They made some suggestions that we had not thought of and we put forward suggestions that we had considered. I talked about my experience with depth studies and why I found them more satisfactory than exams and/or essays, and they were prepared to give them a go. We explored with them, as honestly as we had explored among ourselves, a problem that had to be solved. And so it was with how we might approach the question of teaching practice.

By the second year we had a ready-made programme of assessment that had worked, and to have changed it would have thrown the methods of evaluation out of gear. Hence we failed to cover the steps in our mode of thinking in anything like the same detail, let alone with the same openness that had characterized the decision-making in the previous year. If anything, we set up unwittingly some sort of a model that was accepted but resented. 'Last year's students' became a dirty phrase.

More than that, in staff meetings at the end of 1973, one part-time member of staff, Judy Walsh, had complained of the casualness of students in coming late to seminars or in not coming at all. This she rightly considered impolite, and she criticized our double standards in our treating the students with (very nearly) unfailing politeness while blindfolding ourselves to the fact that it was not always reciprocated. She had suggested that, if students shared our view that examinations were an inferior form of assessment, they should also accept the consequences of taking responsibility for fulfilling their obligations by having the courtesy to notify us in advance if they could not come to classes, and for explaining why if they did not want to come. In that case, if the seminars could not be made more meaningful for them, they should propose an alternative activity. Requirements should always be open to individual or group negotiation.

This seemed to us all to be extremely sound, and I still think it was. But, while the 1974 students agreed to the proposal, some of them silently regarded it as 'covert compulsion'. In fact it was an extremely hard thing to face for both staff and students. Students felt that if they didn't turn up, staff were offended. This discouraged students from voicing constructive criticisms to the individual lecturers concerned. In later years we continued with that policy, with the students' positive agreement; but, with time, staff found it much easier to live up to than students did. It made life considerably easier for me, as director of the Course. If a student complained about the way a seminar course was going I would simply say something like, 'Why do you tell me? The solution is in your hands. Thrash it out with X or Y (the seminar leader) and if that doesn't work, propose something that will give you more satisfaction.'

I had to smile wryly in a later year when the student who was most committed to the idea of autonomy, and theoretically best informed on its importance, failed to come to my seminars. I faced him with his responsibilities to the Course, and would give him no escape. He agreed entirely with the principles guiding the policy and (perhaps because it was easier than saying why his attendance was poor) became a regular attender, though not an uncritical one. Indeed, we spent hours outside seminars pushing around the implications of the idea of autonomy; but, regardless of this, he remained silently absent from another seminar group, and eventually had to submit work of his own devising as a substitute. Theory and action had not properly gelled for him, as he reluctantly conceded.

Student initiative

Even in 1974, however, some students acted on the agreed policy. Following the Airey's Inlet camp, we called a meeting of all students in an attempt to clear up misunderstandings and to resolve conflicts. Bernie and Rod Fawns drew up a list of what they understood to be the main complaints and these were discussed. The air was cleared somewhat, and students were invited to propose courses or activities other than the ones that we were providing. They were assured that we were absolutely sincere about offering them that alternative.

About half an hour after the meeting disbanded there was a knock at my door and a group of students came to tell me that they were going to run their own study group on learning theory instead of going to Curriculum Studies. They already had a list of the writers they wanted to study – Piaget, George Kelly, Ausubel and I forget who else. They wanted to know if that was all right. I, of course, agreed. Then they asked me if I would join the group. I really gasped, for learning theory was hardly my speciality, as I told them. I thanked them, however, and said I should be delighted, since I needed to do more reading myself on learning theory, and I would regard myself, could only regard myself, as their peer. We talked at some length about who might be studied and what might be read. I told them that, since we had a learning

theorist on the staff of Course B, Terry Werner, I should want to consult him if we came to difficult places, and that anyway he might suggest
a more suitable way in to the various thinkers than we could. It was
agreed that I should consult Terry and pass on his advice. We arranged
to meet in my room the following week, when, much to my astonishment, the rebel leader turned to me and said, 'Well, Gwen, how should
we start?', to which I replied that they couldn't have it both ways, but
please to let me know what reading I should do in time for me to do it.

They were very faithful to their idea and to learning theory. Every
week we met and we painfully followed Piaget or Kelly or Ausubel step
by step until we believed we had really grasped the line of thought.
Each week a different student gave a paper and guided us gropingly
through what were seen to be the logical steps. My main contribution
was to try to give examples, as naturally I could more readily do after
umpteen years of teaching. But if I had given those papers, I should
have been left without a single student.

From that experience I probably learned even more than students
did. They proved that teaching skills were secondary to motivation, and
that motivation can come from defining your own problem, trying to
solve it, and proving that you can. More imaginative and sound teaching
methods would presumably have worked a good deal better, but in this
case there was no need to arouse and hold interest: it was already there.
They obtained great satisfaction from 'seeing the light', when quite
suddenly they would grasp a concept and relate it to their own experiences — what they recalled having happened either to them or to children they had watched or taught. It could have petered out, as many a
pupil-initiated project does after the first enthusiasm; but they went
from strength to strength. By the end of the term they asked Terry,
who was in his first year with us and feeling his way, to join the group.
He kept contact with them the following term, and in third term they
continued informally, meeting at nights, attracting friends from outside their group, and discussing wider political issues.

At least one other group met regularly. Calling themselves an 'Education for Change' group, they set up their own meetings and discussions
at home, and although I was never there (and was never invited), one of
the staff, Rory Barnes, sometimes attended and found them most
stimulating. During the year they had prepared a statement — a cry for
greater involvement of school pupils in their own education. It began:

> We think our task ought to be to allow pupils and teachers to see the
> need for change and explore ways of obtaining it. The direction of
> the change must be towards institutions, classrooms and teacher
> relationships with pupils which help pupils develop their own motiv-
> ation, increase their initiative and reduce their reliance upon the

teacher for stimulation and direction. Schools ought to be places where kids gain confidence in their own potential and want to realize it. Schools ought to be friendly places from the kids' point of view. We believe that now they are oppressive, counter-productive to individuality and personal initiative — at the least, undemocratic. Schools at the moment devote little time to learning, much to discipline, organization and assessment (not of themselves). The authority they may have legitimately has been so extended, complicated, and rationalized that pupils have no rights; and, given the right circumstances, anything could be perpetrated on kids and they couldn't do a thing (and what is worse they probably wouldn't see the need to).

All of this was worthy of discussion, and much of it echoes the sort of thing we were inclined to say ourselves. The intention of the document, however, was to show that Course B did not practise what it preached, and was indeed hypocritical in claiming to offer self-direction to its own students. The Course, it seems, was not radical enough:

What does a pupil do if he finds what he is being taught irrelevant, useless, boring or stupid? In my classes, he mucks around and wants to go early. Here I am at University and I'm mucking around and I want to go early. So crapped off that I can't even be bothered being subtle about it. I resent being told that I'm in command of where this car goes and then being given a particular map and told my directions. Hypocrisy is an insult to my intelligence. I need a taste of freedom if I am to give it to my pupils. Alienation of school pupils begins here, with you. Don't pretend to give me freedom; it would be better if you just took it away.

It is hard to be right. Some students wanted to be given a clear map; some wanted to draw their own; some wanted none at all. We were confused about how to meet such conflicting demands. Both students and staff were as yet uneasy in interpreting and using the freedom we said we offered; and it was probably in the nature of that offer that there would always be some stresses. Tensions and consequent adaptations are what keep a course from ossifying.

It was good, if sometimes discomposing, when students evaluated what we were doing, and related this to what they should or should not do in schools. It was also good when they organized themselves into study groups — and when they did, it was often to probe ideological questions. In fact such groups happened in every year except the first, and that year we were so small a group as a whole that it was happening without our noticing it, largely through social gatherings at various people's houses.

It was good when work in schools absorbed them, but not if they became narrowly engrossed — as some did — in day-to-day affairs. Early in the year many were resistant to theoretical pursuits, feeling relief at having ended three or four years at university and gladly grasping at the opportunity for practical work. It is doubtful if the pressure of examinations or repeated essays would have cured this, whereas there was little chance that they could face up to the practicalities of teaching without feeling the need for reflexion on and study of bigger issues beyond their present competency. And if the push from us did not work, as the year progressed there was a constant push also from their more thoughtful fellow-students.

Chapter 6

A course for radicals?

The ideologies of Course B students

Course B is widely considered — by many University staff, by schools, and by students who apply to enrol — as a radical course and therefore as a course for radicals. Despite that, it must be said at the outset that most students who apply for admission do so not because they are radicals but because the Course is school-based. Working on definitions and terminology provided in 1973 by Dr D. S. Anderson,[1] a professorial fellow in educational research at the Australian National University, I estimated that our intake of students in our first year was roughly divided between 'radicals' and 'traditionalists'. This, as I used it, was a fairly blunt instrument and very impressionistic, and I was not very serious in applying it even in that first year. But it can be said that every year our students covered the whole political range; that, in later years, as the issues of conscription and Vietnam receded, concern with politics tended to recede too; that every year the one bond students shared, almost without exception, was a distinct preference for continuous school practice rather than stop-start experiences in schools; and that, so far as they understood it in advance, students thought they would prefer a course that based academic work on school practice. Politically they continued to be divided between radicals and conservatives.

What took rather longer to emerge for them was that professional questions were answered not merely by mastering classroom techniques but by seeing the whole contextual framework in which particular skills might or might not be effective, let alone justifiable. I have already said, and it is worth developing further, that the question paramount in students' minds at first was 'How do I establish my authority?': this soon became a question of 'What is the basis of my authority?' and this in turn became an ideological question of 'What is the nature of proper authority?' That gradation, however, is an oversimplification. It merely suggests where the emphasis lies in a rough sort of hierarchy of urgency, and should not conceal the fact that each question is ever-present in the others. All three are to a greater or lesser extent intellectual questions, which, along with many others, it was our academic and professional responsibility to examine.

Ideological issues arose most forcibly as practical problems especially in schools that created a 'culture shock'. Professor Austin, who was Melbourne's Dean of Education, always reminded students in the introductory session at the beginning of the year that they must keep in mind that they were, by definition, the most successful students of formal education, and that most of the children they taught would not be like them in their response to school. The students always visibly 'sat up' when he threw out this challenge. Some of them might have been from working-class families, some of them from migrant families, some of them from small rural communities; but many came from none of these groups. The radicals among them had strong views about equality and freedom; but for many this was still armchair or 'caf' politics. The reality was but distantly perceived.

Sonia, for example, one of the academic 'heavyweights', chose a community school because it accorded with her radical leanings. It was a school whose children were mostly from Italian and Greek migrant families in an industrial area. Sonia had first of all to rethink her entire response to her main subject, English, and then to discover that her leftist sentiments were by no means shared by her pupils. She was terrified, she said, of alienating the pupils from literature before they had had a chance of learning to enjoy it. It came, she said, 'with a thud' continually to discover that academic attitudes won't work; 'but we have gotten so used to them over these last three or four years that we have forgotten to trust our first fresh intuitions.'

A very reflective girl, she became dominated by the difficulties, and thus for a time her analysis of them became increasingly academic and distant, and she became increasingly lonely as well as shut out from better understanding. She saw the need for closer contact with parents; but, if they became mobilized, their influence would be 'right-wing conservative'. Their high ambitions for their children, she observed, were epitomized in the example of a thirteen-year-old who wanted to work in a zoo, but whose parents were determined that he should be an architect. 'Hell!' she exclaimed, 'he already has the worries of a twenty-year-old.'

Then she and another student were upset by male domination in the school. It was noted that the girls chose different options from the boys; they played different games from the boys; they left the talking in committee meetings to the boys, yet were always willing to become

173

the rubbish monitors — all too true, but also seen by Sonia too much from the outside looking in, which made one of Sonia's Italian fellow-students ask, 'Why the concern to change people's lives when they are happy and content?' When the question of the sex roles of the pupils was raised in staff meetings or class discussions Sonia couldn't understand why the class groaned, 'Women's Lib. again!', and she asked herself sadly why discussions always end in political labels. It is interesting that she did not begin to understand her pupils until she joined a drama workshop for much younger children in a high-rise industrial area. Suddenly the truth of those children's lives broke through vividly to her.

Mark, who was at the same school at the same time, pondered over the problems in a somewhat different way. Was the answer, he wondered, that schools should confront children with values different from the home, and thus present a paradox? He summed it up this way:

The Parents
Mostly migrants, concerned with materialistic success for their children, seeing that their kids don't end up doing what they are doing; the Protestant ethic, strict, authoritarian, non-permissive.

The Kids
Caught in the middle between the teachers and the parents, between the clash of the cultures of homeland (of parents) and Australia, between the permissive, liberal, free, hip society and the societal values and attitudes of the family home ... combined with their own adolescence, their confusion about their sexuality, about getting a job, about school.

The Teachers
Socialist, liberal, educated, progressive permissive, libertarian. Anti-materialistic, nonconformist, radical.

Maybe the important thing about the school is that it poses the alternative to the kids: i.e. it forces them into tension — conflict — decision — resolution — serenity?!!?

My own experience with school — rigid, authoritarian, strict, conservative, catholic. Yet it has produced Mark — the radical!

Must it be this way? Must you get the alternative [if you are] to grow — change — develop — mature? Is it fair to say that [the school] is a success because it is this kind of alternative, regardless of its success or failure in any other area? NO. It must produce —

readers
writers
survivors
crap detectors

individuals — seeing themselves in the world
seeing themselves in relation to others.

THIS IS WHAT SCHOOLS MUST DO

And I take it that Mark, while approving of some degree of ideo-logical tension, saw that the school had a prior, primary educational task. It seems implicit in what he writes that he has some serious criticisms of the priorities of the teachers in their preoccupation with social criticism and their neglect of educational goals.

At the same school, in a different year, Helga went through the same intellectual dilemmas as Sonia and Mark. It could be that, like Antonio whom we met in earlier chapters (asking similar questions though in a different context), Helga did better at acting upon her theorizing because her family had been migrants — though not Italian, Greek, or working class. When she knew that two of her Greek girls wanted to join a netball group, but were held back by their families' reluctance to allow them out at night, Helga was able to make all parties to the conflict happy — and perhaps more thoughtful. She respected the protectiveness of Greek parents towards their daughters, and she set out to allay their fears:

> The plan was that I was to ask their fathers if they could go to training on a Thursday night … I went around to see both parents and both said their daughters could go, which was amazing. I'm going to drive them there and pick them up … which will be a bit of a tie, but the girls are so thrilled about being in a team … that it shouldn't be too much of a problem.
>
> It was really interesting visiting the parents of the girls, they seemed a little nervous of meeting me, and I was a little nervous of meeting them.
>
> Athena's parents offered me a drink and gave me this Greek sweet stuff, which was made from quinces and looked like jam. They eagerly asked me if I liked it so I couldn't say anything else but that it was beautiful. In actual fact I thought it was terrible, it was just so sweet it made my skin creep.
>
> After meeting Athena's parents I went to Celeste's place only to be offered a beer which I thought was funny on a Sunday afternoon. Celeste's father was obviously very proud of his daughter as he brought out all the trophies and things she had won …

Although Helga's family was not Greek, she obviously understood the importance of having one's values and customs, however strange, accepted. It was not hypocrisy, it was a genuine effort to get 'inside' others' lives, and it is not surprising that, good though Sonia and Mark were, Helga was a more inspired teacher — and no less rigorous than they.

Lorna and Bill Hannan, both of whom know the community schools and Course B fairly well, commented that it showed lack of imagination for middle-class students to come into working-class schools that had a big migrant intake and to start with 'trendy notions' about Women's Lib., or to offer units (as one student, not Sonia, did) on alternatives to the family structure, at least until one had really made the effort to see the virtues in the extended family for people who live that life. Really difficult ideological and strategic questions arise. Given that one starts with the children's assumptions and develops their understanding of *their own* values, does one lead them beyond that, as Mark suggested, to confrontation with other views and experiences? If the answer is Yes, how does the teacher do that without imposing *his own* values? These questions are related to the language question that bothered students: does the teacher start by looking for the vitality and richness in pupils' own idiom? Clearly, yes. Does he then impose an acceptable 'standard' English usage, or does he leave that alone and aim to get greater fluency and richness within the child's idiom? In my view, he should do the second, and *then*, when the child has attained greater command, present the alternatives, but not impose them, any more than he would unnaturally adopt the idiom of the child.

These are basically ideological questions, and, by starting with respect for, and a greater understanding of, 'where the children are at', we do not have to abandon our own values — in Sonia's case a dedication to the idea of sexual equality and a rejection of domination, sexual or other. In the process of gaining insight into other's values, our own are likely to be refined and indeed modified. But what is to be done when the children's beliefs are bigoted? What would one do in the situation — the confrontation — that Ruth, a migrant, faced? She was talking to her pupils in a big co-educational high school about an Australian film, *Caddie*, that she and the pupils had been to. 'Caddie' was the name of an Australian barmaid in slum areas during the Depression of the 1930s who had a deep love affair with a relatively well-to-do Greek migrant. The discussion that follows, as reported by Ruth, could, with very few changes, unfortunately, have occurred in an English or American school:

Ruth: Did you enjoy *Caddie*?
John: Oh it was okay, Miss, I liked Jack Thompson [who played the Australian rough, sharp but nice guy] the best.
Ruth: Oh I didn't. I thought the Greek man was really good. He was such a beautiful looking man ... The Greek dancing was so full of life. Didn't it make you want to dance?
John: Greek! I thought he was horrible ... and the Greek dancing was so stupid ... All bastards — Greeks, Italians — all the

176

same ... They eat stupid food – I like pie and sauce. That's
the best.

Ruth: I love Italian and Greek cooking. It's so full of spices and so
tasty.

John: All stupid! Bloody Wogs – Japs caused the war – they're
dirty and stupid and should go back to where they came
from. Take two jobs – they take all the jobs so they can
make so much money.

Maria (an Italian girl who was becoming more and more upset) ...
[and wanted John to know how criticism hurt her] : I hate it
even when the others say that you're stupid. John.

Ruth: John, can't you see that it really hurts some people in the
class if you say that?

John: ... They should all go back. It's not their home. We're Australians ...

Ruth: 'Dirty Australians' – how would you like to be called a 'dirty
Australian'?

John (even more aggressively): Australians are the best. They take
our jobs ... They have two jobs going so they can get a lot of
money.

Jill: They come and beat up people in the fish and chip shops.
Wogs beat up people ...

Jane: Wogs killed my brother. It's true – you ask anyone – they
shot him.

Ruth: ... I thought kids were supposed to be open-minded and
tolerant – But you're so bigoted.

Luigi: I'm not a wog. I'm Australian. I was born here. Do you like
Italian food, Miss?

This whole episode was taking place in a typing class after the prepared work ... Joanna decided to type out everything that was going
on to put it into the school paper ... She had already typed out –
'Ruth said kids are supposed to be tolerant. Bastards. Ruth called
John a dirty Australian. John called Ruth a jew ...'

Perhaps readers will have better ideas of how to handle such a situation than I have. In fact, Ruth's account was part of her depth study
on multi-cultural education in the school. She did a detailed study into
prejudice, school policy on migrant children, migrant parents' lives, occupations and the like. She concluded that nothing short of a massive and
deliberate policy, a change in school organization, and a concerted
effort by staff, could even begin to overcome the problems that *that*
school faced.

What a tangled problem Ruth uncovered, and any slick political
wisdom that we might have offered would only have over-simplified

177

and distorted a problem that nothing short of profound thought and action could meet.

The 'how to' as training for conformity

In 1973 we had begun the year with a fairly heavy concentration on introducing students to such political questions as authority, autonomy and equality. This did prove a strain on some students who were unfamiliar with such discourse, and, the following year, political questions seemed to cause even greater agitation. No doubt the students' agitation was caused by a combination of difficulties, of which the introduction of political and ideological questions formed just a small part, but the reaction was strong enough to make us question ourselves very seriously.

In 1975 we took note of our critics and soft-pedalled, giving more emphasis at the beginning to contact with schools, meeting pupils and concern with teaching methods. For this, students chided us too. During the year we discussed a controversy that was going on in a little paper called the *Educational Magazine*.[2] It concerned itself with contemporary issues such as deschooling, 'learning networks' and community schools, and it began to turn its attention to teacher education. A group of students, Jill Barnes, Graeme Hoy and Trish Thomson, decided to write an article on Course B, and it was eventually published. Graeme brought the draft to me one Sunday so that we could discuss it. They had chosen to take the theme of 'Teaching as a Political Activity', and criticized the Course for not being political enough. Why was this so? they asked (and I quote from the draft): 'Partly because this year the Course started off concentrating on "how to", owing to general staff/student disquiet with explicit political challenges extended last year.' Our treatment of political questions was 'so implicit this year that many people have managed to avoid a confrontation'.

It is interesting that, while many students clamoured for an early concentration on skills (and it runs repeatedly through diaries), Jill, Graeme and Trish saw this as an evasion of the main issues:

While the real challenge of Dip. Ed. ought to be 'what to teach' and not 'how to teach', everybody gets carried away with merely 'surviving'. What does this 'surviving' mean? Surviving is about the exercise of authority — get the kids under the thumb, 'control' the class, and you are O.K. But what do you do then? It is obvious: follow the pattern and do the things you have seen your supervisor do.

And there is the crunch; the hidden curriculum is indeed hidden! Teachers/Dip. Ed. students 'manage' classes and do lots of nice things which fill in time and unconsciously preserve the educational muddle because they are not thinking about their teaching, about 'what to' teach, but 'how to' amuse the children, to keep that precious control. This whole situation comes about because teachers ignore, or are unconscious of, the fact that their teaching is a political act.

Through schools, kids are introduced almost subconsciously to the idea of an institution, an institution created by the society it serves. And not only introduced to 'institutions' but taught to conform uncritically — to accept unquestioningly the power wielded. Teachers are respected and obeyed — not because of the personal qualities they may have or because they help kids to learn about themselves and the world — but purely and simply because of the power invested in them by the institution.

This sharp divide between the 'how to' and the 'what to' bears some examination, for if it were true that we encouraged a narrow preoccupation with 'survival', Jill, Graeme and Trish would surely be right.

The 'hidden curriculum' alluded to in their second paragraph raises interesting questions. We are indebted to Ivan Illich for popularizing the notion of the 'hidden curriculum', and for the emphasis he gives to what is 'hidden', as distinct from the 'explicit', in curriculum; but his assumption that the 'hidden curriculum' is always bad carries with it the possibility that it could, by the same token, be good — a possibility that does not explicitly enter into his exposition. If it is true that what you do, rather than what you say or even what you think you do, is profoundly important, it follows that what you do may be better than what you say, instead of necessarily being worse. In this case the 'how' is as important as the 'what', and is indeed part of it. If we genuinely gave students personal practice in exercising *their* autonomy instead of imposing our authority, it would indicate that our 'hidden curriculum' was good, even if some of our explicit curriculum wasn't.

In schools there is much more encouragement of critical thinking allowed in debate than in questioning the way the school is run — that is, in the 'what' rather than the 'how'. The powerlessness of children is learnt, I would suggest, less by children's being discouraged from challenging a teacher's intellectual view than by its being assumed that they will conform to the way in which the school is run and the learning (or, more accurately, the teaching) is organized. In short, Jill, Graeme and Trish, have made an untenable, or at least exaggerated, divorce between content and method. At one point they see this:

> Moreover the 'how' — tactics of teaching and survival — should be defined by the ideals internalized while discussing 'what to'. For example, an understanding of freedom for kids leads to such teaching methods as discovery learning.

179

Nevertheless, they are correct in charging some students with 'how-to-ing' it too mindlessly. They criticized those students who applauded the Course because of the scope it gave for teaching without their having to bother with what they called the 'bullshit' of Methods and Curriculum Studies. They saw such students' political indifference and anti-intellectualism as pressures that the Course had to resist, and they deplored the fact that some schools, too, abetted the students in trying to minimize theory and make practice all important:

> The schools involved in the Course, and sad to say even the community schools, tend to see the fact of a two-day-per-week basis (instead of separate three-week block teaching rounds) as a better way to learn 'how to'. They see it as an easing-in of the teacher into the first-year 'problem' of survival, and some of them would even like to see school practice extended to four days per week.

And it is true that there was sometimes this pressure on us, from schools as well as students, to divorce content and method unjustifiably (and against our principles) by dwelling unduly on the mechanics of teaching or class management.

'Work harder to please me'

For Ronald, whom we have seen (pp. 69-71) trying himself out with different styles of teaching, the exercise was soon translated into ideological questions. First, he asked himself if his pleasure in developing children's writing ability was guided primarily by a concern for them or the sense of success it gave him — the question that might well have been asked by the students who worried about crushes (pp. 85, 90-1, 95). Trying to answer this filled him with such uncertainty that he lost direction in his teaching, and decided to put off the question 'till next year'. Bernie visited his class at that point, saw what was happening, and 'forced me to confront the reality of what I was doing, which was to incite the kids into producing writing as a commodity to satisfy teacher demand'. Jill, Graeme and Trish saw preoccupation with the 'how' as too limiting, not unlike Ronald who, quite separately, saw himself as guilty of conceit that was limiting in a different way:

> Instead of seeking to promote real confrontation and consideration of the topics provided, I was like a football coach, dancing around and putting on a show, a one-man cheer squad, urging them to greater efforts in terms of production. Instead of setting a topic because of its intrinsic importance and its impact on the kids in terms of the development of their own thinking and world view I was

180

choosing and introducing topics according to their probable efficacy in generating the desired produced 'writing' which was the
material evidence of my success.

Ronald was making a nice distinction. He saw, though he did not
quite put it in these terms, that the slogan, 'start where the kids are at',
is too often interpreted as 'stop where the kids are at'. He also caught
himself out at playing a subtle power game as a teacher. He found himself meeting tensions in the classroom with 'a few sensitive words from
the teacher', and being pleased at his ability to entertain and interest
them:

Are teachers on an ego trip tempered by a sense of humanity and ...
the 'social-worker' type role they can and do play? Is school simply
an institution to assist pupils with personality and development
problems fostered by the environment? What the hell are we trying
to teach pupils? If becoming a teacher means that I am simply
coming to serve as a socializing instrument for the capitalist or any
other state then I don't see myself teaching for long.
   What produces the schizoid element in the attitude of pupils to
school work that divides it off, no matter how socially important or
topical the subject, from the real forming world view? I mean the
sort of situation where it would be possible to imagine a kid writing
sympathetically about the problems of migrants and yet in his
private life still retaining such abusive terms as wogs, yids, chocs etc.
... Is the school helpless against such social pressure? ...
   Suddenly here I was, confronted with the undeniable and brutal
evidence of my own inadequacy as a teacher and human being in
that I had been reduced to doing exactly what I would have wanted
to avoid. For the first time I see the real dimensions of the problem
in its full complexity and immensity. I must confess I find it daunting for it seems to demand a sort of moral commitment and dedication
and self-honesty I have always shied away from ...
   Genuine exploration requires a situation where the kids have a
chance to shape what they look at. Total pupil control can sometimes lead to a situation of anarchy from which no one benefits
other than in a social sense. It seems necessary to confront and
stimulate. I have found from my brief experience at a community
school that this can be very difficult in the very free situation. I
believe that in a slightly more controlled situation it is sometimes
much easier to generate genuine learning. The balance can only be
found by experiment ... Opportunities ... are missed because education is teacher-directed however much it might try to avoid being
teacher-centred.

'Consciousness-raising'

What Ronald came to see is similar to what Jill, Graeme and Trish were leading on to — that the essence of learning is what the students chose to call 'consciousness-raising', or what Freire even more clumsily called 'conciêntização'. In one way or another, each student quoted so far in this chapter had something like that in mind; and they came to see that it was not a matter of imposing set values on children or motivating them with a desire to please teacher, but rather of getting them to take pride in their own development and to see themselves as active agents in their own destiny. For Jill, Graeme and Trish, 'extending the kids' was seen as *the* political act, and who would quibble with that?

> With the [present] trendy mish-mash in educational practice, they [the pupils] are ... subtly told their world is as it is and teachers are there to help them adjust ('New words for old deceptions' — to borrow a phrase from Kozol). The alternative exists — kids could explore their world, 'name' it and question it for themselves with the teacher using his/her insight to extend them ...
> We should concentrate on 'what to' — talking about what is worth knowing ... so that kids can understand how things (including society) work rather than being 'little living libraries' of facts.

The value in what these three say lies in pointing to a widespread willingness of pseudo-progressives to rest content with entertaining children and to confuse this with educating them. Countless students were distressed by such soft pedagogics, but we shall have to be satisfied with two or three other illustrations. Antonio, for example, at a large co-educational high school noted that

> getting children ... to be self-motivated or attentive is very difficult since the teacher is competing with television, cafes and the 'good things in life'. A teacher has to devise ... strategies to make the children interested, or become apathetic to the whole situation. It is absolutely amazing to what lengths teachers go to captivate the children ... fifth-form children draw and colour in maps rather than answer questions because it somehow soothes them and makes them less excitable. When such strategies and 'tricks' to keep 'the natives quiet' take precedence over actual, outright teaching then I feel education is not a high priority. Now, I'm not arguing for the 'chalk-and-talk' teacher, but rather something else, something of a more honest approach. If I knew what that something was then I would have solved the entire problem, but I don't, and neither does anybody else.

Several months later he suggests that the answer does not lie in just being 'good' in the classroom: children need to be aware of themselves as part of the system — they need 'political consciousness'. Course B, he suggests, cannot give the answers but it does give scope for students to become aware of the problem: 'Initially I was concerned with surviving in the classroom ... Now my main concerns are general educational issues such as equality, assessment of kids, Higher School Certificate, school rules, etc.'

Stewart came close to the same conclusion from a different experience:

> Without wanting to sound too melodramatic, I think the events of yesterday played a very significant part, in fact a turning point, in my attitude towards schools and schooling. We went (the Sci. Method Group) to observe a class.
>
> ... I remember finding [my schooling] interesting (to a point) but more importantly, getting something from school — learning. But I'm quite sure the class seen yesterday got absolutely nothing from that 50 minutes — despite the fact that the teacher did all the 'right' things.
>
> This showed the incredible futility of compulsory learning situations.

He concluded that, despite the fact that community schools were not perfect, at least they didn't bore the kids stiff and turn them off 'possibly for life ... I'd send my kid to a free school'. But five weeks later he was rethinking that:

> My position has changed somewhat from a virtual free school entirely [based on] electives [chosen by pupils].
>
> I think perhaps there should be all this, but also an effort must be made in the field of 'consciousness-raising' (which, re-reading, sounds terrible). Somehow emphasis must be placed on English. Schools must play a part somehow of stimulating man to question, and dialogue is necessary here. I think that it is necessary to <u>attempt</u> to encourage people to think above the trivia ...
>
> I can't see what form this 'dialogue encouragement' will take, but I believe the Community Schools are more conducive to such a process than conventional schools.

But what these students are hinting at, and sometimes saying, is that there is no easy road to freedom. Dialogue can be self-centred and arid, children's interests can be fickle or specious and not really generative, yet force can 'turn them off — perhaps for life' — and simply reinforce apathetic defeatism in accepting that learning is 'not for me since I'll never need it'.

By the end of second term Raymond seemed to have struck a commonsense balance while teaching at a community school:

> Once I have overcome the problem of whether I can get on with the kids and work out to some extent what they are interested in, the problem is then to push them — to get them to extend themselves into the area which they choose to study. There is a basic fallacy in the Elective System. Just because the kids choose what they want to do, [it] doesn't necessarily mean that they will push themselves. Thus we had Jim dropping out of Criminology saying that although he was interested in it he thought it was going to be a discussion subject. We tried to deal with this problem in a way which wouldn't compromise the work we wanted to do — if you didn't want to work you didn't come, and if this meant that no one would come then the class wasn't worth holding anyway. I think this is how the system should work ...
>
> By applying the pressure and having some kids walk out I endangered the friendly relationship I had enjoyed with them. However, apart from the advantage of being able to do better work in the classes I took I also found that you don't have to pander to the kids to still be friends with them. You really have to learn to demand things of the kids and take the consequences as well as having them demand things of you.

Raymond saw that discipline lay in the task to be done rather than the whim or ego of the teacher, thus, to use Ronald's term, avoiding being 'teacher-centred'; and he also saw, I think, that in rejecting the conventional dominance of the teacher a new topsy-turvy power structure could grow up in which pupils dominated each other and the teacher, what another student working with him described as 'a tyranny of freedom'. But this school was genuinely experimenting with freedom, as were Lloyd and Carole (pp. 76-80) in a quite different type of school. It does not come from soothing children, pampering or indulging them, and it certainly does not come from forcing them. It comes from leading them to new insights and to their being able to order those insights by expressing them in one way or another. This experience they will never get effortlessly, and the art of teaching lies in helping them to discover the fruitfulness of effort by going beyond frustration, bewilderment and their own sense of failure — getting over what Dewey called the hard places of learning. I am sure that Jill, Graeme and Trish were right in pointing to the political element in this — a sense of powerlessness and unimportance is the enemy of learning, and many things in our society conspire to make many children feel worthless.

Perhaps the best testimonial to successful teaching came from a sixth-form pupil's angry grievance against the staff of one of the community schools. 'You have made me believe that my ideas are important and are worth listening to. But when I leave here I'll be a nothing, like all the people who live around here and who have no influence on anything, who work to eat, and find contentment in resigning themselves to drifting the way that things go because they know they cannot change them.' It so happens that that particular pupil did gain admission into a university; but he was right that for most of the children, including him, the chances of a life that encouraged intelligent living were remote; but should the school also have resigned itself to that sense of helplessness? Surely not.

Catch-22 is how does one give the courage and the appetite for learning before some of the rewards of it have been tasted and some sense of the worth of effort has been experienced? It is this dilemma that leads us sometimes to offer meaningless choices. When the student lacks sufficient background knowledge, a preview of electives gives him no real idea of what the detailed study will be like. Even graduates, who already presumably had some experience of effective learning, needed to be introduced to some of the complexities of the topics available before they could make informed choices.

At times, in avoiding prescription, I tended to abandon structure, as if something we could build on would spontaneously emerge. This was a beginning-of-the-year problem, as I have already indicated; but it was an absurd retreat from the realities, for I did not need to be convinced that generative thinking is essentially a structured pursuit, though structure *per se* does not guarantee generative thinking. It cannot be said too often or too forcefully that the tendency to confuse radicalism with being unstructured (see p.62) bedevils 'progressive' education and accounts for the ease with which its opponents can discredit it if a mood of bigoted reaction prevails.

We use terms like 'radical' and 'progressive' somewhat too loosely, and it is not my intention to try to define them strictly here. Course B's concern with fostering generative thinking and with 'consciousness-raising' may be taken to be 'progressive' and 'radical' in that we acknowledge, as Jill, Graeme and Trish believe we should, that such educational achievements are allied to questions of power in education and society. While, as educationists, it is beyond our province to change society, it is certainly possible to examine the exercise of power within the educational system as well as the limitations that the power structures within society impose on what we can achieve educationally. In this sense, Course B students were confronted with radical issues. Many reacted radically, many conservatively, but all but a few were stirred by the increasingly perceived complexity of the problem as it unfolded.

185

Students' and staffs' political awareness

Jill, Graeme and Trish, I believe, made too rigid an antithesis of the 'how' and the 'what'; but they were right in seeing that the pressures on the Course to teach skills divorced from academic content were a constant danger and that we did sometimes err too much one way or the other. Yet the sort of radicalism they wanted from the Course was the encouragement of open confrontation on political questions. They were critical of the number of students who were politically indifferent; but they admitted that, for the three of them, our approach, which was to challenge and provoke deeper thought rather than to run any political line, had worked:

> ... the staff do not present a unified front concerning the way to teach. In fact it is emphasized that individuals must learn their own style (through trial and error) and must teach in a way which is coherent with their own character and ideals.

This, I take it, was said approvingly. They added that, despite a preoccupation with the 'how to', 'the kind of consciousness about teaching, that a few of us have now, *is* a product of the way in which Course B challenged us and stimulated us this year.'

Some other students made similar points. Brenda, writing at the end of the same year (1975), found real value in our tolerance or forbearance.

> As far as being 'radical' is concerned, I expected Course B to be more radical than it was, to have more of the feeling that was around in the last 2 weeks. What Course B did for me – well, what some of the Course B 'reactionaries' [students] did for me – was to help me to form ideas that were floating around in my head and to help me formulate ways of expressing them verbally. I didn't realize this until I looked at how I felt at the beginning of the year. Where I didn't know before, I know now, why I want to teach and what role in society I can play as a teacher. In this respect I've got clear ideas that were nothing but cloudy random ideas to start with (so don't get rid of all the reactionaries)!

Yet another welcomed the tolerance of conflicting views:

> I have just realized why I can be grateful to 'Course B'. It is because there is such a complete lack of dogma – everyone is free to express their own opinion and to give vent to criticism (myself benefiting from this ...)

Even Barbara, our cynic from chapter 3, the condescending critic of the Course and the students, felt some self-doubt about why we had sent her to the school we did, and why we had correctly guessed that she would find it congenial:

> Well, it did suit me, and I like organization, order, respect and con-
> genial conditions. My physical being is utterly bourgeois in its tastes,
> my mental being or intellectual being to phrase it differently, con-
> stantly rejects this. I'm a typical example of a sunday revolutionary,
> something I'm struggling with myself to reject and overcome.
> ... [The school] couldn't have suited me better – initially. A
> change was to develop. Remember, I entered without a real thought
> in my head as to what Education in Victoria was about.

It may seem odd to equate 'organization, order, respect and congenial conditions' with being 'bourgeois', but we shall let that pass.
Barbara had correctly picked up the ideological muddle that thinking
about the authority of the teacher could induce:

> Some students' consideration revolved around such soul-searching as
> was reflected by the following attitudes: 'I have no right to put
> forward my view as this will only influence the pupils, and what
> right have I to act in this way on another person?' ... This type of
> philosophy solves little and gives way to the 'Let the kids do their
> own thing' thinking ...
> It was not until the close of 2nd term that I began to venture out
> – I visited schools in preparation for my depth study and a whole
> new horizon unfolded before me ... I had shut myself away in the
> proverbial Ivory Tower. The contradictions inherent in the system
> slapped me in the face.
> I began to read more. Political considerations, social inequalities,
> the status quo, it had always been there, I had sensed it, felt it but
> never faced myself with an understanding of it. Suddenly I could
> equate the relevance of my 2 methods, Social Studies and Economics,
> with the real issues. That is, of bringing politics into Education. And
> it was not until third term that I found other Dip. Ed. students
> feeling exactly the same way as I. With other value judgements to be
> sure, many of which I am in basic disagreement with, but neverthe-
> less, that awakening had reached them and they were trying to come
> to terms with it. The pity is, that it is too late now to reverse the
> clock and start again. Knowing now the questions I would raise.

And, boiled down, this is exactly what Jill, Graeme and Trish had
asked – that students should confront one another with their differences. They were not asking for a political line; they really only wanted
students to stop shying off political questions. Students, they thought,
were too chary of 'taking on their colleagues in the Course'. But things
changed, and there was lively confrontation in third term. Political

187

debate dominated the end-of-year discussions. Our cynic Barbara came to a very different conclusion about our intentions and effectiveness from that of Jill, Graeme and Trish:

> Yet this much I know. It was never meant to be a course which taught one how to cope in the limited situation of the classroom. I feel it was about bringing students to cope with themselves, their ideals, their shortcomings, their hopes, their better points. All this in the perspective of interaction with younger people. Perhaps the aim was not to provide the answers but rather to throw a spanner in the works. By this I mean, to propose certain views which might attract or deter students, but at least to challenge their complacency and sense of security. Once these ideas were manipulated and thrown at students, it was left to them to reject or accept them, by such a synthesis to enable students to reach their own answers, individually ...
>
> It was as if we were a stream of tourists passing under the watchful eye of an official observer. 'Anyone can pass through the barrier as long as he isn't smoking dope in too obvious a fashion' ...
>
> Nevertheless, the things I have come to realize about forming a certain philosophy will, hopefully, remain intact enough for me to progress further. For I see it as a first mental step, one that I must build upon, one that gives me a certain basis for further thought and development.
>
> And if this is what Course B has done for me, then that alone was its worth ... still so much I do not understand ...

Students, particularly as the year progressed, wanted the cut and thrust of ideological argument as a means towards defining their own positions. For Barbara, investigating a variety of schools, after a fairly long period in one that she found comfortable, made her see 'contradictions inherent in the system' sharply. She was suddenly able to focus on some of the issues that had been raised in seminars, and she sought a further testing ground in the political debate that stirred students during the last term.

But our hidden curriculum was meant to be the best political teacher. It was Graeme who said at a party late in the year, 'I have never experienced a year until this year that has restored my sense of personal responsibility. Throughout the Uni., the responsibility and the decisions have always been in others' hands.' The essence of participatory planning of curriculum lies in the respect that one has for the students' integrity and the willingness of the lecturer to recognize that his way into a question may be quite wrong for his students and has to be changed. We hoped that there was both a political and an educational lesson learnt from this, and that students would come to see, through their own experiences, that pupils are at least as variable as the students themselves. Breaking new ground does require, both in schools and at university, the creation of a shared endeavour; but, beyond that, we found that students could be trusted not only to see where they were going but also to help determine the way to get there, and it is exciting for university staff to discover that the end might not be exactly what they had predicted.

To see how this once worked in practice there is no better account than that of Jan Deamicis, a sociologist who spent 1975 with Course B. After leaving Melbourne he went to Massachusetts and wrote me the following letter, which is worth quoting in full without any modification. Since I am not quoting from students' diaries this time, I have left the names of the students he refers to unchanged:

Dear Gwen,

I have reached a breathing place in my dissertation work, with only the conclusion to write now. I have had this sitting on my desk for months, it seems like, and I don't even know if you're still interested in it. I found it a little too restricting and precocious to try to write a formal summary of my Course B impressions. I mean, I had it all blocked out and outlined and it suddenly started to sound like a scholar's report instead of my feelings. A letter comes much more to those points I would like to make, in a way I would prefer to make them. I expect you will want to liberally modify this epistle to accord with your book's style, which is fine with me.

Let me begin by noting some important differences between my experiences and those of the rest of you in the program. First, I rather backed into it. I was hired by the Education Department to teach 2 courses per term to Dip Ed Students, and that is all I was scheduled to do. And quite unexpectedly I was approached by some unidentified fellow who wanted to know if I would like to lecture to some students about institutions. Sure, I said (I was eager to lecture to anybody on anything, and I am often accused of lecturing in ordinary conversations instead of talking). But I thought, who is this guy, and where did these students come from? This is the Course B program, someone told me, they do things a little differently. Experimental, really, trying out a new style. But, they said, be careful, they'll try to grab up all of your time. Don't be afraid to say no if they get too possessive. Warily I awaited new overtures. Meanwhile I delivered the lecture, a fairly uninspiring event for most, I gather, but a treat for me — I like to lecture. So I taught my formal courses and began my informal affiliation with this funny group.

The second important difference is that this was my first year of full time teaching. I had tutored for several years, but had never confronted groups of 'my' students in 'my' courses. I was cocky and overconfident, and frightened to death that people would see through my inexperience. More intimidating was the prospect of trying to teach people who were learning to teach others, for surely they would know more than I about what teaching was all about. Well, I figured, see it all as a chance to learn how to teach. Teaching was something that I had always taken quite for granted as a graduate student, assuming it would just happen if only I copied my former lecturers. I had never heard of teaching as an issue. I believed that learning was automatic, a given, an implicit assumption whereby lecturer + student = learning, right? Well, I thought as much, until I began to confront people who were taking quite seriously the very task of teaching. You were all pretty experienced hands at this thing, I was a novitiate trying to learn how to teach and how to test out my assumptions about teaching.

And third, I am writing this whole thing in my study in a 2 storey house in Massachusetts, in the U.S. of A. My affiliation with your program is long terminated. It was a 1-shot deal. I have no stake in Course B's success or future. My livelihood is totally independent from its continuation. My ideas and memories are removed from any kind of reminders, for there are no people around to talk with or ask about, no reports to read and criticize, no plans to discuss. It is long since over and done with, and I am trying to draw together into coherent form what lies scattered over different fields of my memory.

Fourth, I was not a full time participant in the program. I attended some Friday sessions, visited a few schools, went on a campout, listened to some English folk songs, and played some games. Save for my social myths and the media elective in the last term, I was an informal and irregular member of your staff.

What these points mean is that I have a perspective that is distinct from any of yours. Course B affected me in ways that must differ substantially from you who have worked with it from its inception and who are organically affiliated with it. I am the stranger and you the veterans. I came and went, you are rooted there and can yet draw on each other for friendship, ideas, information, and support.

Having qualified all that I might say about my responses to the Course, I should now tell you that overall the most interesting, powerful, intellectually stimulating, personally meaningful, and perhaps lasting associations I encountered at Melbourne University were within Course B. My year at Melbourne was tremendously rewarding. I met many fine people, taught some very good students, felt good about my work, gained immense satisfaction from all of my courses. But I learned more about learning and teaching in my peripheral affiliation with Course B than in most of my formal course work.

This is not to disparage these other university experiences, but to indicate my valuation of the Course's worth. And it had to do as much with the structure of the Course as with the people within it.

I mean, the Course was so arranged that I confronted students more as individuals than as students. While on a few occasions I played the lecturer (I like to lecture), most of my time was spent sitting with everybody else, listening to people talk, drinking coffee or beer, walking somewhere, laughing, joking – not lecturing. I learned to drop sharp distinctions between teacher and student, and found intellectual and emotional satisfaction in relative anonymity. Now I know I wasn't anonymous. I mean, I was a yank, and I was a lecturer, and I did like to talk a lot. But I didn't feel the student-teacher gulf after awhile. I didn't sense that students were looking to me for lessons, data, or specialized information. That was both good and bad.

It was good because it taught me something about listening to students as equals; taught me not to rely on titles and position for gaining others' respect for my ideas; and taught me to see students as thinking individuals rather than intellectual dependents, to eliminate the role distinctions and thus learn to deal with them as colleagues in learning and teaching; and to respect students rather than distrust them as I had grown to do as a graduate student.

But bad because I was new at teaching and felt some need to rely on props and titles to maintain my position; felt threatened when my brightest ideas were sometimes knocked back by students' irreverent differences of opinion; and felt rather unsure of just what I was doing with these people if I was to be apprehended as a partici-pant rather than a lecturer. Of course, as any new teacher will agree, the crisis of confidence is one of the major battles of the first year.

All of this was not 'bad' so much as doubt-provoking, and thus became some of the most valuable lessons learned all that year. I mean, I learned something about the differences between pontifi-cation and teaching, something about the authoritarian and uni-lateral nature of what commonly passes as teaching and learning. I learned that one of the major differences between teachers and students in educational institutions everywhere is that of power, and my loss of power was a unique insight into what education is all about. I didn't learn to deal with this loss of control quite so quickly as I pretend here, though. There was a period of humiliation and I can recall the event that crystallized the lesson. It was the time when we were all engaged in lining up electives for the final term of the year. Bernie, I think, had suggested that I come up with a few ideas for some elective courses, and the students would select from among them.

So I thought and pondered and wrote, and finally came up with 4 or 5 ideas for courses that sounded good to me. I mean, I was enthused about teaching them. They were all plainly inherently interesting, I knew everyone would want to sign up. So the meeting began, all were assembled, and one by one we were asked to list our 'offerings' on the board. I was first, and I wrote them down. And then came time to vote to see how many would line up for each proposal. My list came first. There were about 50 students in that room and not a single one voted for any of my topics! I was demoralized. How could I have so miscalculated? Why didn't everyone think that they were fascinating ideas? Were they not clever enough? What did they want? I thought I had really blown it and I felt humiliated.

But then something interesting happened. As voting continued it became funnier and funnier because nobody's ideas won more than 1 or 2 adherents. Most received no votes at all. The students didn't much like anybody's ideas. It was a fascinating situation for me. I had never seen students so much in control of their program. So a period of negotiation began, compromises were made, new courses blocked out, more voting, and agreements finally reached about who was teaching what to whom.

Except that what I was now in charge of 'teaching' was as much the choice of the students as my own, and I didn't know anything about it. I was supposed to teach about something of which I knew virtually nothing. And I like to lecture so much. The topic was social myths and the media. What would I talk about? And that began the best educational experience I ever had.

I think if I tell you something about this elective I can best describe what I consider most important of my Course B experiences, and what I think is most valuable in the program as well. It will also serve as a personal message of gratitude to 'my students' who worked with me.

I cannot say 'my students' without amusement and embarrassment. For they were not 'my students', I was not their 'teacher', it was not 'my course'. These terms and the relationships they imply became meaningless within minutes of our first meeting. I lectured to them in my office for about 20 minutes, until I discovered that I had nothing more to talk about. From that point onward we became collaborators trying to learn about something none of us knew anything about. We adjourned for coffee and tried to decide what to do next. We never met in my office again.

I tried to stay in control of the course by guiding its direction, if not its content. Time after time I offered suggestions about 'What to do next', strategies of investigation, and what I thought were good insights into the problem at hand. But I could not impose my ideas.

There was no authority to do so. And so they were accepted or
rejected with about equal facility. But so it went with everybody
else. Nobody intended to listen to me more than others, and another
lesson in humility was learned. So we gathered together every week
or so, mostly at Jill's or Ron's and Graeme's, at Julie's once, and my
place one time. Sometimes we thought we had mastered our topic of
social myths and the media. And then we would grow frustrated
when we realized that we had only raised new and more troublesome
questions than before. We undertook various projects, tried alternative strategies, devised arguments, elaborated theoretical constructs,
and we talked for hours, it was easy to talk, to forget about time or
conflicting appointments (Vicky never learned about scheduling her
appointments).

It took time to relinquish my hold on 'my course'. I feared for its
life, worried that nobody would take it as seriously as I, that people
would lose interest, that it would fade away. Those meetings attended
by only 3 or 4 of us made me doubt everyone's commitment to it.
And yet there was nothing to be done, I could control its outcome
only so much, and only for so long. But it never died out, never
really came close to dying out. Because I finally realized — believed
— that everyone was as committed to their/our course as much as I.
We were seriously interested in learning something in common, and
we needed the ideas of each participant as much as any other's. I can
honestly claim that I contributed no more to the course's success
than anybody else.

'Success'. I really do mean 'success'. There were no exams no
papers or reports, no evaluations, no objective measures of progress
or failure. And gradually I overcame my academic need for intellectual
closure. We didn't have to decide anything or accomplish any goal or
reach any culminating conclusions. We often talked about putting
something together at the end, a social science unit of some sort. We
didn't but I doubt that any of us feels cheated or disappointed. Anyway, that is not what I mean by success.

The process of our work, not the product, was the measure of our
success. The very activity of collaborating in an honest intellectual
effort to learn taught us as much about learning and teaching as
about social myths. Learning emerged from our efforts to 'produce'.
We came to like each other, to respect and trust each other — I for
each of them quite strongly, and for some very deeply.

The term ended. We all decided to continue our meetings none
the less, still half-heartedly intent on producing something tangible,
but not really caring if we did. We knew we weren't finished, that
there was more to learn, the time restrictions of a university term
seemed irrelevant. So we pushed on. And then came a climax, all the

more climactic because it was so unexpected, so sudden. It was in Ron and Graeme's kitchen that we finally got a grip on social myths, what they are, what they do, how they can be recognized, all the questions we had probed so long. Social myths, we decided it emerged, had the effect of forcing people (us) to apprehend others (each other) as <u>kinds</u> of people, imbued with label-imputed characteristics. That is, social myths have to do with personal relationships and effectively force people to deal with each other as stereotypes. They lose their impact the more we learn in detail about each other. Myths make us nervous and uncertain before others, and others before us. They keep people apart. Intimacy and friendship is the elimination of mythical conceptions of others.

Regardless of your opinion of these conclusions, it must be understood that this was an emotional and intellectual pinnacle for us all. We had gelled as a group, had rearranged our questions into a new perspective, if not quite answered them all. We were excited with the sense of discovery. And it had somehow happened without anyone knowing how or why. The process had itself become the outcome by seeming to produce one.

There were perhaps 1 or 2 meetings more, during one of which some efforts were made to codify our findings, with some promising results. This served as our official termination. Time had expired, everyone was going separate ways, and I to America. We had tired ourselves as well.

It was the least academic course I had ever been involved with, and probably my most intellectually valuable. I had learned much about teaching and learning; about students as teachers and teachers as students; about intellectual honesty; trusting students; humility and authority; about how and why people learn; and quite a bit about social myths and the media. Not the least of all, I had grown close to some wonderful people. Now, what has this to do with Course B?

Everything. For the course and its staff have certain philosophical orientations that made our/my course possible. First there is a strong trust in students. Not only is it assumed that students want to learn (an assumption not universally shared), but also that students are valuable resources for each other. Forced to rely on each other, students take themselves more seriously, grow in confidence, and learn to resist the preachings of academic authority. To the extent that they learn this, they become better teachers and learners. Which, of course, is what education is all about, isn't it?

Second, flexibility and creativity are encouraged. I was continually amazed at the range of imagination displayed at each of our meetings. I think Course B students learn to use imagination in teaching and learning.

Third, contexts outside the classroom for student-teacher associations are encouraged — campouts, excursions, parties, wine bottlings, workshops, conferences, pub jaunts, simply visiting — the distinctions between staff and students, classroom and living, were largely eliminated. And perhaps most important, students became friends with each other, and with the staff. Thus assured of respect, they were able to challenge each other in the classroom without threat or uncertainty. Confident among friends, we all felt free to accept rebuttal.

And fourth, there seems to be a commitment to challenging what is 'known' about teaching, learning, and education, about power and institutions, about methods and curricula, about everything affiliated with the activity of knowledge. The atmosphere in Course B encouraged questioning about how, what, and why to teach.

This covers most of what I would like to say. I would add one further comment, though. I have the deepest respect for those of you who designed the course and strove to keep true to its ideals. I did not work with many of you. I watched Bernie Newsome and Rod Fawns perform quite a few times, though, and always came away admiring their professional integrity and commitment to their work. The rest of the staff — Gwen, Rory, Rod Foster, Terry — command my respect, as they did the other students'.

I cannot discuss the Course's efficacy as a teacher training program. I suspect that the only way to learn to be a good teacher is to teach. But I learned about teaching without really intending to. Surely those in training must have gained in proportion to their intent.

So there you have it. I am proud to have worked with you all. And I treasure the friendship I feel for many of you. Thank you for this opportunity to unload this all on paper. And cheers for now.

Jan

Seldom did students show quite the amount of initiative that Jan's group displayed (and he was brave, if not typical); but seldom did they entirely lack it if their lecturer was sufficiently receptive. Stephen Murray-Smith, for example, began by offering an option in Curriculum Studies in, I think, our first year. It was one that he had tried with other groups and was well prepared to give: 'Children in Literature'. His students very firmly convinced him that what they really wanted to study was 'Children's Literature', and Stephen had the grace — and the energy — to scrap his well-planned material in order to work out a different course, which he continued to run each year. It was popular in its first year, and continued to be so.

For us all, staff quite as much as students, the Course was a continuing political education. We have heard this from Jan Deamicis; let us conclude

195

with the words of two other lecturers in the Course. Ray Daniels, who shared the history method with me in 1975, and who has remained with the Course on part-time secondment from his school, wrote at the end of 1975:

> The direction the course takes in seminars is <u>open to the interests, needs and decisions of its students</u>. This seems to promote a sense of the course as a cooperative experience rather than something imposed. The <u>flexibility</u> of the course and its limited formal requirements encourage students to work out their own commitments, responsibilities and reading.

And, among the other things that Terry Werner wrote in a letter to me, after two years (1974 and 1975) with us as a part-time psychologist, was his comment on his own political education. Perhaps I should preface this with recalling one of his memorable early comments after Freire had been discussed in several seminars he attended: 'Am I right that what Freire is saying is that any word you don't know screws you up?'

> In the beginning I wondered how the hell anyone could get excited about Freire and Illich. All the talk about Ideology left me feeling very inadequate because I thought I didn't have 'one' ...
> Psychology paled into insignificance against all of this.
> The first year was a kind of lonely one. An actor without a script — a script without an actor — which was it?
> During 1975 I began to write a script in my own head, but I didn't ever get it finished. I think it began to come together when I read Rod and Bernie's theory and practice paper and during the 'equality' option with you.
> I thought I had a script in the beginning — a good knowledge of psychology. I even believed in it. Course B took me apart really. I have a theory now that to be a good psychologist you have to go through a kind of disintegration process. This is the theory/practice thing again — you put all you know through a reality-testing process and watch it disintegrate before your eyes — pull yourself up again etc. It's really nothing new, but until you have actually experienced it you don't know what it's like.

It would be quite wrong to suggest that it was a one-way process. As staff we all learned from each other, just as we saw students learning from each other too. An essential feature in this educational and political programme is, as Freire would emphasize, that dialogue and a willingness to change — to be flexible — are necessary ingredients.

Chapter 7

School teachers as educators of teachers

The centrality of teachers

If teaching practice is the linchpin in a course of teacher education, it follows that teachers in the practice schools have a central place. It is not only inevitable that this should be so: it is also desirable. However lavish a staff–student ratio might be — and it seldom is in schools of education — the staff at the training institution cannot give the time to the student in school that the supervising teacher can give. Very talented university staff might have a lasting influence on their students; but for a teacher-training institution to believe that its independence is a safeguard against educational conformity is self-delusion. Independence is to be treasured, to be sure, but not if its corollary is the kind of separateness that gains for teacher trainers the reputation for being out of touch — the usual metaphor being the ivory tower. The student will be most influenced by what he remembers of his own education reinforced by teaching examples that impress him favourably or unfavourably. It is either folly or arrogance for university staff to believe that what they do in one year can have a more lasting influence than twelve years of schooling, three or four years of tertiary education and then a career back in the schools.

Again, the teacher on the spot has the initial advantage of greater credibility than the lecturer, who is seen only to talk about what should happen rather than to have to make it happen. It is rare for university or college lecturers and tutors to be actively engaged in educational programmes in the schools. When they are, they need to be in close partnership with the school staff and to be seen by their students to be so if they are to be convincing. The student is likely to take his lead from what he sees happening in the schools quite as much as in the classes he attends at his training institution, and the influences on him may be positive or negative. As already suggested, this 'hidden curriculum' will be just as good or bad as are teachers and lecturers in action. While part of the value of the 'hidden curriculum' lies in the variety of teaching styles that students encounter, it is nevertheless important that teachers and lecturers support one another.

Although we have formally abandoned the old master-teacher or pupil-teacher form of apprenticeship in most modern countries, in a sense it persists informally. Realizing this, many universities and colleges have established a very close working relationship with their schools — a tradition that is highly developed in England, though far from universal even there. Leicester is one of the universities that acquired a world reputation in this regard, yet Professor J. W. Tibble, who may take a good deal of the credit (though now retired), considered that too often the good relationship between schools and training institutions may be likened to someone's comment on the marriage relationship — as one 'based on mutual misunderstanding'.[1] He went on to point out that the tutor or lecturer who visited the classroom as 'a non-participant observer' was quite inadequate for the task.

The accepted practice of university staff coming to sit in the back of a classroom to watch one lesson in isolation from the total programme of the supervising teacher was one that had always embarrassed me in the past: it seemed to be discourteous and patronizing, to say the least, and, as well, it betrayed a trivial, artificial attitude to what teaching is about. It is small wonder that schools are renowned for telling their students and first-year-out teachers to forget all the hot air they'd heard 'up there' and to get on with the realities. Variations on the theme abound, such as the remark by a teacher when she noted that the student was carrying a psychology textbook: 'The only application for that is hard on the child's bottom.'

Such scorn for theory (and for children) is countered by charges of teachers' anti-intellectualism laid by lecturers and of cynicism laid by students, to which the schools readily retort that the universities and colleges are unpractical and ignorantly idealistic. And so mutual recriminations get built one upon the other, and the student can be trapped between two seemingly hostile forces.

England's National Association of Schoolmasters/Union of Women Teachers in a recent report gained some Press attention, including a quotation in *The Times* of 20 June 1977:

> Many of the misfortunes which have befallen schools in the past 10 years or so are directly attributable to the inept theories eagerly, and often sincerely, preached by teacher trainers who had lost contact with the real school situation.

The Association deplored the fact that practising teachers were kept on the edge of teacher training, having 'minimal' or 'non-existent' influence on training courses.

An influential educator and academic such as Professor R. S. Peters, who could never be interpreted as being anti-intellectual or anti-theory, observed in a recent book[2] that if, as teacher trainers,

> we were bent on bringing to bear some fairly solid influence on practice during teacher training we might be wise to experiment much more radically with the systematic apprenticeship of students to experienced teachers whose practices had been shown to be effective ...
>
> The fact ... that there is little evidence for the immediate influence of theory on practice should not unduly depress us ... most of teaching involves a highly subtle moralized interrelationship between persons which cannot be reduced to a collection of techniques without debasing the relationships involved and making them less than personal. The effect of theory should therefore be long-term – the gradual transformation of a person's view of children, of himself, and of the situation in which he is acting.

Many students agree. Among students' comments reported in a newspaper article was this sort of remark that confirmed Professor Peters's point:

> You attend college and then you go out on your teaching rounds – you visit schools – and the idea is that there is a culmination. The two processes are there to make you a teacher.
>
> I've found that they are completely different. There's a feeble attempt to tie them up, but it doesn't work.

And a group of professional social investigators, in a report, *Youth Needs and Public Policies*,[3] made the same observation about the divorce between theory and practice, between formal education and the child's world as permeating all forms of education – academic, technical, professional, including teacher education:

> of the [Education] students who assisted us in our interviews, two-thirds had been disillusioned by their academic teacher training courses, feeling an urgent need for more school and classroom practical involvement. They were being given answers to problems and questions they had never faced or asked, and much of the course seemed a waste of time.

The thrust of such evidence, and much more could be cited from headmasters and headmistresses, from teachers and from students, is that teacher training is remote and out of touch, but so too (and perhaps the two things are not as unrelated as they might at first appear) are teachers — though not all of them. It was partly the realization that the drive for reform was coming from some schools rather than from universities that convinced us in planning Course B that we must work with the teachers and schools that were initiating educational reform. This was to risk the possibility that our students would eventually find it difficult to adapt themselves to conservative, less adventurous, schools, if that is where they were later employed; but this seemed preferable to being criticized by the innovative schools for failing to produce teachers who could contribute to intelligent policy-making, curriculum planning and to the fostering of independent learning.

It was essential, we believed, that we should offer the schools real help rather than being beholden to them for 'putting up with' our students. With the proliferation of teacher-training institutions that so many countries experienced in the 1960s the schools were hard pressed to meet the demands that the training institutions were making for school practice. The extra burden that teachers were accepting tended to intensify the breakdown in communications and even the hostility already described. A blockbuster had to be found.

Why, we wondered, shouldn't students be an asset rather than a liability, especially after their first few weeks in a school? What could we, as staff, offer the schools that would be of real help? Both students and staff had to be of service to the schools if we were to reverse the growing disaffection between the schools and the training bodies — the entrenched defensiveness and mistrust between colleagues who, after all, had a common purpose. The core staff of Course B were, all three, school teachers at heart. We enjoyed university work because it gave us more time to think about what we were doing, but at the expense of doing less of what we believed in. As ex-school teachers we were well aware of how many teachers crave and need more time to think and read. It was up to us, then, to sense how we might best be of service to the schools, and by that we meant both to the teachers and to the pupils. But old suspicions die hard, and we saw the task ahead of us as being to allay them.

Starting with only twenty-three students gave us a good beginning. We were able to place a reasonable number of students in each of the three schools that were affiliated with us, to give the schools a good mixture of subjects so that undue strain of supervision was not placed on any one teacher, and for our part, to be able as staff to keep in close contact with each of the three schools. Sydney Road and Swinburne Community Schools, each with only about a hundred pupils, welcomed the help that they expected students to be able to give. All three schools approved the direction that they thought the experimental course would take. In sharing an interest in educational innovation, we had a ready-made bond, albeit one that was perhaps a little fearful, sensitive, and defensive on both sides.

It was not until the next year, 1974, when our numbers increased to fifty, that we were able to move into less unusual schools, but we tried to avoid those schools that were most hidebound and most rigidly organized — for obvious reasons. But the paradox that confronted us was that the more enthusiastic and exemplary the schools, and particularly the teachers, the more we had to battle at the University for the students' time. *They* wanted a form of apprenticeship; they responded enthusiastically to the schools and teachers that gave them increasing responsibility; *we* wanted students to give their school practice highest priority; but we also believed that the work at University, especially the seminars that brought students of diverse backgrounds together, had a contribution to make that schools could not replace. It was not until 1976, the fourth year of the Course, that I began to understand the full force of the paradox.

We were so determined to prove ourselves to the schools that we tended to give way to them in any conflict. At times we were distressed by the weakness, comparatively speaking, of our appeal to students; but the law of diminishing returns began to operate, and by 1976 what the University had to offer came to be prized and sought by students who felt they were becoming too involved in the schools and demanded us to rethink how we could bring the focus back to the University.

We had often wondered if a better system would be to place students in schools on probation for six months or a year after graduation, and then to begin their Education studies with a good deal of experience behind them; but students firmly rejected the idea. I am not sure that they were right. Few, if any, of even the most school-bound students would have forgone their connexion with and support from the University in that first professional year. Just where each institution had to fit in, to the best advantage of the students, was something that only experience could teach both staff and students, and that is what we shall examine now.

The pull between schools and University

After the first fortnight of the year, students spent two days a week in school during first and second term — or that was the formal arrangement. When schools were near enough to the University it was not unknown for the most committed students to be in their schools, even if only for one lesson or a staff meeting, for five days in the week. We usually offered a Bruner workshop for a whole week at the University in second term. That was optional, though well attended. In third term students usually had three full-time weeks in their own school, and then spent the final five weeks at the University. There were variants of this.

One country town, for example, where the technical school was trying to establish a small annexe on community school lines, sought our help. For several years we sent volunteers to live for three weeks in the town, usually hiring a house, and they offered what help they could to the parent school and in the annexe. This was an ideal arrangement in that it gave the school staff an opportunity to catch up on things they had been forced to neglect; we sent only students who wanted to go and whose teaching was already sound, and it gave them the chance to round off their training by planning and trying out team-teaching if they wished. It was an excellent example of how we could fulfil our intention of making the University and schools mutually helpful.

Some of the community schools liked to have the opportunity to try out students before the academic year began and asked us to send students ahead of time. They usually specified what they most urgently needed — for example, a Greek- or Italian-speaker or a student with a keen interest in art or music. Our admission procedures worked in two stages. A group of students admitted into the quota was given a first offer. We interviewed them, and if any of them were certain that they would take the offer and wished to try working in community schools, we offered them the chance of starting early. We could not make a universal practice of this, for there was usually a big withdrawal of students in the first category, many of whom took up higher degrees or academic posts instead of Dip. Ed., and it was, for those who were given second or third offers of University places, too late to teach before the University year began; but that more than a handful took on this offer showed the keenness of the schools to take students and the early commitment of the students to teaching and to Course B. The system worked very well, and the students who were part of it made the most valuable contributions to the University programme at the beginning of the year.

But many students were less fortunate in their schools, and there were tremendous discrepancies in the kind of reception given them, not only between schools but also even within schools. By the time we were using thirteen schools we were finding that some students had taught twenty-five lessons in first term while one had taught none. At one school we did not discover until half-way through the year that a student still did not know who her supervisor was. She had picked up odd lessons here and there by using her own initiative with teachers, and neither she nor the school realized that the system had completely failed to work, for the co-ordinator of teaching practice in that school had either not understood or had ignored our request that each student be attached at first to one teacher. On our visits to the school we had not realized that the supervising teacher of the lesson we saw was not *the* supervisor of that student.

We had a special arrangement with one school, Mount Waverley High School, from 1974, arising from the request from a senior master for four students to be attached to a group of teachers who were especially keen to have our students. The senior master, Keith Creed, had had a lengthy association with the University, and he undertook not only to co-ordinate the teaching practice, but to supervise the students on our behalf. We did visit that school, but knew that the students were in good hands, and with the excessive demands on our resources it was one school where we needed to spend little time. Another school made a similar arrangement with us, but it worked out so badly that we spent an undue amount of time at the school, usually unable to find the students, the supervisors or the lessons.

When we had a combination of committed teachers and students, it was common for students to teach eighty or ninety lessons in the year. Prue (see pp. 25-6), for example, taught seventy or more lessons, an additional fourteen in team-teaching, and, during her teaching practice, she gave continual help to three sixth-form pupils at the school. Much of her teaching was in sixth form, which was a measure of the confidence her supervisor had in her, for the examination sixth-form classes were seldom entrusted to any but the most capable students.

Another student at a newly-formed community school began before the University started, and continued with a heavy load of English teaching, much of which was individual remedial work, and, in addition to her other commitments such as University tutorials with the English Department, she chose to attend, with our blessing, a demanding course in remedial English that was being offered that year as an in-service course. For her depth study she devised her own resources of remedial readers in her attempts to get one child to read and write. She wrote this up as an article: [4]

> A session of one to one teaching with J. will inevitably be disrupted by his desire to chat, by complaints of tiredness, headaches, itchiness or hunger, irritability, anger, or a flat refusal to work. Like any human being J. 'has his moods', and if I am to be of any use to him as a teacher or 'get through a lesson' I must adapt or 'tack' in response to this volatility ... To ignore that individuality, to try and rough-ride over the fact, say, that J. has been in trouble at home that morning and is in a 'bad mood' ... is to come up against a blank wall, a limpness of response and the dismissal of one's teaching efforts. To acknowledge and make use of it is to be continually discovering new and useful teaching tools.

Gwyn Duncan, the author, found that with bigger classes of poor readers and writers there would often be enthusiastic discussion. There was what she called 'verbal readiness' shared by the pupils, but a strong

203

resistance to trying to deepen their thinking through writing. With J., her most resistant pupil, the problem of lack of self-esteem was most pronounced, and she tried to restore it by writing a story in which he was the central character, using his own words and style of speech. Her first purpose was to raise his sense of importance and to provide him with written words that he 'knew'. He was well aware of being 'conned' by becoming a central character, but he liked it, and she found that he enjoyed learning to read his own words, for he was confident when he read ones that were familiar to him.

When she discussed this with her English Methods lecturer and talked to me about doing a depth study preparing reading materials centred on the children in the fashion she had used with J., she was advised to read Sylvia Ashton-Warner, who had tried similar methods with Maori children, and then to study Freire's writing on teaching literacy in Brazil. Her Readers are now being considered seriously for publication.

The point at issue here was the sort of pull that she felt and that we at the University felt about the balance of her year. The school's need of her and her commitment to the children in it made some of the University's offerings pale by comparison; but if she had been a regular attender at Curriculum Studies, we should have been well pleased by the amount of reading she was doing around her central interest. There was a danger that she would neglect whole areas of educational theory, but she was in the midst of a political/educational problem of the severest kind and she was making an imaginative, thoughtful contribution to it. Was she missing out on class teaching of the ordinary kind? She did teaching with small classes at the school, and part of her teaching practice was, we recognized, her contribution to University tutorials, which was highly praised. There was a good deal of versatility here, but not orthodoxy in the usual terms of a teacher-training year. Until the reasons were well known, it was hurtful that she more often than not skipped Curriculum Studies; but when it was all weighed up, and account taken of how hard she worked, it was perfectly legitimate to regard her as one of the students who had accepted our offer of 'writing their own tickets' and having their self-initiated programme accepted. It would, I believe, have been extraordinarily narrow and inflexible of us to have deflected her.

A constant problem for us was that, the more successful the school, or indeed the student, the more University commitments seemed to be sacrificed, and not all cases were clear-cut like the one just described — as the account of Prue testifies. The students themselves were often in conflict, as Brian McFarlane noted. He had been co-ordinator of teaching practice at Trinity Grammar until his resignation late in 1975. Before Course B began, he had been the teacher who had first welcomed the 1972 pilot scheme of trying out two-day-a-week school practice with a handful of students. From that first year, he never doubted the superiority of the scheme to the stop–start teaching rounds of which he had had many years of experience. He was, thus, a great supporter of Course B from its inception, and a close colleague who, at various stages, worked with the Curriculum Studies team, especially with the component that was concerned with depth studies, several of which were studies of various practices at Trinity.

In giving his evaluation of Course B, as he knew it from the school end, Brian wrote in 1976 of the personal and professional gain to students in a course that blended theory and practice by a close relationship between school and University:

> By personal gains, I mean that the students had a real chance to establish themselves as people with both staff and pupils. They weren't just 3-week visitors to be borne with, baited or bored by, as far as their pupils were concerned. The Course B system enabled them to work closely with pupils, to detect individual weaknesses and to give individual help towards overcoming these. I remember a Japanese pupil ... for whom one of the Course B trainees devised a special programme, whom he met regularly, and to whom he gave a great deal more confidence than would have been likely in the ordinary class situation. In their relations with staff, Course B students often made close friends, were accepted in the staffroom as if permanent staff members, and often involved themselves in excursions ... with other staff members.
>
> ... What I really meant by 'professional' development, though, was the way the course made it possible for its students to be truly involved in the planning of curriculum projects, in carrying these through and assessing them. This was challenging, of course: if they made mistakes (e.g., miscalculated the level they were aiming at, failed to introduce enough variety of treatment), they were forced to work, as a permanent teacher is, to make good these mistakes. It's a good deal easier to leave a school at the end of three weeks, secure in the knowledge that the regular staff will repair their errors.

Brian then proceeded to explain how much more satisfactory it was as a supervisor to be able to pass over a whole topic of English to a student instead of having to find short projects which upset his own programme. It was administratively more convenient and educationally less disrupting; it also led to discussions between him and his students about the interpretation of literature and proper academic discussions that students on a three-week stint would not have been sufficiently confident to enter into.

There were some students, 'a *very* small number', who were elusive;

205

there were some who found it difficult to continue teaching with classes they'd had trouble with; and there were a very few who did not become involved in the life of the school; but 'most of them overworked: they did far more preparation, teaching and assessment of work than student teachers I'd been used to.'

Clearly, from the school's point of view, the school-based programme was seen not just as the lesser of two evils, but in many ways a positive asset. Our students at that school, although some of them had real troubles and needed a great deal of support, enabled the school to undertake projects that would not have been possible otherwise, and they did make some serious contributions to curriculum innovation as well as to the evaluation of some of the school's own innovations. Students could be important agents of criticism in their schools.

The first year of Course B was the high spot in our relations with Trinity in this respect, and there were several chance reasons for this. One of the advantages of a school-based course was the possibility of placing a reasonable number of fellow-students together so that, as a group, they could support each other.

This could work extremely well in one year and not so well in another. In 1973, there were seven students at the school, and they included several who had considerable problems with teaching; but that year the group was tightly knit and did support each other. With only three schools to be cared for, there was more University back-up that year than there could be in later years. It was something of a mystery why one year the student group would be strong at one school and the next year it would be so at a quite different school.

Changes of teaching staff and particularly of co-ordinators could account for this. Changes in the place of accommodation for students were very important. In 1973 most of the students at Trinity shared a study for lesson preparation and spare periods but the next year the room was needed and they were scattered. But other chance things, beyond University control, were influential. The tragedy that Footscray High School experienced in 1975 when the school was burnt down had a miraculous effect in bringing the student group close together, and more than that in cementing their relationship with staff. Students brought in their lecture-notes, their books, any aids that they could find to help the teachers whose lesson plans and teaching resources had gone up in flames. The students themselves became indispensable resources and colleagues. Moreover, at Footscray and later at Deer Park, transport was difficult, and a shared car did more than any structuring of groups could do to bring the students together. Nevertheless, although we learned that informal structures were better than any that we could devise in advance (and certainly we had no desire to see any more of our schools burned down), having a group of students from the one

206

small Course together in each school, reducing to a minimum the number of schools that we had to use so that our students were not scattered all over the map, meant that we, as University staff, were in close contact with supervisory staff, we grew to know our schools well, and the students had a far better chance of working closely and supportively together as well as with the teachers who supervised them.

After 1973, with numbers doubled, we met the increase in schools by attaching one member of the University staff to each school, at least for first term. Although this meant some science or maths students had the disadvantage of being supervised in their teaching by me, and some of my history students had the disadvantage of being supervised by Rod Fawns, a biologist, this was more than offset by the fact that each of us became intimately known to all the supervisors, to the students, and indeed to the pupils. Our regular visits formed a nucleus around which the students clustered, perhaps informal discussions at lunch being more important than anything else, and our contact with school staff became much more natural and more easily accepted. We knew that the Course had become too big when our University resources would not stretch to make this arrangement possible in every school we used. The Course was as strong as the link between school staff and a member of University staff.

The pulls between University and school were most serious and least corrigible in the schools that we had, of necessity, to neglect. By 1974 this was the case with Trinity. Knowing that we could not give all the time needed to all of our new schools in 1974 and thereafter, we calculated that the students at Trinity would manage all right because the school by then was so experienced in our ways; but Brian McFarlane's lucid criticism shows that a price was paid. Some of the students, he noted,

> spent *far* more time at the school than they were required to, and I know that some of them got badly behind with their theoretical work.
>
> Perhaps the organizers of Course B are working on this problem: that is, making the theoretical part of the Dip. Ed. course seem more relevant to the needs of the committed students whom Course B attracts. In most cases whenever there was a clash between work required by the University and projects in the school, the latter seemed to win.
>
> It may be that the degree of their commitment to the school – to pupils, teachers, projects – exerted too much pressure on them. However, if this was so I think it points to what they saw as the most important demands being made on them. I don't think it could be said that the school made more demands on them than it should;

in fact, on a number of occasions they had to be discouraged from involving themselves in more school-based work than we felt was in their interests. This sort of theory-practice clash has perhaps been resolved since I was associated with the project; in a sense, it was a defect which grew out of the virtues of a valuable system.

In truth there were some students who were, to use the students' phrase in the previous chapter, 'how-to-ing it' too well, in some cases because they had 'had' academia, in others because we failed at University to get their wavelength. There were some, like Prue, who became so absorbed in her teaching that it was only late in the year that she began to regret having missed much of the theory and to see too late the need for it in her teaching; there were some who were so impressed with talented teachers like Brian that they saw their discipleship as being in the school. Perhaps the 'theory-practice clash' that Brian referred to indicates a failure in some of the schools to take full cognizance of the fact that theory at the University was *not* divorced from practice, whereas we more readily recognized that those students who were supervised by teachers like Brian were acquiring a great deal of valuable theory from their practice. Yet Prue, who was one of Brian's students, discovered too late that she had missed many studies offered at the University that she later saw would have been valuable.

It could be argued that a major part of the 'discipline' (practical and academic) that a year of teacher education could give came from thoughtful and scholarly practice; but the schools were not fully apprised of what went on at the University, and this weakness in communication was difficult to remedy. Clearly our supervisors, especially the co-ordinators of teaching practice, needed to be far more familiar with our intentions in running University courses, and they needed to be a party to our planning if we were to avoid this so-called 'clash'. As we shall see in the next section, we began to make positive moves in this direction in 1976.

There was a further difficulty in that schools that were used to block practice rounds often failed to realize how important it was for our University work that students should gain classroom experience early in the year. Some students had to fit into the slots the teacher offered them, and this was reasonable enough when they were totally inexperienced; but the provision of consecutive teaching was sometimes delayed far too long and led to frustration, both at school and University. By contrast, other supervisors possessively 'took over' the students, giving them the implicit (sometimes explicit) advice to 'forget what's going on up there if it clashes with what you can get here'.

This sort of tension was less acute the closer our contact with the school, and the force of this was intensified by the fact that our

University teaching was greatly enriched and made considerably more relevant if we knew at first-hand what was happening to the student in the school. I may perhaps give one or two examples. Ronald (pp. 70-1) had been a regular attender at my history Method seminars throughout the year. His diffident references to his uncertainty about class management — and it presented serious ideological questioning for him — never became at all clear to me or to the seminar group until one of the Course B staff, Rod Foster, decided in consultation with Ronald that he should be transferred to another school, Flemington High School. For the first time, I actually saw him teach and began to understand his conflict. He had the gift of arousing most of the pupils' interest and sparking off a lively discussion, and then suddenly he would stop himself and his pupils with unaccountably peremptory demands in case the class got out of hand or his supervising teacher thought he was likely to lose control or to seem too permissive. They were restive pupils at the best of times, and certainly Ronald needed to change tack while he still had their interest; but he could not see quite how to do it.

Fortunately, Doug Robb, our geography Methods lecturer, who taught at Flemington, and Carole Buhaj (see pp. 76-80) were working with him and were able to help him to see where his difficulties lay. No tricks of the trade, no slick advice in the history seminar could help Ronald, but discussions about authority became much more meaningful to him once I really understood his ideological dilemma as I believe he saw it. Carole, Doug and I were able jointly to give Ronald more help than he had received earlier in the year, and there was the further dividend that Doug, in a Methods staff meeting early the next year, was able to argue from the school floor, as it were, against those staff who wanted us to centre the Methods programmes on survival skills. They might have provided a palliative, but the palliative would simply have been an evasion of Ronald's main concern. It was originally a visit from Bernie (p. 180) that made Ronald realize that he could not shelve the ideological issues that were inhibiting him. Here we have a good example of University and school staff all supporting each other.

Another example, from the same school, was a girl, Elsie, who was so nervous early in the year that she could not be pushed into teaching and should not have been. She, too, was in one of my classes, and it was difficult, if not impossible, to engage her interest in the kinds of issues that the other students, with some teaching experience behind them, wanted to pursue. Then one day at Flemington I went into a sex education class with Lloyd Jones. The class was divided into several small groups, one of which Lloyd took; a student took another, and I went in ready to take any overflow. I became so absorbed in the discussion with one small group of pupils that it was only after about ten minutes that I looked up to see Elsie occupied with a small group who were obviously deeply interested in their discussion. Elsie was poised and totally at ease, so it seemed; and when I eventually moved from my group to hers she so little noticed my presence as a 'supervisor' that she carried on and drew me into the discussion as if I were one of them. From then on I was on sure ground in trying to build up her confidence, not only in my personal discussions with her but also in University seminars. Far more important, Lloyd was able to help her to become an effective teacher — indeed, a very different person — in a miraculously short time.

Whether teachers worked with us, or as occasionally happened, unintentionally or deliberately worked against us, there was a constant pull on the students. Sometimes it was a productive pull, as it proved for Gwyn Duncan, in that students had to establish their *own* priorities: sometimes it was debilitating and damaging, causing resentment against either University or school staff. It was by no means a totally one-way pull favouring the schools (as Brian suggested), though the school pull tended to be stronger, as I think it probably should be. Students in the least satisfactory schools or supervised by the least satisfactory teachers tended to be relieved to get back to the University and its demands.

Meg was one who saw point in commitment both to school and to University. After the first month she wrote, 'It is difficult to work out the balance between course work and school work. After teaching geography a bit it has set a new tone to ... enthusiasm and potential, as now I am not so petrified about taking a class.' Six weeks later:

> Being in school two days a week gives me freedom to move out of a tension-filled situation into a more relaxed framework for objective viewing of the school situation. I'm sure I would shelve many of the difficulties if I were only in a school for a 3 week stint.

Two months later, she feels the pull rather more strongly, partly because of tensions with her 'bloke', partly because of the depth study, and partly because she is starting to think more deeply about what is involved in teaching. As the informality of her language suggests, she used her diary to talk to herself:

> This time of year is devastating especially when one includes other activities on top of teaching. I'm ... screwed up because I can't handle the dichotomy ... As far as teaching goes ... the kids do the work cos its kinda interesting but it is [also] cos of the inherent work ethic ... There's little interaction between kids and teacher ...
>
> Complete dichotomy between doing my depth study effectively and maintaining my stability, cos the whole thing questions my assumptions about life ... I bet it appears I wrote it without even thinking ... HELP

I've moved a long way. I feel quite relaxed in the soc. studs. context and yet the whole thing is crapping all over me ... Can I be a teacher? Tolstoy — no one has the right to educate any one else ... Really getting slap-hazard with the teaching and quite unconcerned about the kids. This could happen any time ... but especially with so much other work / with depth study ... but I gained many new skills which will help in the classroom. Lots of conclusions that one makes one day are forgotten the next. I guess you learn over and over again.

That would seem to be a healthy state of unease, a good rhythm between thinking and action.

At the end-of-year stock-taking session with students in 1976, much of the discussion revolved around the lack of balance between school and University. Freddie, for example, had formed such a sense of dedication to his community school and its teachers that he commented on the Course's value entirely in terms of what it had enabled him to do in the school. Here are my notes on the discussion:

Freddie: Old Pathology [our building at the University] wasn't the focus of Course B to me. Course B is terrific because it enabled me to focus on the community school.

Pat: Those who have come to Old Pathology really really got something out of the Course. It has produced thirty generative teachers — probably a bigger percentage.

Cecile: Freddie should have said what he wanted from the University staff and not merely taken out of it what suited him.

Freddie: I'm not criticizing Course B. I think it's fantastic.

Nick: There's a lack of fire at University. I take fire at the school but not up here. There's a prejudice against institutions; you can only make them good if you fight for them. The fight for me was in the schools.

And the final reaction against the Nicks and the Freddies was expressed by Cecile in her retrospective diary:

If I were to give a general assessment of this year for me, I'd say it was one of agonizing soul-searching and utter confusion. I felt split between university and school — and felt very isolated from university, since I couldn't even go to some of the activities. I was very disappointed that I couldn't do the option on children's literature — because on Friday mornings there's the school meeting.

... All in all, I feel I learnt a great deal, perhaps because of my personal agonized frustration and confusion, although this prevented me from really letting myself go in having experience at the school.

211

School-based Curriculum Studies

There is a good deal of the law of cussedness revealed in these opposing reactions. When we pulled too hard, and the attraction of the school was strong, the students resisted us. As Nick suggested, they liked to have something to fight for, but perhaps he meant something to fight against, and students constantly complained that we made it difficult to fight against us, though it is clear that when some of us tried too hard to win them, they not only fought against us, but rejected us. On the other hand, when the school pulled too hard, the students, even the ones most loyal to the school, wanted more of the University. Teachers, both at University and in schools, had to learn that possessiveness tends to destroy that which it most passionately desires.

The schools had the trumps, as they should have, for they were 'the heart of the matter', but, as I suggested earlier, when we gave in to this too much we became for many students the much desired scarcity. They wanted more of us, and greater contact with each other. We learnt this from an interesting experiment we conducted in 1976 in trying out running our Curriculum Studies course in four of our schools — Trinity, Sydney Road, Swinburne, and Flemington High — rather than at the University.

At the end of 1975 the staff at Syndey Road Community School proposed that we extend the school-basedness of the Course by moving Curriculum Studies out of the University into the schools. All teachers were interested in contributing to such a project, and the school was prepared to release Chris Hansen from part of his other commitments to be co-ordinator working with University staff. Chris had been a Course B student in its first year, 1973, and had kept a close contact with us both as a teacher at the community school and as a constant attender at what we called our 'in-service' sessions that occurred twice a year between former and present students. He was also doing a higher degree at Melbourne, and Course B often called on him to help in sessions at the University.

After detailed discussion, we arranged that Rod Fawns from Course B and Chris would run the Curriculum Studies jointly, and that Rod would do the major part of his supervision at that Community School. We approached Swinburne Community School, which also agreed, and it was arranged that Rob Lewers, another 1973 student, who was also doing a higher degree with us, would co-ordinate the Curriculum Studies at Swinburne, with Ron Toomey, a lecturer in Course B, who, for his part of the agreement, would supervise the students at the Swinburne Community School and the Annexe, and would undertake some teaching responsibilities to relieve Rob. The State Department of Education agreed to second Lloyd Jones to Flemington High School, as a joint

212

appointment to the school and to Course B, and we appointed Doris Cosopodiotis, a part-time lecturer with the Course, to be attached to Flemington and its Annexe. John Brennan, at Trinity Grammar School, it was arranged, would run a course there; but we were unable to give him back-up comparable with what was arranged at the other three schools. This arrangement meant that half of our students — thirty — were to have their Curriculum Studies in the schools, and only the other thirty at the University.

There were dangers in the scheme, not least of which was the consequent difficulty of giving enough time to the remaining schools except by using support staff rather than core staff — a difficulty that was exaggerated by our old problem of being too much staffed by newcomers each year who were quite unfamiliar with our ways. The advantages we foresaw were, first, that the problems we had early in the year at the University in tying academic work firmly into school experience would be much less severe at the school, and, allied with this, the students would be less worried by the pull between school and University. We also believed that such a scheme would demonstrate beyond question our faith in the schools and would bind us much more closely to school staff on the basis of shared work which is the best foundation for shared understanding.

This long-range aim we could not hope to have immediately and miraculously realized, and it was particularly difficult at the very large schools where the size of the staff, school organization and administrative complications interfered with the co-ordinators' attempts to involve as many staff as possible. Though schools might be unwilling to admit it, they obviously recognized that University staff could be a resource to school teachers if for nothing else than in the obligation to keep abreast with current literature; but even this was a delicate matter. Nobody likes to be told what he *should* have read, and no teachers have the time to do the reading they might wish. It is hard enough for University staff to do so. It might seem a simple division of labour for schools to take responsibility for teaching resources and University staff to cull educational literature; but fewer than a third of our schools had adequate resource centres; the resource centre at the University was in its infancy; and the community schools knew that the price paid for their desired smallness was that they had to tap resources from outside. As an aside, it might be mentioned that it is a strange paradox that an Australian State like Victoria, previously so rigid, had developed a network of small community schools and school annexes despite the lack of highly developed resource centres, which the small school desperately needs, whereas in England, with its highly developed resource centres, the small breakaway schools are rare in the extreme. It is hard to equate demand and supply by administrative decision.

There is no denying that schools staff resented any suggestion that University staff could have anything to offer by way of ideas, wider knowledge of a conspectus of schools, reading, let alone research that could be valuable to the schools. One slip into the ivory tower jargon of educational literature and University staff lost what little credence they might have built up. To recognize this is by no means to blame teachers, as I hear them blamed frequently in England and Australia, for anti-intellectualism. It is merely to acknowledge the fact already described that the suspicion between schools and teachers is so ingrained that an attempt to restore understanding is fraught with difficulties that can never be lessened while universities remain remote. Students, of course, were aware of the tensions, and some of them felt a wry amusement at its manifestations. One student, however, noted in her diary:

> Diana Heath [the social studies lecturer] handed out a fantastic magazine of the social studies teachers' association but I lost mine to John. He shares something in common with all the teachers at the school — that they are very interested in what we do at University. I think that they feel that they are missing out on new stuff, and so I am always being pounced on for handouts.

A shared task, such as Curriculum Studies in the school, was seen as at least a move in the direction of bringing schools and University together, with neither of them in a superior position and each able to enlighten the other in action, and where 'academic' ideas, if they were to carry any conviction, had to be shown to contribute to the solution of actual problems and to the development of more effective practices. This was the challenge that University staff had to face.

It would be pretentious to suggest that we achieved this in one year, 1976; but that we made some progress is indicated by a comment Lloyd Jones made a year after his appointment. Until 1976 he had always, as a school teacher, been at the receiving end of teacher training. In 1976 he was suddenly thrust into the position of being both a school and University teacher. In January 1977 he wrote, among many critical comments about Course B:

> My criticisms of teacher training have been considerably modified as a result of 1976. I came to realize fairly quickly the complexities involved — not only for students, but for staff. I had previously failed to understand or appreciate the demands, the conflicting roles, and the subtle yet extraordinarily contradictory factors at play which affect, even inhibit, decisions for staff.
>
> Yet a major criticism still prevails. I feel that even in Course B there is profitable pay-off for all concerned — in particular the students — by increased presence of University staff in schools ...

Something has to give if the present self-perpetuating syndrome is to be cracked. Clearly Course B has made significant moves in that direction, yet more is needed.

And more *is* needed, though to make that practicable is another matter. What is significant about Lloyd's comments is his recognition of the 'distance' separating the major partners in the educational endeavour, and the accretion of understanding that he gained by being put in our shoes. One of his complaints was that he was thrown in at the deep end, without a supporting structure and with what he called an excess of liberalism that called on him to work out not only his own strategies but also his total programme. It was not ideological laissez-faire that accounted for this but the intolerable pressures on University staff that prevented us from suggesting guidelines and common goals to those starting Curriculum Studies in the schools.

But at both Swinburne and Sydney Road, where University staff were partners in the project (though Ron Toomey was in his first year with us, he had full recourse to experienced members of staff), as well as at the other two schools, the groups encountered exactly the problem that had bedevilled us at the University. Where to begin? Cleo Macmillan, from the Centre for the Study of Higher Education, was the only person who tried to keep in touch with what was happening in all four schools. Her report after the first half of the year is studded with questions about how to break in. Schools on the outskirts previously could say, as Brian McFarlane in effect did, 'You'll have to learn to be more seductive in your University offerings.' Now schools were discovering that they, themselves, had to be more seductive. The theme recurred early in the year — whether one should start from the school floor and then move into theory, or the other way round.

Let us take a few examples of comment from students, staff or Cleo on how our innovation in moving Curriculum Studies into the schools worked in its early stages:

Swinburne

The framework for beginning was set by a document prepared by the three staff members ... a discussion of A. S. Neill's *Summerhill* ... A series of questions was suggested as 'focal points for discussion and reading' ... In fact the first session did not concentrate on *Summerhill* but ranged over a number of ideas generated from reading, prior thinking and the immediate experiences within the schools. (Cleo)

It might be better once I start teaching. We seem to repeat a lot of work ... all at a verbal level ... As I haven't done much teaching yet I'm not meeting problems in practice so it's not meaningful. (student)

215

I am learning the basics, reaching upwards ... Curriculum Studies is up in the air ... working down ... I'm caught up with immediate teaching ... wanting to fix those problems. (student)

Sydney Road

The first discussion was based on the question of what students saw as the main 'dilemmas' in the school ... This was followed by two sessions at which discussions were led by two teachers ... who were involved in establishing the school ... Commenting on this last session, a ... staff member said: 'any number of significant issues were raised' but the students 'seemed silent' ... 'the significant things ... didn't make much impact on the students at the time'. At the 4th session ... proposals included a division ... into two sections, the first focusing on teaching problems, the second a discussion of readings and Depth Study Research. (Cleo)

I'm in two minds. It's great to have a theory to cling to ... It means nothing in terms of classroom practice at present. (student)

There's not nearly enough reference to what is happening in the school ... particular kids, and the problems in handling ... (the basic) philosophical questions [that] arise ... We should work from the kids up not from Graubard down. (student)

(Cleo notes, 'It was not that she didn't want to read. On an earlier occasion she said: "every time I find a book like Graubard I eat it up."')

Trinity

The first discussion was based on an exploration of their own educational experiences which helped to get some perspective on things valued. The following two were based on impressions and observations of teachers within the school and the issue of 'language across the curriculum' was raised in this context. Next came a discussion of some scripts of recorded lessons and science teachers' texts. At this point, a sense of absence of enthusiasm led to a decision to ... draw up a plan as a co-operative effort. This began with a discussion on Illich's ideas which were of particular interest to the student who led it and according to three informants was a very worthwhile session ... (Cleo)

It is noteworthy that two students who were uncertain about the value of C.S. sessions both found the early discussions on language across the curriculum very valuable ... they drew on their own observations of language usage ... and this is one of the staff member's areas of special interest and working knowledge. The following session based on scripts from an unfamiliar context was less successful. (Cleo)

Flemington

The two initial sessions were concerned with getting to know one another ... and on exchange of past educational experience and of present aspirations as teachers ... The staff member regarded the exchange of autobiographies as critical in developing the basis of group work. The students I interviewed confirmed its importance. Following sessions helped students to become familiar with the school and its area directly ... For example, video-tape of a simulated 'class lesson' with 'F2 recalcitrants' made by Doug Robb ... provoked a worthwhile conversation about management ... and its connection with the ... content of courses. (Cleo)

The early sessions in the schools were thus not without their difficulties, and those difficulties were of a similar kind to the ones we had experienced at the University. Cleo, for example, produces eloquent evidence of the split in student opinion about structure. In all four schools the staff were in as much conflict as we ourselves had been on this issue. Like us, they all knew the importance of structure and a sense of direction, but like us, they were also feeling their way toward attaining this without imposing their own firm ideas too heavily – without making students feel there was no room for their own influence.

Despite the inexperience of the school group leaders (who were in much the position which we had been in in our first year), they had the advantages of smaller groups with a ready-made basis for cohesiveness in that they were all working together in the one school, and they were surrounded by the more commonly identifiable problems faced by each particular school. There can be little doubt that our conclusion over the four years was strengthened by the new departure – that students, however academic, wanted to move from practical towards theoretical concerns, not the other way round; and the best starting structure was found by drawing on the students' own memories and knowledge, and guiding their observations towards extending their knowledge in a way that was available to them all – for example, at Trinity by listening to the classroom language and at Flemington by seeing a classroom lesson on TV.

Beyond that, as Cleo observed, the community schools offered a cohesive structure in themselves, and all teachers felt themselves identified with the new programme in the school. In the two big schools this was not so. At Flemington, for example, one student noted that 'for the 1st month we all felt isolated from the rest of the school'. Another said, 'Among supervising teachers there is a great variation in commitment to teacher training – can see the need to hold a meeting with them.' Alas, a desirable and constructive idea, but one which was

217

unlikely to do much, for the whole structure militated against its success. In such a big school, cohesiveness of staff would be found in pockets around some concern that bound only a particular group, and our students would have been moving in and out of various 'sub-communities' within the one school. The effect on the Curriculum Studies group worried Lloyd, who was new to the school, and, as one student commented, 'Students' interest is closely centred on their individual work hence it is important to get a corporate thing going.' This meant, I think, that each student found himself in a number of separate sections, or 'sub-communities', and was so busy trying to find his place in each that it militated against the cohesion of the student group as a whole.

Cleo noted that John Brennan felt the same difficulty at Trinity. Each student, he observed, was self-conscious about his personal commitment and what excited him about teaching. The way to discover these things was by working with a teacher who had found the answer for himself; but, John added, 'a group is needed so that students are not "dominated by supervising teachers".'

A further difficulty arose from too strong a 'discipleship'. The schools, as Cleo observed, had varying success in 'capturing the students'. At Trinity, they tended to be captured by the magnetism of individual supervisors who had a great deal to offer. At Sydney Road they tended to be captured by the magnetism of the school as a corporate body that presented the absorbing problems of a small group committed to its pupils and to an experimental educational endeavour; but the interesting thing about the seductiveness of the schools was that, once we placed Curriculum Studies in them, there was an intensification of the appeal to the students of what we were offering at the University. My most faithful attenders at history Method were the students from these two schools, and at the end of the year it was students from these two schools who insisted that we must set up a structure within the University that would draw them to it. This was *not* a criticism of their schools, but a feeling that the University could and should offer something more than Methods that would bring together University staff and the students from various schools. The earlier tendency in some cases was reversed. In some schools the students tended to 'skip' Curriculum Studies in the school in order to attend options that were offering at the University instead of the other way round.

None of this is to cast doubt on the wisdom of making Curriculum Studies school-based. Despite my experience of it for only one year, I should not reverse that, and my successors have not done so. What they have done instead is to provide a new focus at the University – a Tuesday morning session for all students, in which students from each school take responsibility in turn to run a session for all the others, and this, I hear, works very well indeed. The suggestion came primarily from the 1976 students at Sydney Road and Trinity.

It may seem worrying that, by giving each school curriculum group so much control over that central component of our Course, Curriculum Studies, we risked the possibility that absolutely crucial areas of study would be ignored. It was a risk that the staff of Course B took. It is a quaint worry, except when one is dealing with the lunatic fringe, yet it is a worry that occupies a tremendous amount of time, thought and energy in Britain at the moment. The central government, it is said, must make sure that children are not short-changed in their education. It is their right to learn the 'basics' − the three Rs − and the cer.•.al things about their society that will enable them to operate effectively in it, and they must also understand the role of science and technology in making the world as it is and as it will be. At that level of generality surely there can be no dispute − and no need for dictation from the centre. What school would argue against all or any of those things? Certainly none that I know.

In the more rarified atmosphere of teacher training for secondary teachers it is similarly said that every prospective teacher ought to know about child psychology; learning theory; the determinants of the culture; the democratic and political constraints to innovation; the moral issues such as indoctrination, academic freedom, and equality; the techniques of evaluation of learning; the modes of school and class organization; and certainly the essence of his own teaching subjects − to name just a few of the things that 'EVERY TEACHER OUGHT TO KNOW'. What teaching institution would argue against all or any of those things? Certainly none that I know.

But come down to how do you do it and what do you select as the best exemplars and we must all fall apart. It's like a questionnaire. The best answer could be revealed by asking everyone every question that mattered, and we'd end up with a census that tells us a great deal about statistics but nothing about how Lou Soccio feels living in Australia or England or America as one of a migrant family. Similarly one could make an exhaustive list of what everyone ought to know, make sure that nothing slipped through the net and end up with a shadowy conspectus but 'a little learning'.

In curriculum planning, as in learning to teach, one must be prepared to live dangerously and to risk gaps, rather than to plan safely and to plug all gaps come what may and thus spread the coverage very thinly indeed. Those who are critical of my approach, if they have read as far as this, will now be critical of our concern to draw on student opinion. Certainly the danger we ran was of being unduly influenced by passing moods and fickle criticisms; but experience helped to remedy our misreading of student opinion. Even so, our greater worry was the tendency

219

of students to endure politely and to sit through boredom uncomplainingly. Few ever thoroughly unlearned this habit that school and university had made second nature, and it would have been blind arrogance not to take note when our most academic students pointed out that they gained most by moving upwards from actual behaviour or from incidents that set them thinking.

What is interesting is that different lecturers and teachers, working dynamically with their own particular groups in school-based Curriculum Studies, tended to take different routes but ended up with much the same destinations. Let us take two Curriculum Studies programmes — one from a community school, Sydney Road (SRCS), the other from a large high school, Flemington:

Sydney Road
Term 1
A   *Dilemmas in teaching at SRCS*
 (i) Indoctrination and commitment
 (ii) Education for society/individual
 (iii) Pupil responsibility — the will to learn
 (iv) What experiences are educative?
B   *The origins and development of the school*
 (i) Traditional schooling — the hidden curriculum
 (ii) Community access and curriculum reform
 (iii) Freedom
 (iv) General Studies
 (v) Process of change — role of theory, General Studies, critical analysis, bureaucracy and survival, forms of government
C   *The Romantic Tradition*
 (i) Childhood
 (ii) Freedom as an aim and method
D   *The developing political purpose*
     The cultural group, cultural consciousness, curriculum as practice, 'social judgment is political knowledge', the 'how' is also the 'what'

Term 2
E   *What to teach: the disciplines*
 (i) Social origins of knowledge
 (ii) Objective reality — logical structure
F   *The process view*
     Syntactic/substantive
G   *Moral education*
 (i) Stages of development
 (ii) Values and dogma

220

(iii) Teaching of a unit by the team
H   *Expressive arts in a free school*

Term 3
I   *The committed teacher in a 'participatory democracy'*
  (i) Beyond Freire
 (ii) The working-class curriculum
(iii) Alternative sixth-form courses [i.e. not for Higher School Certificate]
J   *Language and learning*
      The 'expressive function'
K   *Personal ideologies*

Flemington (in less detail)
Term 1
A   *Getting to know one another*
  (i) Educational autobiographies
 (ii) Present aspirations as teachers
B   *Getting to know the school*
  (i) A tour of the Flemington area
 (ii) Different sections in the school, with meetings held in those different areas
(iii) Issues raised by the school experience as a basis for future planning — Form 2, the relationship between class management and the content of lessons, literacy problems and the possibility of language across the curriculum

Term 2
C   *It's a big wheel to move*
  (i) Some ways in which the word 'curriculum' is interpreted in secondary school
 (ii) Changing attitudes towards curriculum in Victorian secondary schools 1947–77
(iii) Equal opportunity for education — a bigger mess than ever?
D   *'Conformity is the main subject taught'*
  (i) Discipline in the classroom — some short cuts
 (ii) The hidden curriculum
(iii) School politics
 (iv) A little sociology is better than none
  (v) Deviance and deviants — at the governor's pleasure
E   *'A drop in the ocean?'*
  (i) Alternatives attempted in schools — General Studies and 'soft-cops'
 (ii) Some alternatives attempted at other schools

(iii) Panel discussions with teachers who have helped set up community or free schools

Term 3
Topics from which to select
The total school curriculum. Will you have a say?
Planning one's own courses in practice. What will you be trying to do?
Radical educational thought in practice
'How is also what'
Assessment
Future shock: teaching in the 1980s
The literacy issue: Panic or panacea?
Somewhere over the rainbow
              or,
There's a grey lock or two in the brow of her hair
There's some silver in mine too, I see
I've been sent to the wrong school
              or,
Ways of staying sane in 1978
It's easier in the country — visit to a country high school

Note that both courses began with an examination of the school and moved outwards to put curriculum and educational change into an historical setting. Both were concerned with freedom and conformity, and the sociological, political influences on change. Both were concerned with curriculum planning. Both were concerned with the 'how' and the 'what' as two sides of the one coin and not, as so many educational platitudes would have it, as a dichotomy. Both were concerned with language development (and both schools happen to have a large migrant intake as well as Australian-born children with grave literacy problems). And, if it looks as if Flemington was less concerned with psychological and ideological issues, this would be because the school-based programme was being run in conjunction with University-based weekly sessions which included both these studies. Of course the two groups of students would not end the year having given identical emphasis to identical things, or having covered an identical reading course — but why should they?

Reading a programme tells only a fraction of what actually happened, and one of the inevitable variables will be that their teachers' style and interests would not be identical. What, however, importantly emerges is that in their quite separate ways they shared so much. It may appear that Flemington's programme was more practical and personal, in, say, its concern to prepare students for their first year out, yet it was a Sydney Road student who related his own development to Brecht's, showing (as the student put it) an early sceptical, anarchic, bitter, romantic dilettante and condescending attitude being replaced later by one of classical restraint which embodies deeply felt values:[5]

I'm polite and friendly to people. I put on
A hard hat because that's what they do.
I say: they are animals with a quite peculiar smell
And I say: does it matter? I am too.

and in a later poem:[6]

Who built Thebes of the seven gates?
In the books you will find the names of kings.
Did the kings haul up the lumps of rock?
And Babylon, many times demolished
Who raised it up so many times? In what houses
Of gold-glittering Lima did the builders live?
Where, the evening that the Wall of China was finished
Did the masons go? Great Rome
Is full of triumphal arches. Who erected them? Over whom
Did the Caesars triumph? Had Byzantium, much praised in song
Only palaces for its inhabitants? Even in fabled Atlantis
The night the ocean engulfed it
The drowning still bawled for their slaves.

By putting Curriculum Studies in some of the schools we did, to a large extent, achieve what we thought we would. The unexpected result of the first year was that a positive proposal was put forward by many of the students in those schools suggesting the kind of help they wanted from the University. A planning group worked on this and out of it grew a fairly precise demand for the University to provide a regular forum and some connecting theoretical threads, and so the Tuesday morning session began. This, too, I understand (during 1977 I was not there) was carried out with the closest collaboration between school and University staff.

Supervision

The new structure of Curriculum Studies helped to clarify in our minds what students saw as the academic role of the University, but there was always one facet of our work where there was more demand for us than we could ever meet – and that was as supervisors and consultants in the schools. Some of us might have had less credibility for students than some of the teachers, yet our school visits were for students an important link with the University, and mostly we appeared to bring in something of the world they were familiar with and to be welcome even when their supervising teacher was exemplary.

Our visits were most profitable when we could work effectively with the supervising teacher and the student in joint consultation. Our visits were crucial when there was hostility or even lack of confidence between student and teacher. This inescapable role made school visits extremely delicate if we were not to intensify the suspicion between teachers and University that we were so anxious to combat. It was Lloyd who talked about the importance of increasing our contact with schools if we were to break through; but this meant broadening the old role of supervision. As Lloyd put it, it would no longer do for the students and schools to see 'uni staff (apparently) blowing in to scan a lesson'.

The perceptive comments of staff who were closest to actual school teaching, like Lloyd, were invaluable. Ray Daniels, who in 1976 was given a half-time position with us, the other half being as a teacher at Williamstown High School, spent much of his time with me in history Method, but backed up his Method work by undertaking a great deal of school supervision. He applauded our approach to supervision. One of the reasons why he found Course B better than other courses he was familiar with was that

> it doesn't do some of the unpleasant things that other courses do – assess students competitively, observe students from behind one-way glass, prescribe masses of reading in educational theory before students know what a classroom smells like ...
> The school-based nature of the course encourages students to work closely together in schools. The concern among students in some schools for each other's teaching and well-being in the school was remarkable.

And when we had a close relationship with a school we could help to foster that, though we could not force it. Despite Ray's appreciation of the way we went about supervision, he still found it the least satisfactory part of his work:

> It was a simple matter to visit a student in a school and offer an opinion on the lesson, to offer encouragement, sympathy, or advice on how to deal with difficulties over a supervisor, a text-book, an excursion or a class. Although the students were always glad to discuss such things, in some way it never seemed enough. Students were aware of the course's assessment policy yet it was difficult to break down the sense that some judgment was being expected and offered. The solution to the problems I discovered in this area seems to me to lie in actually working with the student (or a group of students and

their kids) so that the role of the visitor for whom some sort of 'performance' is put on has to be eliminated.

This was so right, and reminded me of a funny but revealing incident during my first visit to Flemington. I visited one of our students who was taking a third form for elementary economics. When I walked out of the class, I stood by the door trying to work out where to go next, and I heard a small voice inside say, 'Don't worry, miss. You can relax now she's gone. Who *is* she anyway?' It was extremely unlikely that that could have happened the following year when I was fully attached to Flemington for at least a day a week in first term. Then I gradually came to know the supervisors; I would take my share of the teaching when the classes were engaged in group work; and I was regarded as part of the furnishings by pupils, students and teachers. Even so, that is only part of Ray's point. When one of our most dedicated and scholarly students, for example, was having trouble, as he himself put it, 'getting out of the university syndrome' — lecturing, failing to see when the pupils lacked the background knowledge to make sense of abstractions, and burdening them with a logically presented array of information that they could not possibly grasp with the speed of the exposition — no amount of supervision from the teachers, from Ray or from me seemed to have any effect, although the criticisms were all apparently understood. Ray then took him to his school for a term. The pupils were far less academic and the student would have come a cropper, after the patience and motivation of the pupils he had been teaching, if he and Ray had not taught together, planning every move and encountering every difficulty in action together.

As university staff we became more credible both to students and to teachers in the schools when we taught with the students, both in the planning behind the scenes and in the actual teaching. Need I say that although it was a hard test it was also very good indeed for *us*? It was Rod Fawns of the core staff, at the beginning straight from school teaching, who adopted this role most naturally and gave the lead. He so loved school teaching (as all the core staff did) that he could not resist it when it offered — or resist finding ways to make it available when they were not already there. Thus in the first year of the Course, he, the supervising teachers (John Brennan and Brian McFarlane) and a team of our students at Trinity 'took over' a large portion of fifth-form General Studies in third term and devised 'the Island course' that became legendary. They shipwrecked the class on an imaginary island with a chest full of belongings. The class divided itself into groups, each one setting off in a different direction, and, as each group moved out, further information about the island was disclosed to them by the staff. They did mapping, they kept logs, they learned how to survive with the natural resources they found, they bickered, they re-formed their group-ings to restore harmony, they fantasized, they evolved their own enter-tainments — what did they *not* do? Footnote to *Lord of the Flies*, perhaps, but it was a most generative and imaginative programme, though not without its faults. The project was written up and evaluated in a depth study that ran into hundreds of pages.

We have never again quite equalled that as a team-teaching project; but we did become engaged in many school activities. Bernie, bravely following a visit of Dorothy Heathcote, tried to adopt her drama methods with pupils. This was valuable to students early in the year, for they could see what worked and where difficulties lay, thus feel-ing less threatened themselves. Rod and Terry Werner worked with a group of teachers and students at Bentleigh High School introducing a first-form General Studies programme based on the materials available in Bruner's 'Man: a Course of Study'. I taught sixth-form social studies at Sydney Road with a student who was an honours graduate in Political Science. Rod did a good deal of science teaching at Sydney Road, and in 1976 and 1977 was working towards linking science with drama, starting with Brecht's *Galileo*. In another case, Flemington's deputy principal asked the Course B staff if they would work with a panel of teachers who hoped to link an intensive first-form programme for language development with the main subjects in the curriculum. Doris Cosopodiotis, our English Method lecturer, Elizabeth Dines, a socio-linguist, Lloyd Jones, the staff and I started with preliminary planning and conferences, and despite Elizabeth Dines's difficulty in construct-ing a satisfactory research design and of obtaining the research support she needed, the work is now taking shape.

Some of the schools attached to us would be astonished to read all this, for in some of them we did not get beyond the point of ordinary supervision, and with a few our communications were very poor. It was only natural that, with our sensitivity about moving into schools, we grasped appreciatively the schools that made us feel that we had a con-tribution to make. Terry Werner's diary, for example, shows that he spent at least half a day each week at Bentleigh, not only planning the Bruner classes, but sometimes spending an hour and a half with one student who was seriously disturbed, and turning up for meetings between teachers and students. The diary also includes references to night phone calls from troubled students (don't I remember them!) and, in general, hassles. To be realistic, for the University staff to be able to meet the demands of proper contact with schools, Education staff-student ratios at the University have to be improved, and the schools have to be able to appoint more people like Lloyd and Ray, and to give supervisors the conditions that make it possible for them to take seriously their responsibility toward students — their future colleagues.

Even when supervision from the University and from teachers is of the most traditional kind, the problem of what makes for good supervision is an extremely elusive one which is as subtle for the teacher as discovering one's teaching style is for the student. Schools kept asking us for precise specifications of our expectations of supervisors. We did, from time to time, say that we expected the student to have taught X number of lessons by the end of first term and things like that. But to lay down the principles of good supervision was another matter. The good supervisor could have told us as much as we could tell him though his methods might not have worked for other sorts of teachers. With the bad supervisor it was like being asked to write soufflé recipes for somebody who couldn't make white sauce and didn't want to learn. Prescriptions from us would have insulted good supervisors and would have had little influence on the rest. We resisted this request, fearing that it would have disaffected our best supervisors, thus decreasing our chances of establishing really good relationships with them. We did eventually write a sort of pragmatic document for discussion, based on our understanding of what students found helpful or unhelpful.

Students wanted to be part of the normal life at the school, and seldom objected to taking extras or even unpleasant duties; but it is hard to be definite about the wisdom of schools which suddenly, without warning, give our students lessons, simply to fill a gap. It is deplorable, for example, to give students the idea that teaching can be done 'off the cuff', even though all teachers are sometimes forced to do this. Certainly with students early in the year it is a brutal thing to do unless they have something already prepared that they can use and adapt. Students' reactions to being treated as a normal member of staff in this manner will vary. A teacher who was constantly dobbing students in for impromptu lessons could make them most resentful about being 'used' selfishly, and being exploited. Janet, for example, within her first fortnight at school, was initially contemptuous but later pleased – not with the supervisor but with herself – when called on to take a lesson. She felt totally at sea at the school. Nobody had shown any interest in her subject, and she felt utterly lost and useless: 'They are "dead", and I do not feel as if I should have to become one of them.' She found it difficult to raise enough enthusiasm for going to school. 'I can't understand it!' she commented in her diary. 'I am never half-hearted about things.' The next day her entry read:

> My reaction to these people has not changed. Because there is no
> one to look after a certain class, I have been asked to take the lesson
> (15 minutes notice, mind you! Completely impromptu). I treated
> this as a challenge.
>
> The lesson which dealt with graphs was very successful, much to

my surprise. I am pleased because I have achieved this on my own.
These pupils … keep asking me am I going to be their new teacher!

The resentment remained; but her ability, when so green, to take an
impromptu lesson such as this was founded on her familiarity with, and
confidence in, her topic — though that was the last thing that had concerned the supervisor. It was sheer chance.

It was perhaps also chance that set Penny up — a misunderstanding
between her and her supervisor (Alec) about the time of the lesson. In
this case she and another student, Maureen, had prepared to teach
together. Penny commented:

I became really bubbly and happy — feel really good. I suppose this
all started off with Alec arriving in 2nd period saying, 'Hey, aren't
you taking this lesson?' So Maureen and I went to the lesson and did
part of what we'd talked about last night — it was really great. Alec
left the class and we got on really well with the kids — really super.
Spent some time later discussing how we would continue.

Possibly Alec was shrewder than Penny knew and deliberately sprang
the lesson on her so that she did not have time to be anguished, for
Penny was an extremely diffident student. This was a very different
story from Janet's. Alec and Penny had been working together for
several weeks. Penny knew his classes a little from observation and from
taking some small groups for parts of the work within his lesson.
Maureen, her friend and a more confident girl, worked with her. Alec
had perceptively seen that Penny would move less nervously into teaching if she and Maureen taught together, and he had the sensitivity to
leave the students to it once he had introduced the lesson to the class.

In a community school it was easy to teach in tandem with the
supervisor and to observe him with shared classes, showing in action
how some of the pitfalls the student experienced could be avoided.
This, of course, can be done by good supervisors in any school, and in a
big school the use of parallel classes can be very valuable. Students
found that being a participatory observer was most helpful, for it is
while the two are in action together that the student is more likely to
notice some of the finer points in teaching that might escape him as an
inactive novice. Just sitting in the back of the class can be fairly meaningless or, with a specially talented teacher, somewhat intimidating. We
gave students sheets with pointers to guide their observation, and we
discussed these from time to time; but the most valuable sort of observation comes from a partnership between student and supervisor;
and students often gained a great deal from going in pairs to observe,
and from observing each other.

Eric, at one of the small community schools, pointed to the help he gained from team-teaching with his supervisor who, early in the year, took the major part in the lessons, thus naturally and easily providing meaningful observation:

> I have been fortunate ... to have been under the continual supervision of an experienced humanities teacher who is always approachable ... and exceedingly informative about subject materials and resources. When team-teaching [with her] she is normally the one who does the most work in actually preparing the lesson and teaching ... I draw an immense amount of energy through witnessing her teaching technique.

Knowing when to stay and when to leave is a matter of fine discrimination for a supervisor. Another very unconfident student, Helen, was greatly helped by Jim Noonan, an inspired teacher and supervisor at Williamstown Technical School, who asked Helen first to take small groups within his classes and, as she gained confidence, small sections of his lessons until eventually she was ready to take whole lessons. He planned carefully ahead of time with her, and he helped her to use strategies that would save her if she suddenly lost her nerve. He did this by having materials available and planning possible tasks should she 'dry up' or the class become too restless. He had detailed and encouraging discussions with her after every lesson until she was adventurous enough to try very difficult lessons on her own — running a whole discussion period with unruly boys.

'Jim', she said, 'is a terrific teacher ... because I am constantly able to learn from him. After every lesson he tells me how I went and fills me in on what I should do. I am no longer as nervous as I used to be.' Jim was so good that the best thing for us to do was to keep out and not to increase the ordeal, but Helen then asked for us to come and see her:

> X came out on Wednesday morning. I wasn't overkeen on having an extra person sit in on the class, but ... I wanted someone from the Course to see how I was going. X was really beaut. She saw that I was nervous and so went out and came back when the lesson had got started ... She was very encouraging after seeing my lesson and criticized things that I knew myself I was doing but hadn't actually verbalized — like using words that were too long. Things will straighten out with experience, I was told.
>
> Anyway that week at school was an enjoyable one. I had a terrific teacher in Jim who always has something nice to say to encourage you along. He even knows how to criticize without making you feel bad. I have learnt a lot from him and I couldn't be more grateful.

It is comparatively easy for a visiting member of University staff to sense when his presence is making a student speechless; but for the class supervisor it is not so easy. He has the worry of whether the class will get out of hand and then of how he is to restore calm without undermining the authority of the student. Jim seemed to know intuitively just what to do by gradually setting up a lesson that would work for both student and pupils. By anticipation and prevention he avoided having to interfere in the lesson. Early on, he organized the lessons so that Helen took over from him, as planned, and this made it perfectly natural for him to resume before things started to fall apart.

It would be misleading to pretend that this is an easy thing to do. Nearly every school Principal is bothered by just this problem with new members of staff who have difficulties with class management. With students it is easier to set up a workable plan, but students did complain of feeling demoralized by their too helpful supervisors, as the following diary extracts from five different student show:

1 First week back I have a history class with whom I am dead chuffed. The lesson was so undisciplined (my fault — let them get away and couldn't put the brakes on) that the teacher got up and gave a Don't be cruel to the student teacher type speech which was full of subtle threats. Anyhow I struggled on till the bell went having lost all enthusiasm and just wanting to get out of the place ... Last week I went in and sat on the desk and told them a story about Rommel and Hitler, followed by an explanation of why and how power is such an important concept in history. They sat in silence for 20 minutes and not an alien silence that had followed their teacher's tirade two weeks before but an interested silence. After that they split into their play-writing groups.

2 Lesson commenced. Peggy hadn't arrived and so I had them to myself (which I haven't often had) and there was no Peggy to undermine my authority by stepping in and disciplining the class (which she often does when I'm satisfied with their behaviour anyway).

3 Straight after that came 6C form again. I dictated the questions on Education and *Dibs*, and then Paul simply took over the lesson, which made me feel really foolish. I think he felt I couldn't cope because of the experience in the period before, but all the same I felt as if I had to put my hand up to contribute to the class discussion.

4 K tends to stick up too much for me, not realizing that I am not as unresilient as I may seem. He threw one boy out for muttering something under his breath that K could not have even guessed

at ... It is embarrassing to have someone superior make a scene ... I settled down after about a quarter of an hour.

5 None of the kids behaved ... and my supervisor was away and so another fellow came in to take the extra. This fellow is supposed to be the school's 'ideal' man — all my little 1st form twitty girls just about went into raptures when this fellow walked in — the boys were just plain scared ... they wavered between chaos and cowering silence ... One revolting little girl kept saying, 'What are we keeping quiet for now he's gone? We should scream and yell' (her words faithfully recorded), whereupon several delightful children screamed and yelled.

These comments are, of course, just one side of the story; but there is no doubt that students feel belittled by a supervisor's unplanned intervention, however well-intentioned it might be, as it presumably was in 1 and 4. Example 2 shows, as an earlier example has done, that a student may sometimes benefit when the supervisor is out of the room and that class management might be better — not worse as predicted. Example 3 I know most about, and can imagine how anxious the supervisor might have been to avoid a second catastrophe; but to proceed from one disastrous lesson to the next, without having worked out some strategy for unobtrusively helping the student, and then just to take the lesson away from him seems insensitive to say the least.

Subtle points like this require far more examination and discussion than they are usually given. Supervision is a highly complex form of teaching, but one that receives little attention. Some students' diaries are studded with comments about the constructive help that supervisors give, as Jim Noonan gave Helen. I can recall one where the student had a nervous tic that made teaching extremely risky and painful. His supervisor not only supported the student and guided him into techniques that safeguarded him, but she did a great deal towards helping him overcome the nervous tic itself. By contrast, there were (fortunately extremely rare) examples of the supervisor who was an incorrigible cynic or sadist.

With the cynic, the student is possibly better protected than are his pupils — witness this, the worst example that I encountered:

Our first full day at school. I was assigned to Mrs S. for the whole year. She gave me some hints on how to teach: namely to be harsh and stern, to correct essays by reading the introduction and conclusion and to be as little involved with the children and geography as was possible. I could see that we were going to get on splendidly (wrong!). After recess I sat at the back of her first form class whom she had told to read p. 8 of the rather simplified account of the Nile in their book. She then asked some questions of the class, drew a picture of a pyramid on the blackboard and the period ended.

Her double period in the 5th form was even more enlightening: she spent the entire hour writing notes on the blackboard. This woman, I could see, was determined to make geography as dull and irrelevant as she possible could without jeopardizing her standing as the senior teacher ...

I was irritated and infuriated by her mistreatment of geography. She gave me the twelve class essays to correct (the 5th form) and I am to take a double period tomorrow. Her instructions: to spend the first period returning the essays and the second reading a chapter from a book. My God! So much for 4 years at University seeking a meaning to geography.

Need it be said that teaching from pupils' written work can be a most valuable learning experience? But to make it so required a close examination of the pupils' work, decisions about the weaknesses that needed remedying and the strengths that might be commended, and some suggestions for a new student about how to conduct the lesson.

This supervisor did not harm the students, who tended to learn what they could from her by negatives; but the full weight of supervision fell on University staff. The students could see what was wrong but they found it difficult to replace it with anything constructive. It was the pupils who were most to be pitied, for this teacher was headed for promotion, and I cannot resist mentioning that her close friends in the school were those who were most active in the movement for 'restoring educational standards' in Australian schools — the Australian equivalent of the English Black Paper movement.

One advantage with the cynical, selfish teachers like Mrs S. is that they tend to ignore students, while at the same time using them. Thus they are less likely to tread on explosive ground than are the bitch supervisors, who also, fortunately, are extremely rare. There was one supervisor in our four years who persecuted and nearly destroyed a capable and apparently confident student, Brigit. A few snippets from her diary throughout the year tell the story:

18 April

3P were next and at this stage I was feeling slight nausea. I marched into the classroom ... determined to be on good terms with the kids no matter what! And they were so good ... I strutted into the staffroom feeling absolutely terrific only to be reminded that the children didn't really know anything and weren't interested in the work. What can I do? I was overjoyed that for me they weren't a discipline problem; but after talking to Sadie ... my enthusiasm was almost down to zero.

232

<u>10 May</u>
John [a fellow-student] gave me a vivid description of what had
gone around the night before. Apparently Sadie has 'spread the
word' that I'm lazy ... Me lazy! You can call me everything else but
that. I nearly cried except for the fact that ... kids were having a
meeting in the same room.

<u>10 June</u>
Searched for Jean and Sadie, for they had a search party out for me:
found them. Talk about a session with the gestapo! YES it was so
bad that my health was inquired after, I was so pale ... At least now
I have my time-table.

> Sadie: I hope you work as hard as John. I had a great time last
> term when I had him, I got so much work done.

We can skip the repeated jottings of this kind, and go to the finale:

<u>18 July</u>
Sadie beckoned me to her [room] and there we went through all the
lesson plans of the ... year and she insisted on reading <u>every</u> one of
the comments after each lesson. Talk about no respect for one's
privacy! ... I was purple ...

Later ... Sadie walks in with her report all typed out ready to
hand in. She asked what I thought and I gave her my opinion on
some things. [The other teachers] read it too and I later found out
that both were shocked and thought, 'It's the most negative report
I've ever read.'

A few of Sadie's written comments after Brigit's *first* lesson in the
subject will suffice to show what a negative report can look like. The
opening statement reads:

You asked 'Has there been a change in this sentence.' Of course
you'll get 'the boy ... they'. Elicit more information from the class
... You told Mark the adjective for 'feast' after you had asked him
... Beware of the blackboard organization – you can erase, you
know.

Compare this with the supervisor who writes:

One of the hardest things to do with a class is to wait for answers
and to be prepared to reword your question if you suspect they have
not understood or cannot answer. When Mark seemed not to know
the adjective for 'feast', you might have tried him with an easier one,
such as 'response', to encourage him and then have seen if the class
could have worked out 'festive'. You could have used the blackboard
to help you further by listing sentences with nouns that take the '-ive'

233

ending in the adjectival form, and under them have had sentences with a blank for pupils to try to fill in the adjectival form.

Sadie's comments presuppose the application of skills that no teacher in her first lesson could be expected to have or even to understand unless they were well spelt out. Anyone can talk in generalities, for example, about organizing the blackboard, but one needs more than generalities, let alone sarcasm, to learn how to do it. Brigit was in deep trouble which got worse, not better. The criticisms confused her and seemed so unjust that she had no help in putting her finger on where her troubles lay. Unknown to Sadie, during the year Brigit visited eleven schools and attended a university conference, all in search of up-to-date and effective teaching methods in Sadie's subject. Brigit knew that she was not lazy, and so how much credence could she place in the other comments? She became so rattled that when a sympathetic supervisor, Rosemary, took her over and noted that her trouble was lack of confidence, she was relieved.

Brigit's diary also reveals that Sadie had discussed her before fellow-students, behind her back. It can be profitable for a student's difficulties to be discussed with other students, but only if the student in difficulty knows that the others are all on side, all have similar sorts of difficulties, and it is not a matter of 'holier than thou'. In this case, personal comparisons were made — indeed mischief was made — that were hurtful and that threatened to split the group of students at that school. They, themselves, transcended it, thus showing rather more maturity than their supervisor; but although that example, I must stress, is very rare, it points to the danger of appointing teachers, let alone supervisors, who are so lacking in tact and sensitivity — and who resort to hasty moral judgments as well as to destructive criticisms based on personality.

We have seen how a later supervisor rescued Brigit by recognizing that her trouble was not laziness but was undermined confidence. Because this assessment was true, just, and so much less defeating than false judgments, it helped Brigit. But even such a personal comment must be used warily. An extract from Penny's diary shows the razor's edge that we tread as supervisors, and that personal comments should always be made in a constructive, friendly way, concentrating first on what happened rather than on what sort of figure the student has cut. This would seem to be the best approach with an aggressive student; was so with Brigit, who to an imperceptive supervisor seemed abundantly confident; and it was certainly so of the reticent, shy student like Penny, who described Bernie's visit to the school in these words:

> [My] lesson was OK but lacked any clear questions. Also different sections didn't relate to one another very well and overall purpose only became evident at the end. Bèrt, Bernie, Maureen and I talked

about the lesson in detail which continued through lunch and got on to objectives of Course B — really quite heavy and topped off by ob-servation and recognition of my unconfident manner which may lead to hassles next year — being 'introverted'. Shouldn't really have affected me but recently have been basically pretty depressed and this tipped me completely because I've really been trying to resolve my personality ... Bernie was really great and incredibly sensitive realizing what had happened — took us to coffee — really appreciate this as it gave me time to get back on an even keel. Lesson in after-noon was better in so far as the kids were asking more questions and our questions appeared to be generally understood — really, really tired and exhausted at end of day, a day full of thinking and ques-tioning of myself.

Personal comment, especially when it has strong moral connotations, can be deeply damaging to students just as it can to pupils and, unless it is based on an analysis of what happens, it is useless to boot. I have referred in passing to the following incident, but the student's sense of helplessness is evident in this diary entry:

Received Sam's report on me. Almost cried. In effect, it said, 'How the bloody hell did he ever get in to the teaching profession? Needs to be more mature, far too cavalier.' Does he realize I am supposedly learning how to teach?

If we only asked ourselves what good our comments could do, we could be frankly critical and yet constructive. How can a student improve when laziness is wrongly diagnosed as her weakness? How can a student suddenly become more mature except by the effluxion of time, which he cannot control? What he needed was not the judgmental label but examples of how he might have better handled situations that he did not understand fully.

There is not much doubt that teachers learn to supervise well in just the way the students learn to teach well, by centring their imagination less on what they are doing themselves than on what is happening to their students/pupils. Good supervision is simply another kind of good teaching. A good supervisor might require the student to submit a lesson plan in advance. Usually this was helpful, though not necessarily by requiring it to fit some usual formula like: Objectives, Materials, Method of Presentation. Similarly, a good supervisor might make a detailed written critique of a lesson. That usually helped, but what mattered much more lay in what was conveyed to the student after-wards in writing *and* by word of mouth.

The good teacher is skilful in the techniques he uses, he knows his material, and he also cares for and is positively aware of, his pupils' learning. Without this last quality he might have partial success but that is all it will be. He may be very bad at analysing why what he does succeeds; but that matters far less than a sensitive intelligence and artistry which he demonstrates in his own teaching both of his pupils and his students. This does not mean that to be a good teacher he has to be inspired, let alone charismatic. Very often the teacher who has had to overcome nervousness (or, worse, dullness) may be the best teacher of pupils and of students. The inspired performer can too easily be satisfied with entertaining pupils, whereas the nervous or dull one has painfully persevered, and through that has much to impart — so long, of course, as he is not a dull *person*.

School organization and school life as educators

Students often found that things only indirectly connected to their actual supervised teaching helped — or hindered — greatly. At some schools, for example, the Principal welcomed them and they were properly introduced to the school and their supervisors: at a few their arrival appeared to be unnoticed, and some did not even meet their supervisors. At some schools they were welcome to attend staff meetings, but not at others. Staff meetings that were concerned with school policies and practices, or considered pupils' progress, stimulated the students' interest in educational theory, and somewhat unexpectedly also seemed to give them something very important to latch on to in thinking about their teaching. Meetings about trivialities — e.g. loose-leaf folders, length of hair — by contrast, foreshadowed for the students a lifetime of petty concerns.

It is a problem in a large school to hold any one sort of weekly or monthly meeting that covers the major matters of school life. Discussion tends to be decentralized into subject meetings or 'year' meetings — or no meetings — and a student teaching across all the years and in two different subjects is hard put to it in the network of organizational discussions to find profitable ones that he can attend. The small community schools, with their soul-searching staff discussions about everything that the school is doing, proved to be one of the most educative things in the year for many students.

Paula, for example, found the weekly meetings at her community school invaluable, for the week's problems were discussed until they were resolved or the staff gave up in exhaustion. 'One gets the impression', she wrote, 'that there is not much likelihood of attitudes or policies ossifying here.' A mature student, and a mother, she compared what happened there with traditional schools: 'there is none of the authoritarian structure that usually dominates relationships' between staff members and even more between staff and pupils. 'The pupils are encouraged to be self-evaluative.' While she found that pedagogical strategies were left very much in the hands of individual teachers, she also found that maths and English teachers, for example, came to each other's help and the barriers that seemed insuperable in many schools were broken down informally by close collaboration. At the end of one meeting that was concerned with pupils' progress and was based on their own evaluations of their progress, she observed, 'This is no child-minding centre.'

At another community school there was a fierce debate about whether the pedagogics in the school were 'going soft', whether there was enough structure in the teaching or too much 'spontaneity', and about the whole question of how one respected migrant or working-class cultures without being inhibited about pushing children to explore wider understanding and unfamiliar values. Some of the student-teachers at this school were extremely intense about these issues, and they prepared a very carefully considered series of statements for the night meeting called to discuss the issue. It went on until morning, and the students could talk of little else for days before and days afterwards. Some of them made a real contribution to the standard of the discussion, and few of them were totally uninfluenced, unchanged, by the very powerful debate.

One of the community schools was uncertain about whether students should attend the school's meetings, fearing that they might stifle the frankness of staff or any criticisms of the school. Late in first term they were invited to a meeting, and Des, a student, wrote in his diary:

> This was certainly both enjoyable and beneficial — if we could have attended one of these earlier it would probably have led to our greater participation in the school much sooner ... In the two or three hours of the meeting it seemed we moved so much closer both to the staff and to some appreciation of the school both as a practical 'institution' and as a collection of theoretical aspirations interpreted in very different ways by the individual staff members. At one stage 'Dip. Eds.' were discussed and we expressed our feelings of 'separateness' in the school. This led to Freddie asking for my help on Wednesday and an awareness of our willingness to participate in and help with whatever subjects, units etc. are running. This was probably the most significant day this term.

Schools that encourage pupils to evaluate their own progress and to work with the teachers in planning their own education provide an invaluable feedback for student-teachers: for example, Eric (pp. 228-9) had nothing but praise for his supervisor, but he found even more

237

instructive the too little tapped resource of pupil opinion. The pupils'
response, when negative, he said, showed

> that they don't appreciate situations in which their time is wasted by
> bad teaching methods ... The bluntness of their expressions ... acts
> as a form of litmus paper ... Kids are more ... pronounced in the art
> of criticism than ... of flattery ... Most of the 'heavy' feed-back ...
> stems from the comments of kids ... and I personally think that is
> the way it should be.

In case it should be feared that 'kids' might be more brutal than even
sadistic teachers, it must be allowed that it depends on the whole mores
of the school. Jack could take frankness from his pupils because it was
not a retaliatory exercise of power on their part. The following extract
from a student's report on his own progress indicates how much the
pupils were 'at one' with him and could thus be frank without being
hurtful. Bert's account I find strangely moving:

> Every six weeks each class has to do a self assessment. Because each
> kid had to do a self assessment I thought it only fair that I should
> too. I told them that the main criticism I had was that I had domi-
> nated the class too much, not in discussion, but in the approach that
> the class made to each topic. We agreed that from now on we should
> have a preparatory lesson before we started a topic to decide how to
> deal with it, and to give an opportunity to those who want to deal
> with it differently to do so. These kids pointed out that I was a
> pretty nervous person and that, while this had decreased, it was still
> there. I thought I had got over it by this time. They thought the sub-
> ject was improving as I adopted the way of the school. As time went
> on they were enjoying the subject more. I feel that these pupils'
> assessment of me is a more competent one than that by any other
> teacher at the school.

Sceptics may doubt the sincerity of that report on school practice; but
it so happens that Bert was one of the students I knew well. I often
joined his lessons and I found them interesting because his preparation
was thoughtful, thorough and stimulating. I enjoyed being a member of
his class. The 'kids' respected his care for their learning, and they took
a professional as well as personal interest in his acquisition of competence
and confidence. Why sceptics might question that true report is that it
is so rare for schools to have broken down the we/they hostility. Bert
had no speech impediment, but he was handicapped by a hesitancy, a
more than momentary inarticulateness, that was close to an impediment.
The pupils valued him for what he had to offer, and they, more than
anyone else, helped him to become more self-assured and to acquire

greater teaching skills. I hope that the next school did not kill him. I don't know.

There are other intangible ways in which 'the school' can do its best to make or break.

The feeling in a staffroom is one of the most revealing barometers of school morale — just the way a knock at the door is received says a good deal. It would be romantic to expect seasoned teachers to share the students' interest in earnest educational talk during lunch and tea breaks, but equally an embargo on 'shop talk' or anything remotely related to it, such as plays or films that 'kids might enjoy and profit from', and an obsessive pursuit of recreations as distant as possible from anything to do with school, students found profoundly disillusioning and disheartening.

Unthinkingly bad school organization would often account for lengthy and exasperated diary entries about chasing around for the key to the room with the equipment that was needed, arriving for a lesson after staying up till 2 a.m. preparing it only to find that the class had gone out to sport, profitlessly searching for hours, sometimes days, seeking resources for a lesson to be taught on some topic for which there were no school materials and the supervisor had no suggestions — and so one could go on.

The centrality of schools

I began this chapter by examining the centrality of school teachers in teacher education. To repeat a truism — a course of education will be only as good as the teachers contributing to it, and their contribution will, in important ways, be influenced by the organization and mores of the school. It tended to be flexible and innovative schools that initially we chose — or chose us. But later, as we expanded into a more usual type of school, being school-based was still preferable to the normal organization of Dip. Ed. I think that most of those schools would say that they preferred our Course, and some would say that they benefited in some ways from it. The Principals of several of those later schools became our most loyal supporters.

In whatever ways students might have criticized the Course, there was no doubt in their minds of support for a school-based course. Even Brigit, who had such unhappy experiences with one supervisor, wrote at the end of her diary:

> So officially ends my course. It has been one hell of a year and experience, but I wouldn't have missed out for anything. And as for ever having done another course that is out of the question.
> AMEN

239

Another student, who had chafed under a cynical, unhelpful supervisor, went to a country school for the three-week round in third term.
It so happened that a number of students from another course were
also on a teaching round there, and the two groups mixed:

> Three week teaching rounds are too short and our stint here demon-
> strated to us students the stupidity of [normal courses]. The other
> students didn't notice this and were only too pleased to have finished
> their practical experience and so to be able to get stuck into half a
> dozen essays, assignments and child psychol. projects which, they
> assured us, were what a Dip. Ed. was really about ... By the end of
> the third week we were just getting to know the pupils and some of
> our best work was being done.

One other example will suffice. Towards the end of second term
Caroline reeled with the news that her lesson load had increased from
five to ten hours:

> Actually I wanted and needed it, and it was surprising how uncomfort-
> able I felt in the new classes which lack the easy-going relationship
> of the other forms. 3 week teaching rounds must be the most use-
> less classroom experience ever devised. You must work fully from
> formulated theory of lesson plans without ever reaching the point of
> prepared improvisation. This comes about from knowing your group
> and having a sense of continuity. It also allows for long-range projects
> which can flow over several lessons, like my 2E history.

Criticisms of school practice came from having too little teaching,
hardly ever from having too much. Caroline's phrase will do very nicely
to catch the essence of what continuous teaching can do for a student
— it can give the context in which 'prepared improvisation' becomes
possible.

Conclusion

It was as difficult to decide where to break into this book as it was to discover how best to break into a teacher-training year. Every consideration was contingent on other ones. Perhaps the book should have started with chapter 2, as I had originally intended, for what was of paramount importance to students was the 'Who am I?' question. Yet to start there might have suggested too much preoccupation with inward-looking personal concerns, and it was important that students were shown to come to terms with the 'Who am I?' question best and most quickly by combining reflexion with looking outwards – by becoming less self-absorbed. This they were helped to do in two main ways – by actually teaching and in particular by beginning to see things through children's eyes, and also by becoming aware of the constraints and possibilities that inhibited or encouraged children's learning. To do this they needed to analyse the educational system, the school as an institution, the society in which the school functioned and the culture of which it was all a part.

Our approach to these broader questions was the most controversial and difficult part of the Course, and this is where the book begins. The growing pessimism throughout the Western world about the effectiveness of introducing educational theory into a teacher-training year, or indeed into concurrent courses, has led on the one hand to a tendency to discard or at least to diminish and postpone theory and on the other hand to a dogged insistence on retaining and strengthening such subjects as educational psychology, sociology and philosophy.

What emerges from the story of Course B over five years is that students, in learning to teach, can learn to learn; indeed, they are forced to be more self-conscious and less self-centred about their own learning. The experience of teaching, as the book's title suggests, helped them to learn about *their own* and others' learning. The discipline required in effective teaching is ready made. Action – that is, having to teach – is

241

its own discipline. In the process students ask increasingly searching questions and set about trying to answer them, not to meet someone else's demands but to meet their own. Hence the title of the book, with its deliberate ambiguity.

Our experience, influenced at first by some overseas universities, confirms my belief that the easiest and most immediate route into meaningful educational theory is through concentration on Methods, in which we could take off from where students were academically strongest. We were right, I believe, to concentrate our staff power on Methods work, and to insist that if that was where the 'how' and the 'what' most readily meet for students, University Methods staff had to get out into the schools with their students. This, rather than more pure theory, was the way towards greater rigour in the academic programme.

Where we had our greatest difficulty was in discovering how to introduce a broader knowledge of educational questions to novice teachers, who had often little, if any, background in political theory, sociology, philosophy or psychology. Our mistakes, and the students' reactions to them, have been dealt with at some length because through them *we* learnt, all too slowly, better ways. Ideological and philosophical questions, indeed any of the major educational questions, could not be forced. We impatiently, and with qualified success, tried to make students anticipate them, whereas experience gradually convinced us that they arose meaningfully and of necessity as the students' school experiences widened. The place to see this happening and to seize on it was in the schools. Our pilot scheme of moving Curriculum Studies (or educational theory, if you like) into some of the schools themselves may well prove to be one of our most important innovations.

We knew that a much more enlightened approach to supervision, both by school and University staff, was needed, and that a much closer, more trusting partnership was absolutely essential in the students' interests. Some of our schools were far more adventurous and thoughtful about educational policies than were some of our staff, though our staff were in a better position to keep abreast of recent literature. Here was the place for making the partnership much more rewarding by having a shared responsibility for a large segment of the academic component of the Course.

The way in which schools and University moved towards each other developed from our growing mutual concern for students, our sometimes separate and sometimes shared stock-taking of what we were achieving, and pragmatism as we dealt with one damned thing after another.

For teacher training to gain greater respect politically, academically and with its consumers — the students — both training institutions and schools must be willing to change. Course B was just as strong as its

242

schools and their teachers. School organization and policy-making must be planned with a full sense of the importance of the education of future teachers as well as of pupils, and teacher-training institutions must recognize that to break free from their ivory towers they are utterly dependent on schools. It is not surprising that the best teachers tended to be the best supervisors; but nothing short of a concerted effort on the part of all concerned can lead us towards sounder educational practices. As Bill Hannan observed after reading the manuscript of this book, 'If little of substance is known about the nature of teaching, less will be known about how to organize training. It's a bit like trying to teach relativity before Einstein formulated it.'

There is little doubt that the low status of Education studies (in the eyes of students, in the school world, and in universities themselves) is not because it is too simple but because it is too complex and too subtle. Our ignorance can force us on to the defensive, leading us to seize on new illuminating ideas, techniques or theories and trying to elevate them into profound truths, but in fact too often turning them into dogmas that lend themselves to faddism. The more that training institutions are out of touch with schools, the greater the danger. Many schools, because of the difficulties of their task and the sometimes insupportable demands that sensitive and thoughtful teachers make of themselves, settle for tried ways, the comfort of conservatism, or even at worst for cynical resignation. Contact with training institutions can provide a new stimulant.

I have not tried to make a judgment about whether Course B's ex-students make uncommonly successful teachers. In the follow-up investigation undertaken by the evaluators of the Course (chapter V of their Report), there is evidence that students did have a conceptual framework that strengthened them, though perhaps became modified, once they fully faced the realities of teaching on their own. There was much evidence of ex-students' taking a great deal of responsibility for planning and innovating. But there is also evidence of some students being defeated by the apathy and rigidity they encounter in their schools. Professor Britton, who returned to England late in 1977 after some months in Australia, has gained the impression that many of the most vital and imaginative teachers whom he met, and they included some he had come to know from Course B during an earlier visit, were leaving teaching, perhaps only temporarily, not because they were disillusioned but because they were exhausted and had to have a break. Others, like Antonio, who has just written to me, find a deadness, but are still trying to fight it. He had, he said, been asked to take a post at a community school, but he thought it might be escapism to accept it. 'It's easy there', he wrote, 'because there isn't the bureaucracy. It's easy where I am because there *is* the bureaucracy that insulates one from real education.' Less resilient young teachers, the evaluation shows, who unluckily were placed in uncongenial schools, were planning to leave teaching, defeated by the rigidities they encountered.

There seems little doubt that the mismatch between teacher training and the school system must be met by more school-based courses which bring the two together and help to invigorate both. It is also significant that Course B ex-students, with the help of University staff, set up their own in-service programmes in their first year out. Each year at least two week-end conferences have taken place. As one teacher put it to the evaluators, they act as a kind of 'generator that you can go back and plug into'. The contact between present students and ex-students has proved most fruitful, and the ex-students, in addition to pursuing various studies that they felt they needed, set themselves up as a group to help present students to prepare themselves for their first year out and later to support them at times of difficulties.

Thus the distinction between pre-service and in-service education tends to be blurred. A school-based course makes abundantly clear to all – to students, schools, University – that a one-year course only begins and never completes a teacher's training. Perhaps, as Bill Hannan suggests, 'teacher training should consist of periods of Course B style spread throughout a teacher's life in the schools', accompanied by 'a flow of trainers into schools and teachers into faculties'.

Meanwhile, Course B has shown one way of beginning to equalize and interchange the roles of teachers and lecturers. From this has come a shared recognition of common problems and the beginnings of attempts to formulate them, even to confront them together. A new respect for the skills and abilities needed in supervision is one. The need for schools and universities to co-operate in planning curriculum and organizations that will break across sub-cultures of subject specialists is another that might well help to mitigate the loneliness and sense of isolation felt by so many first-year teachers. Thus policies during training might flow into induction programmes and vice versa, and another damanging division in the teaching world might become blurred.

The distinction between teacher and student was another that our experiment helped to scrutinize. There are some inequalities that cannot and should not be eliminated, notably the (let us hope) greater experience, knowledge and maturity of the teacher; but all students brought to the Course their own experiences, their own knowledge and their own hard-won wisdom – assets to be shared with their colleagues to better the instruction, and at many points to enlighten the teacher. By abandoning competitive assessment we encouraged self-assessment and came more readily to be accepted as colleagues whose prime concern was not to be judgmental but to foster self-knowledge and greater professional mastery. Implicit in such a view was our belief that students should participate in the planning of courses and be able to influence their direction, just as they should be responsible for the planning of and execution of their own programme. To achieve this was one of the hardest tasks of all. Some students, as diary comments indicate, thought that such radicalism was based on faith in spontaneity as the sole determinant of learning. This we had to resist, but our ability to do so was sometimes undermined by our fear of pushing our own 'line', our own way of structuring material on to passive or hostile recipients. To learn how to hold on to structure and yet to be willing to modify it in response to students' reactions was indeed a subtle problem that few of us mastered quickly and that cannot be mastered easily.

I recall drawing great comfort from a talk given by Professor John Nisbet to the Victorian Institute of Educational Research entitled 'Anyone who plans to jump on the bandwagon of innovation should also consider its potentialities as a hearse.' This was published shortly afterwards in Australia and later more widely.[1] Lest any reader should gain the impression that this book is merely a local or domestic story, he should read it in conjunction with the brilliantly perceptive generalizations that Nisbet drew from his British experience. In one sense the book could be read as a detailed case study of the points Nisbet made.

He had schools in mind, but the phases that innovations go through and the dangers they face could apply in almost any profession, and are certainly illustrated by our experiment in teacher education. Nisbet maintained that there are 'four waves of difficulty which the innovator must survive'. First there will be an increase in everyone's work-load, and second a loss in confidence accompanied by an increase in anxiety (for which we might read the chapter 'Being at risk'). The third, he suggested, was an inevitable period of confusion, no doubt partly consequent upon the second, during which the innovation is isolated by outside colleagues and expected to die from its own infections. The reaction to this, Nisbet observes, can be to deal with problems piece-meal, which we did by pushing theory too hard too soon, and then switching topics in an unthinking way as soon as we sensed that students were restive. Often we seemed to (and did) skirt over too many things instead of pursuing a few more effectively. It may be seen, too, in our uncertainty, just referred to, about how persistent we should be in ensuring that we did not lose structure and coherence. Unless one learns to 'tolerate uncertainty', Nisbet suggests, there can be a lethal seeking for 'loyalty' born of undue sensitivity to criticism. Our survival of this crisis has also been told in this book. Finally, he warned with some prescience in 1974, that if these first three threats are surmounted, there will be a rapid backlash coming from far more widely organized hostile groups in society.

Despite these dire warnings, Nisbet's conclusions are positive.

Conclusion

Through innovations, he suggests, we must build up structures that will help the educational system to be 'self-renewing', and we must build in evaluation so that the innovators are a party to the style of evaluation adopted and receive support, strength and enlightenment from it. In this, Course B was lucky indeed. I can conclude the Conclusion with an application of one of Nisbet's final points. Any innovation will have only a passing and temporary influence, he suggests, unless the teachers concerned in it are proper participants who feel genuinely involved. For teacher education this must include teachers in the schools as well as those in the training institution. The future for rejuvenated teacher education and for a 'self-renewing' educational system would seem to lie in strengthening and extending school-based approaches to pre-service and in-service teacher education.

Notes

Introduction

1 Torrey Orton with Cleo Macmillan, *Course B: an Alternative in Teacher Preparation at the University of Melbourne: an Evaluative Case-Study*, Centre for the Study of Higher Education, University of Melbourne, 1976.
2 The schools that were added made the sample more generally representative of the Victorian system than the first three had been. The new schools were: Flemington High School, and the annexe it set up at Kensington; a second Swinburne annexe; Williamstown Technical School, Bentleigh High School, Mount Waverley High School, Deer Park High School and University High School (for one year), Footscray High School, and Kingswood College (an independent school).
3 *Growing*, London, Hogarth Press, 1961, pp. 61–2.

1 Thinking about education

1 Stephen Murray-Smith, ed., Melbourne University Press, 1977.

2 Who am I?

1 Paris, OECD, 1974.

3 Being at risk

1 Orton and Macmillan, *Course B*, University of Melbourne, 1976.

4 Methods

1 *Education and the Education of Teachers*, London, Routledge & Kegan Paul, 1977, pp. 151, 153.
2 Alan F. Wright and Freda Headlam, *Youth Needs and Public Policies*, Melbourne, Australian Council for Educational Research, 1976, p. 20.

3 'Training the Graduate Teacher: an Unorthodox View', *Education for Teaching*, summer 1969, pp. 53–4.
4 Bernard Newsome and Roderick Fawns, 'Theory and Practice in Teacher Education' in Orton and Macmillan, *Course B*, University of Melbourne, 1976.
5 London, 1970.
6 Paris, OECD, 1974, p. 13.
7 London, Methuen, 1977.
8 Quoted from G. M. Dow, 'Clear Thinking', *Idiom*, the Journal of the Victorian Association for the Teaching of English, July–August 1976, p. 25.

6 A course for radicals?

1 In a draft of a paper published in *New Patterns of Teacher Education and Tasks*, Paris, OECD, 1974.
2 The Magazine of the Education Subscription Service and the Open Book, Melbourne, no. 11, September 1975.

7 School teachers as educators of teachers

1 *The Future of Teacher Education*, London, Routledge & Kegan Paul, 1971, p. 101.
2 *Education and the Education of Teachers*, London, Routledge & Kegan Paul, 1977, pp. 162–3.
3 Wright and Headlam, Melbourne, 1976, p. 61.
4 'So You Want to be an English Teacher?', *Idiom*, July–August 1976.
5 From 'Of Poor B.B.'
6 From 'Questions from a Worker who Reads'.

Conclusion

1 'Innovation – Bandwagon or Hearse?' in Alan Harris, Martin Lawn and William Prescott, eds, *Curriculum Innovation*, London, Croom Helm, 1975, pp. 1–14 (originally published in Victorian Institute of Educational Research, *Bulletin*, 33, November 1974).

Booklist

This list cites merely those authors or titles referred to in the text of the book either by the author or, more often, by students in their diaries. Although it is far from exhaustive, it does give some indication of the kind of reading undertaken by students. When they referred to a particular writer, it was a matter of trying to guess from the context which work or works they might have had in mind.

Ashton-Warner, Sylvia, *Teacher*, London, Secker & Warburg, 1963 (also in Penguin).

Ausubel, D. P. and Robinson, E. G., *School Learning: an Introduction to Educational Psychology*, New York, Holt, Rinehart & Winston, 1969.

Axline, Virginia, *Dibs: In Search of Self*, Penguin, 1964.

Bannister, D. and Fransella, F., *Inquiring Man: the Theory of Personal Constructs*, Penguin Education, 1971.

Bantock, G. H., 'Discovery Methods' in Cox, C. B. and Dyson, A. E. (eds), *Black Paper Two*, London, Critical Quarterly Society, n.d.

Bernstein, Basil, 'Education Cannot Compensate for Society', *New Society*, 26 February 1970, reprinted in Rubinstein, David and Stoneman, Colin (eds), *Education for Democracy*, Penguin Education, 1970, and Cosin, B. R. *et al.* (eds), *School and Society*, London, Routledge & Kegan Paul, 2nd ed., 1977.

——, 'On the Classification and Framing of Educational Knowledge' in Young, M. F. D. (ed.), *Knowledge and Control*, London, Collier-Macmillan, 1971, reprinted in *Class, Codes and Control*, vol. 3.

——, *Class, Codes and Control*, vol. 3, London, Routledge & Kegan Paul, 2nd ed., 1977.

Bloom, B. S. (ed.), *Taxonomy of Educational Objectives: the Classification of Educational Goals*, 2 vols, New York, David McKay, 1959, 1964, London, Longman, 1965.

Britton, James, *Language and Learning*, London, Allen Lane, 1970 (also in Penguin).

Bruner, Jerome, Man: a Course of Study (Kit), Connecticut, Curriculum Development Associates (Australian Educational Media).

—, *The Process of Education*, Cambridge, Mass., Belknap Press, 1966.

—, *Towards a Theory of Instruction*, Harvard University Press, 1966, rev. ed., 1974.

Creber, J. W. P., *Lost for Words: Language and Educational Failure*, Penguin, 1972.

Dennison, John, *The Lives of Children*, New York, Random House, 1969 (also in Penguin).

Dewey, John, *Experience and Education*, New York, Macmillan, 1938, Collier Books, 1963.

Dienes, Z. P., *An Experimental Study of Mathematics*, London, Hutchinson, 1963.

Erikson, E. H., *Childhood and Society*, rev. ed., New York, Norton, 1963, London, Hogarth Press, 1964 (also in Paladin).

—, *Identity, Youth and Crisis*, New York, Norton, 1968, London, Faber, 1971.

Ford, G. W. and Pugno, L. (eds), *The Structure of Knowledge and the Curriculum* (essays by Joseph J. Schwab and others), Chicago, Rand McNally, 1964.

Freire, Paulo, *Cultural Action for Freedom*, Penguin, 1972.

—, *Pedagogy of the Oppressed*, New York, Herder, 1972 (also in Penguin).

—, *Education for Critical Consciousness*, London, Sheed & Ward, 1974.

Ginsburg, Herbert, *The Myth of the Deprived Child*, Englewood Cliffs, N. J., Prentice-Hall, 1972.

— and Opper, Sylvia, *Piaget's Theory of Intellectual Development*, Englewood Cliffs, N. J., Prentice-Hall, 1969.

Grene, Marjorie (ed.), *Knowing and Being: Essays by Michael Polanyi*, London, Routledge & Kegan Paul, 1969.

Hannam, Charles *et al.*, *Young Teachers and Reluctant Learners*, Penguin Education, 1971.

Hines, Barry, *Kestrel for a Knave (Kes)*, Penguin, 1969.

Holt, J. C., *Freedom and Beyond*, Penguin, 1973.

—, *How Children Fail*, New York and London, Pitman, 1965 (also in Penguin).

—, *How Children Learn*, New York, Pitman, 1967 (also in Penguin).

Illich, I. D., *Deschooling Society*, London, Calder & Boyars, 1971 (also in Penguin).

—, *Tools for Conviviality*, London, Calder & Boyars, 1973.

—, 'After Deschooling, What?' in Gartner, A., Greer, C. and Riessman, F. (eds), *After Deschooling, What?*, New York, Harper & Row, 1973 (also London, Writers and Readers Publishing Co-operative, 1974).

Jackson, B. and Marsden, D., *Education and the Working Class*, London, Routledge & Kegan Paul, 1962 (also in Penguin).

Jones, R. M., *Fantasy and Feeling in Education*, New York University Press, University of London Press, 1968 (also in Penguin).

Kelly, George, *see* Maher, B. A. (ed.).

Kohl, Herbert, *36 Children*, Penguin Education, 1972.

—, *Reading, How to*, Penguin Education, 1974.

—, *Writing, Maths and Games in the Open Classroom*, London, Methuen, 1974.

Kozol, Jonathan, *Free Schools*, Boston, Houghton Mifflin, 1972 (also a Bantam Book).

—, 'The Open Schoolroom: New Words for Old Deceptions', *Ramparts* (Berkeley), 11 (1), July 1972.

Kuhn, T. S., *The Structure of Scientific Revolutions*, University of Chicago Press, 2nd ed., 1970.

Labov, William, 'The Logic of Nonstandard English', *Georgetown Monographs in Language and Linguistics*, 22, 1969, reprinted in Keddie, Nell (ed.), *Tinker, Tailor ... The Myth of Cultural Deprivation*, Penguin Education, 1973.

McPhail, Peter *et al.*, Lifeline (Kit), Schools Council Moral Education Curriculum Project, London, Longman, 1972.

Maher, B. A. (ed.), *Clinical Psychology and Personality: the Selected Papers of George Kelly*, New York and London, Wiley, 1969.

Martin, Nancy *et al., Writing and Learning Across the Curriculum, 11–16*, London, Ward Lock Educational, 1976.

Neill, A. S., *Summerhill*, Penguin, 1968.

Polanyi, Michael, *Personal Knowledge*, London, Routledge & Kegan Paul, 1958.

—, *Science, Faith and Society*, University of Chicago Press, 1964.

—, *The Tacit Dimension*, London, Routledge & Kegan Paul, 1967.

Popper, Karl R., *The Open Society and its Enemies*, 2 vols, London, Routledge & Kegan Paul, 5th ed., 1966.

—, *Conjectures and Refutations: the Growth of Scientific Knowledge*, London, Routledge & Kegan Paul, 4th ed., 1972.

School of Barbiana, *Letter to a Teacher*, Penguin Education, 1970.

Schwab, J. J., 'The Concept of the Structure of a Discipline', *Educational Record*, Washington, 43, 1962.

Skinner, C. E. (ed.), *Educational Psychology*, 4th ed., Englewood Cliffs, N. J., Prentice-Hall, 1959, London, Staples, 1960.

Stead, Christina, *The Man who Loved Children*, Penguin, 1970.

Stenhouse, Lawrence, Schools Council/Nuffield Humanities Curriculum Project (Kits), London, Heinemann Educational, 1970 –.

Vygotsky, L. S., *Thought and Language*, Cambridge, Mass., MIT Press, 1962, rev. ed., 1965.

Whitehead, A. N., *The Aims of Education*, London, Williams & Norgate, 1929 (also in paperback, London, Benn, New York, Mentor Books).

Index

academic standards, 83; Course
  B's concern for, 2–3, 9–10,
  17, 19–23, 31–6, 37–8, 117–
  18, 137, 180; at University of
  Melbourne, 1, 9
Adrian, 58
Aileen, 111
America, 118, 119; see also
  universities
Anderson, D. S., 172
Andy, 59
Angela, 57–8, 75–6
Antonio, 45–8, 85, 96, 175,
  182–3
Ashton-Warner, Sylvia, 204
audio-visual aids, 141–2; video-
  taping, 61–2
Austin, A. G., 5, 173
Australia, 119, 213, 214, 219,
  243, 245; Federal Govern-
  ment, 1–2, 6; graduates in,
  136
Australian Advisory Council for
  Research and Development
  (later ERDC), 6
Australian Council for Educa-
  tional Research, 247n
Australian Council for Educa-
  tional Standards, 232
Ausubel, D. P., 168–9
authority: moral basis of, 9,
  72, 172–3, 181; parents',
  174–6; students', 73, 79–80,

[authority]
  86, 87–9, 163, 172–3, 179,
  209; teachers' and lecturers',
  73, 78–80, 122, 170, 187,
  191–5; see also freedom;
  schools
autobiographies (students'), 14,
  22, 102, 138, 164, 217, 221
Axline, Virginia, 23, 54, 230

Bantock, G. H., 128
Barbara, 105–6, 186–7, 188
Barnes, Jill, 178–80, 182–93
  passim
Barnes, Rory, 44, 128, 169, 195
behaviourism, 39–41, 45
Bentleigh High School, 226,
  247n
Bernstein, Basil, 25
Bert, 234, 238–9
Betty, 92–3, 95, 97, 100–1
Black Papers, 37, 163, 232
Bloom, B. S., 219
Bob, 101
Brecht, Bertolt, 123, 222–3,
  226
Brenda, 186
Brennan, John, 213, 218, 225
Brigit, 232–4, 239
Britton, James, 25, 243
Bronwyn, 146–7
Bruner, J. S., 25; learning theory,
  27, 30–1, 129, 149, 165;

[Bruner, J. S.]
'Man: a Course of Study',
226; workshops, 50-1, 93,
102-3, 201
Buhaj, Carole, 76-80, 87, 184,
209
Byron, Lord, 131

Caddie, 176
camp, Airey's Inlet, 92-102, 168
Carl, 95, 96
Caroline, 240
Cecile, 211
Centre for the Study of Higher
Education, *see* evaluation;
University of Melbourne
Chris, 51-3
class management, 3, 54-80
passim, 83-92, 144; pupil
control in, 181, 184; and
pupils' conformity, 178-80,
814; purposeless strategies in,
182-3, 236; structured planning and, 127, 217, 221, 230;
supervisors' influence on
students', 230-1, 232-4; *see
also* discipline; pupils
commitment: of students to
Course B, 193, 195, 210; of
students to teaching, 55, 67,
75, 99, 181, 203, 204, 207-
8; of teachers to ideology,
220; of teachers to teacher
training, 217
community schools, 32, 84, 135,
178, 202, 213, 217; challenge
to students in, 82, 173-6,
181, 184; close contact with
pupils in, 59-60, 71, 73-4,
141-2, 160; demands on
students in, 180; innovatory,
100, 222, 243-4; and pupil
interest, 183-5; staff meetings in, 236-7; teaching opportunities in, 145-7, 149,
203, 211, 228-9
comparative education, 21
competitiveness, 12, 50,

[competitiveness]
153-71 *passim*, 224, 244; *see
also* examinations
Cosopodiotis, Doris, 145, 213,
226
Countesthorpe College, 74
Creber, J. W. P., 25
Creed, Keth, 203
Crowther Report, 42
Curriculum Advisory Board, 4,
5, 7
Curriculum Studies, Course B,
10, 13, 34, 41, 134-6, 139,
140, 165; attendance at, 25,
204; background to, 3, 9; at
beginning of year, 17-26, 39-
43, 106-7, 111; interdisciplinary studies in, 3, 9-10, 12,
19-26, 39-43, 118-19, 121,
134-40, 152; problem-
centred, 19-26; school-based,
137-8, 204, 212-23, 242; *see
also* curriculum topics
curriculum topics, Course B, 23,
118, 205; Children's Literature, 25, 43, 53, 195, 211;
drama workshops, 139-40,
174; Equality, 43-9, 107,
196; Freedom and Authority,
43; historical, 109; Ideology,
43, 169-70, 219, 220-1, 242;
Language and Thought, 41,
43, 128, 139, 158-9; Learning Theory, 168; Scientific
Language, 43, 138; Social
Myths and the Media, 192-5

Daniels, Ray, 196, 224-5, 226
David, 102-3
Deamicis, Jan, 189-95
Deer Park High School, 206,
247n
Dennison, John, 71
Des, 237
Dewey, John, 108, 184
Dibs, *see* Axline, V.
Dienes, Z. P., 33
Dines, Elizabeth, 226

discipline through experience,
158–66; by learning from
mistakes, 205; of shared endeavour, 188–9; 193; the
teaching task as, 11, 69, 72,
115, 171, 184, 208, 241–2
Dow, G. M., 248n
Dreyfus, Alfred, 149
Dugan, Michael, 143
Duncan, Gwyn, 203–4, 210

*Education and the Working
Class, see* Jackson, B. and
Marsden, D.
educational administration, 21
Eggleston, S. J., 55
Elsie, 209, 210
equality, 178, 219, 221; class-
consciousness and, 44–9,
71–3; sexism, 64, 173–6;
social mobility and, 46–9,
173; students' attitudes to,
183, 187; of teachers and
lecturers, 244; *see also* curriculum topics
Eric, 228, 237
Erikson, E. H., 108
Europe, 118, 119
evaluation of Course B: by the
Centre for the Study of Higher
Education, 6, 99–102, 133–4,
142–3, 148, 150–2, 156,
167, 243, 244, 247n; by
Course B staff, 134, 189–96,
205–8, 214–15, 224–5; in
depth studies, 32, 35; in
diaries, 15, 24–6, 29–30, 52–
3, 63, 106–7, 170; in *Farrago*,
113--14; by students, 35–6,
63–4, 98, 111, 167, 183, 186,
211, 239–40
examinations and tests, 31–2,
132, 158–9, 219; Dip.Ed., 12,
37–8, 162–3, 167, 171, 193;
secondary school, 110, 129,
154, 222, 232; sixth form,
48, 129, 144, 148, 151, 154,
165, 183, 203, 221

Falk, Barbara, 6
Fawns, Roderick, 63, 114, 195,
248n; and administration,
168; appointment of, 7; and
Curriculum Studies, 33–4,
52, 142; and drama work-
shops, 139–40; involvement
in school teaching, 225–6;
and school-based Curriculum
Studies at Sydney Road Community School, 212, 220–1;
and school supervision, 135;
school visits by, 142, 207;
and science Method, 123,
128; and student anxieties,
98, 101–2, 168; team-
teaching, 139, 248n; on
theory and practice, 196
Flemington High School, 57,
247n; Annexe, 213, 247n;
curriculum at, 33, 137; Curriculum Studies at, 212–13,
217–18, 220, 222; language
across the curriculum project
at, 226; staff of, 76–80;
students at, 209–10, 225
Footscray High School, 206,
247n
Foster, Roderick, 39–40, 45,
104, 195, 209
Freddie, 211
freedom and autonomy, 36–49,
153–71 *passim*, 173, 174,
178, 223; academic, 219; for
Course B students, 8, 11, 36–
9, 55, 63, 98–100, 170, 185,
191–5, 204; pupils', 179,
184, 185, 220; schools', 3–4,
135, 154, 169–70, 183;
students' response to, 98,
168; *see also* curriculum topics
Freire, Paulo, 23, 25; and 'banking' theory of education, 26–
7; and history, 131, 147–8;
ideology, 44–5, 51, 182, 196,
221; influence, 26–7, 28; and
language acquisition, 124,
196, 204

Ginsburg, H., 25
Gita, 49
Goodlad, John, 12
Graubard, Allen, 216
Great Britain, 74, 119, 219;
    see also universities
grouping of Course B students,
    53; and diversity of student
    background, 9, 19, 104, 108–
    14, 152; group pressure, 83,
    98, 102–4, 155, 167–8; in
    schools, 135–6, 137–8, 206–
    7, 217–18, 225–6, 234; size
    of University seminars, 53,
    73, 92, 102, 103, 105, 107,
    217; students learn from each
    other, 36, 43, 163–4, 168–
    70, 192–5; students sup-
    ported by, 50–1, 104–5, 107,
    117–18, 160, 206–7; students
    threatened by, 54, 81, 93–8,
    102–16
Guy, 103

Haley, Alex, 149
Hannam, Charles, 23, 50
Hannan, Bill, 176, 243, 244
Hannan, Lorna, 176
Hansen, Chris, 212
Harris, Alan, 248n
Headlam, Freda, 247n, 248n
Heath, Diana, 111, 214
Heathcote, Dorothy, 226
Helen, 229–30, 231
Helga, 175–6
Higher School Certificate (HSC),
    see examinations
Hines, Barry, 68
Hirst, P. H., 12, 21–2, 42, 55
    60
history of education, 20–1,
    137, 221, 222
Holt, John, 87
Hopkins, G. M., 122
Hoy, Graeme, 178–80, 182–94
    passim
Huntingdale Technical School,
    74

ideology: Course B's, 7, 35, 54,
    68–9, 126, 149, 153, 156–
    7, 166–8, 172–96, 215;
    historians', 133; and indoc-
    trination, 88–9, 128, 151,
    176, 182, 219; of parents,
    173–5; students', 17, 35, 43–
    51, 70–3, 87–9, 111, 168,
    172–96, 209; students'
    clashes, 104–6, 163; super-
    visors', 76, 175
Illich, Ivan, 44–5, 51, 67, 179,
    196, 216
'inert ideas', 27, 126, 128, 133,
    147
innovations, 6, 54–5, 92; in
    Course B, 1–16 *passim*, 153–
    71 *passim*, 189–200, 245–6;
    in educational research, 4–5,
    8, 12, 214, 226; evaluation
    of, 6, 246; in-service training,
    244, 246; school, 3, 4, 11,
    200–1, 219, 221, 236–7, 239,
    245–6

Jack, 105, 106, 113
Jackson, Andrew, 149
Jackson, B. and Marsden, D., 46
Jacqueline, 85, 92–3, 95, 96
James, 144–5
Jan, 111–12
Jane, 143–4
Janet, 227–8
Jenny, 97–8, 99–100
Jill, 24–5, 60
Jim, 71–3
Joanna, 58–9, 103
Jocelyn, 66
Jock, 65–6, 85–90, 91, 96
John, 44–5, 48, 111
Jones, Lloyd: appointment, 7,
    212–13; on subject specializ-
    ation, 134–7, 218; experiences
    in Course B, 214–15, 224,
    226; and school-based Cur-
    riculum Studies at Flemington
    High School, 221–2; style of
    teaching 76–80, 184

Jones, Richard, 149
Julie (Guerson), 193
June, 150

Kate, 50–1
Kelly, George, 25, 168–9
Kennedy, Roger, 128–9
Kes, *see* Hines, Barry
Kingswood College, 247n
Kohl, Herbert, 23, 24, 40, 87
Kozol, Jonathan, 71
Kuhn, T. S., 128

Labov, William, 40
Lacey, Colin, 136–7
Language and Learning, *see*
    Britton, James
language study, *see* curriculum
    topics; pupils; student teach-
    ers
Lawn, Martin, 248n
learning, 1, 11, 22, 25–36, 190,
    241; by exposition, 34;
    rhythm in, 33–4, 158–9; by
    rote 120, 125, 151; and
    scholarship, 118, 121–2; self-
    directed, 11–12, 37–9, 169,
    181, 185, 187, 192–5; spon-
    taneity in, 38–9, 45, 62, 122,
    159, 185, 237, 245; theory
    of, 24, 28, 39–41, 129, 168,
    219
Lee Dow, Kwong, 5
Len, 160–2
Lesley, 107–8
Letter to a Teacher, 46, 68
Lewers, Rob, 212
Libby, 109–10, 113, 141–2, 159
Liz, 84
Lord of the Flies, 226
Lost for Words, *see* Creber,
    J. W. P.
Luddites, 131

McFarlane, Brian, 204–5, 207–8,
    210, 215, 225
Macmillan, Cleo, 6, 130, 149,
    215–18, 247n, 248n

McPhail, Peter, 120
Maddocks, Ray, 7
Margaret, 33–5, 36
Mark, 174–5
Martha, 61–4, 65, 66
Martin, 76–80, 82, 83, 87, 88
Martin, Nancy, 36
Maureen, 53, 105–6, 113, 228
    234
Meg, 210–11
Methods studies, 12–13, 23, 89,
    117–52, 178–80, 242; and
    academic standards, 9–10, 19,
    252; in economics, 187;
    family biographies in, 35,
    131, 138, 147–8; in history,
    104, 111–12, 148–9, 164–5,
    196, 224; oral history in,
    131; in science, 183; in social
    science, 187, 193
migrants, *see* pupils
Milani, Father, 48, 124
Morag, 84–5
Moreland High School, 5
Mt Waverley High School, 203,
    247n
Murray-Smith, Stephen, 53, 195,
    247n
Myra, 65, 69
Myth of the Deprived Child, *see*
    Ginsburg, H.

Neill, A. S., 44, 108, 111, 215
Newsome, Bernard, 63, 195,
    248n; and administration,
    168, 191; appointment, 7;
    and Curriculum Studies, 40;
    and English Method, 128;
    involvement in school teach-
    ing and school supervision,
    226; school visits by, 25,
    143–4, 234–5; and student
    anxieties, 87, 94–5, 98, 114,
    168; and student assessment,
    160–2, 180; and team-
    teaching, 40, 139; on theory
    and practice, 130, 131–2,
    196, 248n

Nick, 211, 212
Nisbet, John, 245–6
Noonan, Jim, 229–30, 231
Norma, 64–5, 66–7, 83–4

OECD Conference (1974), 55, 136, 247n, 248n
Orton, Torrey, 6, 100–1, 247n, 248n

Paffard, Michael, 121
Pam, 111–13, 114
parents, 83, 173–4; and community, 220; migrant, 77, 173–8
Pat, 211
Patricia, 101
Paul, 111, 164–5
Paula, 236
Peg, 150
Peggy, 105–6, 107
Penny, 228, 234
Perth, HMAS, 131
Peter, 90–1, 95–7, 112–13
Peters, R. S., 118–19, 121, 132, 199
Phyl, 145–6
Piaget, Jean, 19, 129, 168–9
Poincaré, J. H., 159
Polanyi, Michael, 27, 159
Popper, Karl R., 128
practice teaching, Course B, 5, 10–11, 17–18, 22, 32, 81, 107, 137, 172–96 *passim*, 197–240 *passim*; *see also* class management; reflexion; theory and practice
Prescott, William, 248n
professional education, 2, 83, 119, 121, 245; theory and practice in, 2, 22, 54–5
Prue, 25–7, 29, 53, 203, 204, 208
psychology, 3, 9, 20–1, 137, 241; of children, 121, 219, 240; in topic studies, 42, 121; graduates in, 24–5, 38
pupils, 1, 16, 18, 37, 54–80

[pupils]
passim, 81–116 *passim*; assessment of students by, 149–50, 238–9; 'consciousness raising' among, 47–8, 182–5, 188, 220; language acquisition by, 36, 57–8, 88, 158–9, 226; language and socioeconomic class of, 46–7, 49, 176; literacy, 222; migrant, 35, 46, 77, 145, 148, 173–8, 222, 237; participation in school policy, 5, 11–12, 137, 153–4, 169–70, 238; reflexion on action, 29, 50, 122, 149–50; self-assessment, 11, 149, 153–4, 158, 237–8; *see also* class management; freedom and autonomy

Ralph, 28, 29–30
Raymond, 184
reflexion on action by students, 17, 21–2, 24–7, 35, 54–80 *passim*, 118, 143, 171, 180–1; diaries' value for, 29–31, 33–4, 37, 50, 89, 110, 210–11; of English, 133, 143; of history, 127–8, 133, 164–6; of science, 108–11, 142–3; on undergraduate studies, 10, 24–5, 173
relationships, 5, 8; lecturers with lecturers, 11; pull for students between schools and University, 163, 166, 170–1, 201–11; pupils' 'crushes', 57, 85, 87, 90–1, 95–6; pupils' teasing students, 78–80, 82–92, 96; between schools and training institutions, 4–5, 8, 11, 39, 156–7, 178, 180, 197–240 *passim*; students with pupils, 5, 23, 37, 49, 54–80 *passim*, 81–116 *passim*, 126–7, 130, 139–40, 145, 159–60, 205–6; students with lecturers, 37,

[relationships]
43–4, 51, 93–9, 134–6, 167–8, 191–6; students with students, 21, 36, 50, 113–14, 187, 196, 224, 244; teachers with lecturers, 11, 55, 129, 135–6, 197–240; teachers with pupils, 8, 39, 56, 73, 76–80, 96, 97, 127, 179, 184; *see also* grouping; ideology; pupils; staff; student-teachers supervisors of school practice

requirements, Course B, 13–15, 29–36, 38, 108, 129, 155; compulsory, 167–8, 196; negotiable, 167–8, 196; *see also* self-assessment

Resource Centres, 151, 163, 213

Richards, I. A., 121

Robb, Doug, 126–7, 128, 209, 217

Roger, 67–9, 104

Ron (Hoenig), 193, 194

Ronald, 69–71, 180–2, 209

Roy, 108–9

Ruth, 176–8

Sandra, 82–3

School of Barbiana, 23, 24, 40, 44, 48, 125

schools used by Course B, 5, 7, 18–19, 49, 137, 157, 180; authoritarian, 50, 89, 170, 174; class size in, 130, 141, 160, 204, 209–10; co-educational, 85, 176, 182; organization in, 177, 179, 187, 213, 236–40; single-sex, 83–5; size of, 59–60, 71, 73–4, 76, 84, 135, 213, 217–18, 236; structuring curriculum in, 135, 137, 154, 218, 244; and teacher training, 135–7, 154, 200, 243–4; *see also* community schools; innovations

school-based studies, *see* Curriculum Studies

school curriculum, 4, 46, 47, 154, 221; art, 202; compulsory studies, 28–9, 37, 129, 183, 219; criminology, 184; drama, 139–40, 149–50; economics, 151; English language, 36, 123, 132, 144–5, 151, 183, 221, 222; English literature, 43, 123, 132, 144–5, 173, 205; family history, 147; general studies, 5, 41, 45, 123, 134–41, 151, 220, 221, 225–6; geography, 48, 123, 150–1, 210, 232; 'hidden', 67, 88, 178–9, 197–8, 220, 221; history, 48, 123, 124–5, 131, 145–50, 230; history dramatized, 149–50, 230; home economics, 123; language across the curriculum, 123–4, 138–9, 216, 221, 226; mathematics, 33, 120, 124, 151; modern languages, 120, 202; moral education, 120, 220–1; multi-cultural studies, 13; music, 202; physical education, 123; physics, 123, 141, 143; psychology, 141; remedial programmes, 13, 46, 145, 203–4; science, 110, 123, 143, 151, 219, 226; science and drama, 226; sex education, 209–10, 221; social studies, 120, 211, 219, 221, 226; structuring of, 28–9, 41, 45, 122, 127, 135, 152, 205; three Rs, 219; women's liberation, 141, 174, 176

Schruhm, A. E., 7

Schwab, J. J., 128

scientific method, 20–1, 109–10, 138

simulation games, 47, 52

Soccio, Lou, 35, 36, 38, 147–8, 219

sociology of education, 3, 9, 20–1, 38, 121, 137, 141;

[sociology of education]
  in Curriculum Studies, 222;
  in Methods, 111
Sonia, 173–4, 176
Spender, Stephen, 38
Spunner, Suzanne, 113
staff, Course B, 6, 7, 16, 160,
  189, 197–240, 244; anxiety
  for, 82, 92–9, 101–2, 116,
  154–5, 162–3, 190–2, 215,
  219, 245; and conflict with
  students, 94–9, 168–9;
  exemplifying educational
  principles, 17, 98–9, 186; and
  in-service courses, 244; and
  Methods teaching, 10–11; and
  structured teaching, 13, 17–
  53 *passim*, 62–3, 72, 85, 103,
  217, 218–19, 222, 245; *see
  also* relationships; supervisors;
  teachers
Stead, Christina, 19
Stenhouse, Lawrence, 113, 120,
  128
Stewart, 30, 183
student-teachers (Course B), 1–
  3, 7, 11, 14–16; fears of, 2,
  19, 53, 56–69, 80, 81–116,
  159, 162; heterogeneity of, 9,
  19–21, 38, 41, 104, 114, 118,
  137, 170, 201, 242; im-
  promptu lessons given by,
  227–8; numbers in Course, 6–
  7, 53, 102, 107; and participatory planning, 8, 11, 36–43,
  99, 153–71 *passim*, 188, 192–
  6, 217, 219–20, 222, 244–5;
  risks for, 8–9, 54–5, 61–116
  passim, 157–62, 219, 235;
  self-assessment, 8, 11, 12, 30,
  35–6, 37–8, 51, 94, 99–101,
  129, 140–5, 153–71, 224,
  244; self-knowledge, quest
  for, 2–3, 54–80 *passim*, 81–
  116 *passim*, 131–2, 141, 159–
  66, 180–1, 188, 199, 235,
  244; subject specialization, 8–
  11, 17, 19–21, 23, 38, 42,

[student-teachers (Course B)]
  108–11, 114–15, 117–18, 125–
  38, 142; *see also* grouping
student-teachers' academic background, 117–52 *passim*;
  biology, 132; economics, 10,
  38, 111, 126, 150–1, 187;
  English, 10, 126, 135, 143,
  151; English language, 86,
  131–3, 139, 203–4; English
  literature, 41, 132, 173, 205;
  geography, 10, 38, 111–13,
  126–7, 250, 209; history,
  10, 11, 35, 41, 126, 132,
  134–5, 145–7, 164–5, 207;
  linguistics, 132; literacy and
  fluency associated with,
  19–20, 38, 108–11, 112–14,
  114–15, 124, 133, 138–9,
  142–3; mathematics, 10,
  124, 126, 151, 160–2, 207;
  modern languages, 10, 126,
  150; psychology, 19, 24–5,
  38, 108; science, 10, 11, 41,
  59, 69, 126, 151, 207; social
  science, 10, 126, 128, 130,
  135, 187, 226
supervisors of school practice, 3,
  8, 16, 134, 197–240; advice
  to students, 55–6, 74, 87;
  educational discussions with
  students, 19, 75, 86, 159; as
  Method staff, 10; relations
  with University staff, 11, 242;
  skills of, 243, 244; and
  student assessment, 52, 156–
  7, 160, 161, 233, 235; and
  student teaching, 56, 61–2,
  178–9
Susie, 30–1, 49–50
Swinburne Annexe, 212, 247n
Swinburne Community School,
  5, 200, 212, 215–16
Swinburne Technical School,
  5
Sydney Road Community
  School, 5, 200, 212, 218,
  219, 220–1, 226

Taylor, Gillian, 124–5
teacher education (general), 136,
    154, 156, 214, 241, 244; in
    traditional training courses,
    114, 117, 137, 199, 239–40
teacher-training institutions and
    schools, 117–26, 135–6, 154,
    197–240, 242–4, 246; *see
    also* staff; supervisors; univer-
    sities
teachers, ex-Course B, 8, 12, 64,
    69, 89–90, 114, 162, 243,
    244; of English, 123; personal
    power of, 70, 74–80, 88, 95–
    6, 155, 178, 180–1, 187,
    191–5, 245; political power
    of, 185–96; *see also* staff
teaching styles, 54, 66–8, 73–80,
    180, 186, 198, 222, 227
team-teaching, 13, 18–19, 28,
    39–43, 137–8, 143, 152, 203,
    225–6, 228–9
theory and practice, 1–16 *passim*,
    17–53 *passim*, 106, 172, 196,
    205–9, 213, 215–17; divorce
    between, 154, 198–9, 214,
    224; practising what is
    preached, 54–5, 98, 170–1;
    students' relating of, 111,
    164–6, 169, 186–8, 241
Thomastown High School, 74
Thompson, Jack, 176
Thomson, Trish, 178–88 *passim*
Tibble, J. W., 198
The Times, 198
Tolstoy, Leo, 211
Toomey, Ron, 32, 212, 215
'tricks of the trade', students'
    demands for, 24, 57, 80, 106,
    121, 126, 178–80, 182–3, 209
Trinity Grammar School, 5,
    204–8, 212–13, 216, 218,
    219
Tulloch, Richard, 139

unions, 155; National Associ-
    ation of Schoolmasters/Union
    of Women Teachers, 136,
[unions]
    198–9; National Union of
    Teachers, 136; Victorian
    Secondary Teachers' Associ-
    ation, 4
universities: Australian National
    University, 172; and teacher
    training, 117–26, 135–6, 154,
    242–3, 244; Bristol, 12;
    Cambridge, 12; Harvard, 4,
    12; Keele, 12, 121; Leicester,
    12, 119, 198; London, 12,
    36, 119; Oxford, 12; Sussex,
    12; York, 12
University High School, 247n
University of Melbourne: and
    Course B, 1–16, 155, 156,
    158–9, 190–1; Centre for the
    Study of Higher Education,
    6, 15, 30, 99–102, 130, 133,
    142–3, 150–2, 215–18, 247n;
    Diploma of Education, 1–16,
    17–53 *passim*, 63–4, 65, 155,
    156, 189, 226; Education
    Resources Centre, 163, 213;
    educational research, 214,
    226; Faculty of Education, 5,
    6, 8, 156; 'New Develop-
    ments', 6; Schools' Com-
    mittee, 5, 8, 18, 156, 157,
    161; staff, 1, 135; students,
    1, 9, 11, 32; *see also* aca-
    demic standards

Vicky (Marles), 193
Victoria, Education Department,
    1–2, 3–4, 7, 44, 153–5, 155;
    inspectorate, 154; school
    system, 213, 221, 241; staff-
    ing policy, 156, 206, student-
    ships, 157, 160; support for
    Course B, 212–13
Victorian High Schools Princi-
    pals' Association, 136
Victorian Institute of Educa-
    tional Research, 245
Vidal, Gore, 54
Vietnam war, 172

Index

Vygotsky, L. S., 108, 129

Walsh, Judy, 93, 94, 127, 167
Wanda, 57, 104, 107
Werner, Terry, 40, 169, 195, 196, 226
Whitehead, A. N., 121, 126
Williams, Morris, 5
Williamstown High School, 224
Williamstown Technical School, 247n

Woolf, Leonard, 15
Wright, A. F., 247n, 248n
Wright, R. D., 138
writing and thinking, 31–6, 58, 70, 108–9, 111, 128, 132, 180–1, 203–4

Yeats, W. B., 143
Young Teachers and Reluctant Learners, see Hannam, Charles